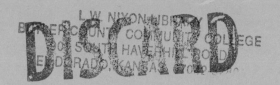

DATE DUE

X

YOUNG
HENRY
FORD

Henry Ford in His First Car: 1896

The picture is pure period—not because of the funny little handmade pioneer automobile, its four bicycle wheels, the doorbell which he rang with a button in the top of the tiller that steered it, and not because of his mustache and derby hat. It is a period picture because the street is empty.

The whole land was empty. There were only 69,000,000 Americans and no traffic. Only railroads joined the horizons. The American road ended at the city limits.

When Henry Ford was fighting the auto trust in 1904, he and three loyal friends said that this picture was taken in 1892, hoping to prove that this car antedated the Selden patent of 1895. The fib turned out to be unnecessary: Ford triumphed after eight years of court fights because of the *kind* of engine he had built, no matter *when* he built it. The picture was taken by John H. Livesey early in October 1896 on Second Boulevard and Ledyard Street in Detroit, with Cass Park in the background. A moment later Henry Ford stepped out of his car and took Photographer Livesey's picture (p. 79).

YOUNG HENRY FORD

A PICTURE HISTORY OF
THE FIRST FORTY YEARS

by SIDNEY OLSON

WAYNE STATE UNIVERSITY PRESS   Detroit

Copyright © 1963, 1997 by Wayne State University
Press, Detroit, Michigan 48201. All rights reserved. No
part of this book may be reproduced without formal
permission. Manufactured in the United States of America.

01   00   99   98   97   5   4   3   2

ISBN 0-8143-1224-1 (alk. paper)
LC 63=Z0162

GREAT LAKES BOOKS

*A complete listing of the books in this series can be
found at the back of this volume.*

PHILIP P. MASON, EDITOR
Department of History, Wayne State University

DR. CHARLES K. HYDE, ASSOCIATE EDITOR
Department of History, Wayne State University

{ CONTENTS }

{ ILLUSTRATIONS }

[FOREWORD]

Sidney Olson's *Young Henry Ford: A Picture History of the First Forty Years* was a labor of love, which helps explain why it was so meticulously researched and beautifully written.

Before becoming a student of Ford's early life, Olson was a *Washington Post* and *Time-Life-Fortune* editor. In 1950 he joined Ford's institutional advertising agency, Kenyon & Eckhardt. Three years later, when promoting Ford's fiftieth anniversary celebration, he examined long-buried papers and photographs in the home of the late Henry and Clara Ford. Fascinated by the oldest of the documents and photos, he set out, as an avocation, to learn as much as possible about the Fords' formative years. In time, magnifying glass in hand, he began interviewing Henry's surviving friends and business associates. All too often, he laughingly told friends, he ran into the kind of oldster who pointed to the same "Mr. Cunningham" twice in the same picture. Doggedly persistent, Olson and his secretary, Pat Maroni, spent years squeezing out the last ounce of information we are ever likely to know about Ford's first forty years. Playing Cupid, Olson also introduced Pat to "the man you are going to marry"—Jacques Maroni, a bright young Ford executive.

A sweet man, Olson was nonetheless a demanding boss. Working days on agency business, he often cleared his desk at 5 P.M. and wrote furiously until the wee hours, expecting his secretary to remain with him to the end.

Olson's highly acclaimed mid-1950s institutional advertising campaign, "The American Road," elicited a handsome job offer from Ford's lead advertising agency, J. Walter Thompson. He was serving as vice-president of forward planning when *Young Henry Ford* was published in 1963, the centennial of the magnate's birth. Retiring at age sixty-five in 1973, Olson died in 1995 in Darien,

Connecticut. His widow, Zembra, whom he married in 1937, survives.

Olson wrote only one book, but what a book. Thanks to its 229 captioned photographs, interspersed by carefully crafted biographical narrative, *Young Henry Ford* clearly shows that its subject did not come out of "nowhere" to organize and build one of the world's greatest enterprises. It also suggests why Ford would retain the common touch that contributed to his folk heroism, while becoming an industrial superman and billionaire. Above all, the book illuminates the youthful inner workings of a man who would become one of the most enigmatic, paradoxical, controversial, colorful, and influential characters in American history.

Wayne State University Press has a well-earned reputation for being the nation's leading publisher of automotive-history titles. In keeping with its reputation, and in recognition that the long-out-of-print original edition of *Young Henry Ford* has become a collector's item, the Wayne Press is performing a laudable service by giving this charming book a new lease on life.

David L. Lewis
University of Michigan Business School
February, 1997

[PREFACE]

This is the story in pictures of the first forty years of an American farm boy who became one of the greatest manufacturers of modern times, and who was, also, a profound radical all his life.

He was a great man, and Americans know most of their great men rather well. He made mistakes, sensational, international, even classic mistakes, and perhaps he is remembered chiefly for them. But if you look through these pictures, and read a bit here and there, you will gradually see another Henry Ford emerge, and that is the real Henry Ford. And you will be dispelling the myths, the legends, that have become attached to him, as they become attached to any great man.

If you think of Ford at all, you may think of him as the originator of the monotony of mass production, of the five-dollar day, and the car for the masses. But things are not quite so simple. Henry Ford was like no one else. He was unique, and original, and there can never be another. He fit no pigeonhole until he became a very old man—and the grave is one pigeonhole we all come to fit.

No easy label describes in any real way the man who did so much to change the whole face of America, of the world. Henry Ford helped change our very habits of living, and that of course is the hardest of all things to do, harder than building dams or bridges or passing laws.

Most books written about Henry Ford either attack him bitterly or praise him with somewhat sickening sweetness. The point of view of this book is simply, see for yourself.

In this book you will see what his beginnings and the beginnings of the Ford car were like and some flashes of what his times were like. Many of these pictures were long buried in old files; a great many have never before been in the public view. You will even see some of Henry

Ford's own snapshots, taken with his first camera before the turn of the century and now printed for the first time from old negatives found in trunks in his home. Many of these were tightly curled up, cracked, shredded, spotted, stained, sticky with dust after having been tucked away and forgotten for more than half a century. The restorations are excellent, but obviously not all the defects could be removed. For each picture I have been able to use, I have discarded a hundred or more.

You will find here again and again, a hundred times over, the look and the clear sound of an America now gone, gone with the buffalo and the Sunday evening band concerts, and women's high-laced boots. But this is no mere lament from an antiquarian: the only importance of these words and pictures lies in the fact that the men and the women pictured here helped to give America the look and sound it has today.

I have altogether dispensed with footnotes, references, appendices, and all the other fine-print baggage so dismaying to the reader. No single *ibid.* or *op. cit.* has been allowed to creep in. Although this may be a disappointment to footnote-fetishists, the reason is wholly practical: the references are so many and so voluminous that their mere citation would force this book into shelf-length. But that the serious reader may be reassured, let me say that behind every paragraph, sentence, and word stands the massed documentation of the Ford Archives, one of the great storehouses of facts on this continent. Often, more than a cotton bale of documents rests in the Archives as proof of a single assertion of fact. For each fact or anecdote I have brought in, I have passed up a thousand or more. I have spent much time among the documents and pictures and can testify that no single set of eyes will ever see the whole of the Archives. And as a further assurance, wherever I have theorized or assumed or conjectured or surmised, I have plainly labeled the conceits as my own speculations.

I am grateful to the Archives staff for every courtesy and aid which they have extended to me, and to members of the company and all other sources involved, to make this book as accurate as history can be. I wish also to record my personal debt to Charles F. Moore, Jr., who initiated the Archives, and to Henry E. Edmunds, who so organized and administered it that it has become a model archives, an institution of profound importance to American scholars. The intense five years I spent among all the documents and pictures were enjoyable and enlightening. The Archives is to be congratulated on the pioneer use it has made of its materials.

Any mistakes are my own, whether in fact, in taste, or in interpretation of all the great, extraordinary, and mystifying events that made up the first half of the life of a man whose history can never be adequately told within the covers of a book.

S.O.
Dearborn, Michigan
7 April 1953

[INTRODUCTION]

For about a dozen years the Ford Archives at Dearborn has been carefully documenting the things that Henry Ford did. The list is still incomplete. Each one of the hundreds of items might represent a lifetime achievement for an ordinary man; for example, "Bought a railroad."

The range of Henry Ford cuts across eight decades. Presidents came and went. But from 1914 to 1947, there was scarcely a day when Ford could not take the front pages from any of them. He was news for weeks and even months at a stretch, year after year, decade after decade. He became a folklore figure overnight in 1914 —and from then on his every opinion and movement had that quality of a living legend which so satisfies the American public. From coast to coast smiling heads would waggle, people would ask, "See what Old Henry's done now?" and everyone knew which Henry.

He was news in a way peculiar to himself. The American people simply never thought of him as a rich man. He never thought of himself as a rich man. Thus we had for a generation the gratifying spectacle of the richest man of his time denouncing Wall Street.

He did not frequent the resorts of the idle rich, Newport and all that. I cannot find that he ever gambled, entered a night club, or saw a horse race. But he could stand on his hands when he was seventy-five years old. There are films showing him—at seventy-two—racing school children across a lawn. Down to his last years he entered open cars by vaulting over the side. He raised his only son Edsel to work—not for money but for people. And Edsel and Eleanor Clay Ford raised their children in the same clear-headed discipline not notable in the complex annals of the American rich.

His power was extraordinary, his influence immense. The Model T—the Tin Lizzie, the flivver —was the very first automobile that millions and millions of people around the world ever saw. The first English word learned by millions of Chinese, Russians, Spaniards, Africans, and Hindus was the word "Ford."

Yet today Henry Ford is forgotten or remembered on hearsay for the bad things. His name is on a motor car unlike any he ever made and on a great foundation whose domain is the social sciences and some of whose activities no doubt revolve him in his grave. His face has not appeared on a postage stamp, although the woman who invented Mother's Day has been so honored, along with Casey Jones, some minor poets, and the Battle of Brooklyn (which we lost to the British).

Yet he made history—and historians.

For Henry Ford almost never threw anything away, even down to ticket stubs. And he was also the greatest single collector of Americana in American history. His taste was more enthusiastic than expert, but as a sheer accumulator he had no peer. If he wanted an early typewriter, an early sewing machine, an old-fashioned stove, a Phyfe chair, out went his scouts and back came boxcars filled, the junk and the priceless mixed.

The older antique dealers think of him as the man who sacked New England: once his buyers bought up every hooked rug that was not being immediately rocked on. And only a regiment can polish and oil all the guns in the Ford Museum.

The Ford Archives represents the same kind of thing on paper. You know how the local paper boy leans his bicycle against the front porch, collects his seventy-five cents, and then gives you a little scribbled slip as a receipt? You throw the slip away, sooner or later—but Henry Ford didn't. The unknown newsboy who once delivered *The Detroit Evening Journal* to 58 Bagley Avenue in November 1894 left a receipt for forty-five cents for the month's papers; and that is in the Archives.

Clara Ford's grocery bills from before the turn of the century, the department store bills for shoes, suits, and hats, the bills for the rose bushes she loved—all are in the Archives.

There are Henry Ford's bills for hardware and tools, for gasoline to use in his 1893 experiments

1

with a gas engine. So are hundreds of thousands of newspaper clippings. So are thousands of documents, the office files from the Rouge and Highland Park plants, blueprints of racing cars and tractors and airplanes, plant layouts for factories all over the world, letters from men wanting jobs, letters from crackpots in and out of asylums, from politicians, farmers, scientists, letters from Franklin D. Roosevelt and Queen Marie of Rumania, from Louis B. Mayer, Eddie Foy, and Harry Lauder, from the Duke of Windsor and George Washington Carver.

There are thousands of pictures, from the first little faded brown snapshots on through the years when photographers followed him everywhere, and millions of feet of old movie films, from the days when the Ford Newsreel ran in 1,500 theaters every week, including many of the first film documentaries and travelogs ever made.

The calling cards people left at his hotels when he went abroad are in the Archives, and all the Christmas cards sent him through the years. There is a bill for $35 due on a gray-streaked toupee made for a balding relative who had paid $10 down and couldn't pay up the rest. (Henry Ford paid it.) There is the coded telegram to the Chase National Bank which released $75,000,000 to be paid to the stockholders he bought out in 1919.

There are dozens of the little black "jotbooks" in which he made notes for fifty years: his ideas, diagrams of machinery, lists of player-piano rolls and phonograph records to buy, lists of hard words he had trouble spelling, and the dry little epigrams in which he compressed his wisdom, such as, "Health is catching."

The whole is a vast mountain range of contemporary Americana, one of the greatest hoards of the raw materials of history ever discovered. Its existence became known soon after the death of his widow on September 30, 1950.

Someone asked, "I wonder if Mr. Ford left any papers?"

A search party went through the fifty-six rooms of Fair Lane, the great stone home on the River Rouge in Dearborn.

The guestbook days of Fair Lane were long past. The blue-uniformed guards had opened the gates only to a friend or two and a pair of servants as the Fords had sunk quietly into the gentle loneliness of old age. The vast house had

steadily filled with the furnishings and memorabilia of a generation; and after the death of Henry Ford the desks and then the rooms, one after another, became choked up with stacks of unopened mail, magazines in wrappers, books, and gifts.

Clara Ford, quietly watching her life run down, serenely locked up each room as it filled, and finally spent most of her time in her little office and on the wicker-filled sun porch next to it, where for so many years she and Henry had watched the birds fly across the still green waters of the Rouge.

The search party hardly knew where to begin. The explorers were confronted with fifty-six rooms packed with tons of material: microscopes, hand tools, clocks, rare books, dolls, cameras, music boxes, racks of test tubes, and scores and scores of huge cardboard cartons and packing cases filled with papers, letters, and notes.

A dozen huge basement rooms were packed so tightly that the search party could only open the doors and gape. A bowling alley was filled end to end with rolled rugs and carpets, one rug so big that twelve men were needed to move it. One whole room was filled with old draperies, another with huge carved walnut candelabra tasseled in red-purple, one room with Hitchcock chairs, and one little basement room had nothing in it but hundreds of wicker baskets.

Heading the party was a professional, Dr. Robert Bahmer of Washington, deputy archivist of the United States. Archivist Bahmer put his hand at random into one of the cartons of papers, found a letter, opened it. The letter:

1. Robert R. McCormick's letter.

Bahmer stood still in the dark basement, trying to remember details of the great *Tribune* suit. (It was in 1919: the *Tribune* had called Ford "an anarchist"; Ford had sued for $1,000,000 and after a spectacular trial won the verdict but collected only six cents in damages.) No one but Henry Ford had seen this letter since Colonel McCormick wrote it.

2. The next random item was a telegram—from Calvin Coolidge.

Now they knew they were in the middle of history.

Introduction

Owen Bombard of Columbia University, an expert in oral interviewing, the new technique of history pioneered at Columbia, was imported with a half dozen tape recorders and a staff of typists. Bombard's assignment: to interview for the use of historians every surviving man and woman who had ever known, dealt with, or worked with Henry Ford. (Bombard's results to date: several hundred blue-bound volumes of memoirs, ranging from those of William J. Cameron and Sir Percival Perry to those of gardeners, watchmen, and mechanics who helped Henry Ford with his first car in 1896. Many other volumes are in preparation, but the real fact is this: more than eight million words of testimony have already been taken—direct eyewitness views of the great and small things that happened over most of a century. Already many of these veterans have died, but their eye-witness stories are preserved for historians.)

Fair Lane was chosen as the logical site for the Archives, which was dedicated in May, 1953. The archivists and their staff set to work. The first task was to clear out Fair Lane and re-vamp it as a scholar's work place. For a year and a half they worked in the old Engineering Laboratory offices—not the huge mahogany front offices where Henry Ford seldom went but the little "farm office" quarters that had been one of his main hideouts for twenty-odd years.

A coffeepot bubbled steadily all day and most nights; the staff spent most of their time as literary stevedores, lifting and dusting and classifying. Hundreds of framed photographs and oil paintings were stacked in rows along the walls; the transfer files poured out of trucks to stack up in brown mountains twelve feet high.

They were under a curious set of pressures: they had to live at once in two worlds, that of the life and times of Henry Ford and that of the future. For their prime task was to establish an archives that would be a model of the modern approach both in the preservation of documents, pictures, and books and in the methods of their use.

And to master the problems presented by the fantastic career of Henry Ford, the archivists had to master the history of the auto industry, to bring the discipline of the modern historian's method to the inchoate, bubbling mass of facts

THE CHICAGO TRIBUNE

Henry Ford
RECEIVED
JUL 3 1 1941
Secretary's Office

July 30 1941

Dear Mr. Ford

It occurs to me on this, our birthday, to write you and say I regret the editorial we published about you so many years ago. I only wonder why the idea never occured to me before.

It was the product of the war psychology which is bringing out so many similar expressions today.

I am not planning to publish this myself, but you are perfectly welcome to use it in any way you wish.

Yours sincerely,

Robert R. McCormick

Mr. Henry Ford
Dearborn
Michigan

m

1.

WESTERN UNION TELEGRAM

Form 1206A

Receiver's No.

Check

Time Filed

NEWCOMB CARLTON, PRESIDENT   GEORGE W. E. ATKINS, FIRST VICE-PRESIDENT

CE DESIRED

k an X oppo-
rvice desired:
E MESSAGE
ITTED AS A
LEGRAM

owing message, subject to the terms ereof, which are hereby agreed to

Government Message
Day Letter   Filed 4:24 PM

White House
Washington D C   Dec 19 1923

Henry Ford:

My attention has just been drawn to your interview, declaring your satisfaction with the present National administration and adding that you would not consider running against the present chief executive on any ticket whatever. It is naturally a great gratification to have you take such a position. Your statement will be accepted as the considered pronouncement of a man of great affairs, wide experience and far-seeing judgement regarding the public interest and material concerns of the nation. To have won, in a very brief period of responsibility and opportunity, such a testimony as you have pronounced, is deeply assuring. Your career of service and achievement is the best proof of your ability to judge what will promote the fortunes of the country. I want you to know how highly significant and influential I esteem your declaration. I appreciate and am grateful for it in proportion to my high appraisal of its weight and of your own good judgement.

CALVIN COOLIDGE

2.

and controversy that is the furious dog-eat-dog story of the automobile in America.

To begin with, the staff knew no more about automobiles than that the emergency brake is usually found on the left. Only two or three of them had ever actually seen a Model T. They had only the vaguest notions about Edsel Ford, Charles E. Sorensen, and James Couzens.

3. Henry Ford's universal peace flag. When they dipped into one box they came up with this flag. And this turned out to be the first sort of United Nations flag ever designed; the flag that Ford took abroad on the Peace Ship of 1915 when he hoped to convince Kaiser Wilhelm II to call off the First World War.

When they dipped into another set of boxes they found themselves at the beginning of the finest collection of Edisoniana in existence.

Day after day the coffee went cold as they made the discoveries that scholarly explorers live for: the discovery that Henry Ford first built an airplane in 1910; the moment when Richard Ruddell found Edsel Ford's letter of December 24, 1901 to Santa Claus; the letter from John Dillinger; the letter from Bartolemeo Vanzetti, from the death house on the night before his execution. By invitation, I was the first to dip into the massed cartons of pictures. The picture I pulled out showed Henry Ford speeding over the ice of Lake St. Clair on January 12, 1904, the first man in history to travel ninety miles an hour.

I can remember the difficulty of proving that the man in the mustache was actually Henry Ford, when every oldster interviewed denied that Ford ever had a mustache.

The full story of the Archives, from the swimming pool that became a two-story document file to the flower-cutting room that became a photographic darkroom, is best told in another place; the simplest way to report it here is that Henry Ford's home, where he lived for thirty-three years and where he died in 1947, had been a monumental storehouse of Americana.

Today the Archives holds thousands of shelf-feet of documents, which is the way archivists measure these things. This figure includes about ten million documents, a quarter of a million photographic negatives and prints, and about ten thousand books.

The collections may be roughly divided in this way: 20 percent are records of the Ford family, 70 percent are records of the Ford Motor Company, and 10 percent are records of other companies and other people.

One way to look at all this is to figure that these records represent a pile of paper that would reach to more than six times the height of the Empire State Building.

Another way to look at it is to think that a whole tribe of historians can dig and delve in it freely for a generation and still not exhaust the pleasures its information can bring to people who like to read about America.

I. THE LAND WITHOUT STONES

*With me always are the burning stumps,
the rail fences, the rough roads, the
corded wood, the gathering of the sap
running in the springtime, the forest
all round, the black crows flying
against a wintry sky, the sound of the
woodchopper. . . .*

—FRANK L. STEVENSON

The Irish were always leaving Ireland. In the nineteenth century whole generations of them streamed out of the tired green island, moved by oppression, by famine, or by their own light feet.

One of them, a good man with tools, was William Ford, born on an estate called "Madame" near Ballinascarthy, in County Cork, on December 10, 1826. At the age of twenty, in the second year of the Great Potato Famine, he packed up his "saws and hammers and various tools" and borrowed £2 from a young cousin, who drove him to the station "in a common cart."

And so it was that the father of Henry Ford sailed from Queenstown for America, the land without landlords, the land without stones. It was 1847, a great year for migration and pioneering; farther west than William Ford would ever see, a man named Brigham Young was making ready his Mormons and his covered wagons at Council Bluffs.

The Fords had not always been men of Cork. The faint trail of old parchments starts in England in the early thirteenth century, with the Fords of Somersetshire. There they stayed until 1585, when Queen Elizabeth confiscated a great piece of Ireland, a 600,000-acre parcel. The Queen, who had a hard hand with Catholics, wanted to resettle Ireland with English Protestants. So Protestant men from Somerset and

Devon came over the Irish Sea to Cork, and among them were the Fords.

The mark of the Fords in Cork is not much —stone cottages, mossy stones in churchyards— a good family given neither to crime nor high deeds. Then in 1832 three Ford brothers, uncles of our William Ford, left Ireland on one of the waves of discontent. The American doings of two of them (one uncle died en route in' Pennsylvania) were the talk of the family for fifteen years, and William was brought up on that talk. The uncles had settled in a place called Dearbornville in Michigan. So that became William Ford's goal.

He knew all about Michigan: the huge trees so thick the sky was gloomy, the fat deer and Mr. Bear and Mr. Wolf (the bad animals were always given titles by the settlers), the grassy bottoms where hay was for the taking, the vine-hung streams swimming with fine-eating fish that held still to be speared, the wheat growing round the stumps of your own clearing—and it was said in an old joke that a good shot could bring down four turkeys at once (if they held their heads together).

The Michigan land was so rich that in 1835 a man had already written: "This is a pretty good loam of eighteen inches, [but] I think some of moving off to Kalamazoo where they have it four feet deep and so fat it will grease your fingers."

4. The bark-covered house. In the woodland gloom, wheat stood short and thin around the stumps.

5. The big clearing meant tall crops, as the sun came in. It meant, too, that a settler had learned to swing an axe so that each stroke cut a clean pie-shaped chip precisely toward the heart of the tree.

6. The first railroad train west from Detroit reaches Dearbornville in 1837.

William sailed with a whole boatload of Fords: his grandmother Rebecca, seventy-one, his father John, his mother Thomasine, two brothers and four sisters, and an Uncle Robert and his family. It is much better not to put down all their names because the result is a wild confusion; on the Ford family tree there are some

4.

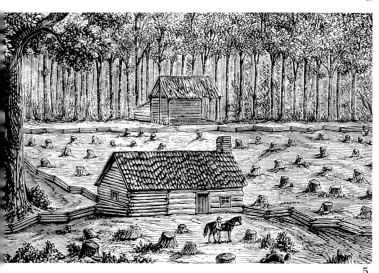

5.

6.

nine Williams, four Rebeccas, six Johns, seven Marys, four Jameses, and four Georges—and at least nine Henrys.

William's mother died just before she reached the Promised Land; one story has it that she was buried at sea, one story says it was at Belle Isle off the coast of Maine, and a third story has it that she reached Quebec and died there in quarantine hospital. Now no one knows or ever will.

The family pushed on west. The route is lost and no guess is very good, but we know the way most people went in those days, the way his uncles had traveled fifteen years before—and things changed slowly then. There were fine roads in the East, great turnpikes made smooth for the Conestoga wagons; there were bits and pieces of railroads; a railroad already led out from Detroit past little Dearbornville on its way to Chicago; and the great canal boom had joined many rivers. But most travel was by waterway and ox team; a horse was too light and fancy to pull heavy wagons through miles and miles of mud.

The route of the Ford uncles had been from New York down across Pennsylvania to Pittsburgh, down the Ohio River to Cincinnati, and then up to Dayton, from there on canalboat by the Portsmouth and Ohio canal to Cleveland, and then by lake boat along Lake Erie to Detroit. It was a weary, long way from Ballinascarthy to the good land.

Dearbornville was eight miles west of the outskirts of Detroit, where already the smoke of factories hung in the air and the famous French pear trees were dying—the pear trees one hundred years old and one hundred feet tall, the pride of Detroit—and most people walked the eight miles. This was 1847, and it was only two years before that the first buggy had been seen in Dearbornville, driven by a wandering missionary preacher named Wells, from River Raisin.

Dearbornville came about because it was exactly one day's journey west from Detroit by ox team. Over the centuries the padding feet of Indians had worn a wide trail from the site of Detroit to the site of Chicago. This, the Sauk Indian trail, became the Chicago Road, then the Chicago Turnpike; now it is Michigan Avenue (U.S. No. 12), 269 miles from city to city.

In those old days the first westering men kept a shrewd eye out along the rivers, looking for a place where the river "fell"; enough of a fall meant riches, for there a man could put up a dam and have himself a millpond and a mill. The shrewd pioneer of Dearborn was a man named A. J. Bucklin. He built a mill on the River Rouge in 1818 and enjoyed immediate prosperity. To Bucklin's mill on the Rouge, hard by the Chicago Trail, came the first settlers on foot, their corn in sacks, dragging their wheat on crude sledges, bringing wool to be carded for the mothers to spin into yarn on the spinning wheels, the black sheep's wool best for brown mitts and wool knit jackets.

Next in Dearbornville came a tavern, nine miles west from Campus Martius in Detroit—the inn on one side of the Chicago Road, the stables on the other side. The proprietor was a British-hater from Albany, named Conrad Ten Eyck. Old "Coon" was a lusty character, hearty, loud, hospitable, and violently pro-American. When the British captured Detroit in the War of 1812, they banished him and forty other men. But years later, in 1838, "Coon" Ten Eyck got his own back. He had become sheriff of Wayne County and a big political figure. Still anti-British, he sympathized with a group of Canadian patriots who were rebelling against the British provincial government across the border. The United States government in Washington was conscientiously neutral; its soldiers at the Dearborn Arsenal and a big militia company known as the Brady Guards stood alert to stop the bootlegging of American arms and ammunition to Canadian rebels.

One day in 1838 Sheriff Ten Eyck had an idea. It came to him on the second floor of a Detroit store. He leaned from the window to shout a loud hint to a group of the unofficial friends of Canada who loitered on the sidewalk. Old Coon roared: "I expect any night that the jail may be raided. We have 150 or 200 muskets in the basement—and the lock on the door is so poor that anybody could break in and get the guns."

This was a sufficient advertisement. The men on the sidewalk looked at each other and drifted away. That night the sheriff was awakened by bad news: a mob had broken into the basement of the jail and seized the muskets.

The Canadian Rebellion failed but jolly Coon Ten Eyck prospered; when oxen and tired guests pulled up at his Dearborn tavern at twilight he would roar to the kitchen: "Sally, put some more wolf steaks on!" (Many years later his daughter Sally rather stiffly denied that they ever cooked wolf meat. "Father was very fond of a joke.")

The tourists today, traveling west from Detroit on Michigan Avenue, can spot the site of the Ten Eyck Tavern; just after you cross Southfield Road you will see in the center of the turnpike a stone monument, marking the old toll house on the plank road. Directly west one hundred yards stood the tavern and its stables. Across Michigan Avenue a little road leads into the woods: up that private road a mile is Fair Lane, Henry Ford's home, and in the basement playroom is a huge brick-and-stone fireplace. Some bricks in that fireplace are all that remain of the Ten Eyck Tavern.

When William Ford trudged into Dearborn on his way to find his uncles, the main buildings in town were three: the Ten Eyck Tavern, Bucklin's mill on the Rouge, and, much more impressive, the Dearborn Arsenal.

II. THE HOMESTEAD

*The natural thing to do
is to work.*
— HENRY FORD

7. *Changing the guard at Dearborn Arsenal,
1867.*

Dearbornville had been named for General
Henry Dearborn, hero in both the Revolutionary
War and the War of 1812 and later Secretary of
War; the Arsenal was a main military depot of
the government from 1833 until 1878, when it
was abandoned because the United States became self-conscious at having a military installation so near its best neighbor.

The Arsenal covered several hundred acres,
on which there were eleven buildings. At one
time there were twelve buildings, but the twelfth
was unofficial: Thompson's Tavern. When a survey showed the Tavern stood on government
land, an officious commandant ordered his reluctant troops to tear it down and stack the lumber outside the boundary. The sober settlers in
the Ford settlement and the Scotch settlement
took this news without a quiver. But thirsty
frontiersmen took the news hard. A mob was
formed of the most distinguished wolf-killing,
bear-slaying citizens; they marched on the Arsenal for a free-swinging riot. As always, the
government won.

8. *Some of Henry Ford's "uncles," not true
uncles, but cousins of his father. These were the
men who greeted Henry's father, William Ford,
when he arrived from Ireland: Samuel and James,
standing, and George, William, and Henry
Ford, sitting. The William above was called William North; Henry's father was called William
South. The Uncle Henry on the right is the one
for whom Henry Ford was named. He helped
organize the first Dearborn band in 1862, and
played the fife. One of Henry's first teachers,
Frank R. Ward, played flute in the same band,
and they paraded and played in the Dearborn*

7.

8.

8

bandwagon, almost exactly like the one below.

9. The Plymouth bandwagon, 1868. This was "fresh after the war," as they said in those days, and all the bandsmen wore Phil Sheridan mustaches or Abe Lincoln beards. The special bandwagons were Brewster green, with yellow spoke wheels and a flag socket next to the whip socket.

9.

Ford, as a collector of Americana, found and restored the Dearborn bandwagon in which Uncle Henry had played—it is in the Ford Museum today. He could not find an oldtime picture of it, but he did find this picture, taken in Plymouth only a few miles away. He must have liked it very much, for he had a huge enlargement framed for the wall of his farm-office hideout, where he could see it every day.

This has the true American look of those times, when Henry Ford was five years old: the hitching racks for the horses, the town square for big doings, the wooden sidewalks, the emptiness, the quiet.

William Ford walked into Dearbornville, the uncles put up the pack of new Ford immigrants, and William went to work. There was always work to be done and not just on frontiers, as his son would preach years later: "More men seek wages than seek work. If work be put first, then we shall get somewhere—for the amount of work to be done is always unlimited."

As was the custom, Father John Ford went immediately into debt, buying eighty acres for $350. The family anxiety was never food or shelter or clothing but simply cash, actual money, to pay the debt. William started as a carpenter for the Michigan Central Railroad and farmed with all his might in whatever time he had to spare.

A few years later John Ford was free and clear, with a house on Joy Road, his sons grown, and his daughters growing. Then William Ford, saving his money hard, went with his cousin Henry (the fife-playing uncle) to do some carpenter work for one Patrick O'Hern.

Patrick O'Hern (Henry Ford always insisted the name was properly Ahern, but he was a poor speller) was another man of Cork, born at Fair Lane, Cork City on March 17, 1804. When times were bad in 1830 he had enlisted in the British Army, which shipped him to Quebec. There he

10.

11.

promptly skipped the Army, took a ferry to Detroit, and found work helping to build the Dearborn Arsenal. He also built a log cabin, married Margaret Stevens, a spinster some years older than he, and adopted a child, Fannie. But all his life he kept secret that he had deserted from the British Army.

Then, on a day before the Fourth of July, only a year or two before his death in 1882, the secret popped out. He and William Ford were in Detroit to get fireworks for the children when William Ford proposed they cross over the river to see some fine horse races that day in Canada.

"It will take but an hour," argued William, who liked a good horse.

"I cannot go," said Patrick O'Hern, though a lover of horse racing.

"Why not?" said William. "We will have time for the chores."

And now, after all the years with his secret, Patrick confessed. "There will be strangers and officers of Canada there, and when I first came to this country I deserted the army at Quebec. I do not want to be recognized." And he stubbornly would not go, though the chance of arrest was remote: so ran the story our Henry Ford told young Ann Hood, a schoolgirl reporter who came to know him better than almost anyone.

Patrick O'Hern loved his wife dearly, but she could not have children. So as their adopted Fannie grew up, they cast about for another child to raise. According to one story, in 1842 two friends, a lawyer, Sylvester Larned, and a Thomas Palmer, told them of an orphan girl.

This was Mary Litogot, born in 1840, who became the mother of Henry Ford. There are almost no other actual facts about her, and this was a heartache all his life to Henry Ford. He spent much money on genealogical research and never found a fact. Mary's mother was dead (no one recalls how and when); her father, a carpenter, had been killed in a fall from a roof (it was said).

Mary had three brothers, Sapharia (also spelled Sophira and Saphara, but the Fords called him Saffarius), Barney, and John. But the O'Herns could adopt only the one girl, and the boys grew up somehow.

10. William Ford, father of Henry, combed to

the nines, with the stern man-about-to-be-executed look that was required by portrait photography in the 1870's: you had to hold still or pay double.

11. Twelve good men and true, a Dearborn jury; the obvious man of substance, the foreman third from the left in front, is William Ford.

12. Mary Litogot Ford, mother of Henry. This is the only known picture of her, although her son tried all his life to find another. We do not even know how old she is in this picture.

13. John Litogot, Mary's younger brother, on the right, in uniform; Andrew Threadgould on the left; and there is a story about them which shows the times.

When the draft came in the Civil War, Andrew paid John Litogot $1,000 to serve in his place. This kind of bargain was common enough; while the contract was fresh they had this picture taken together.

Young John marched bravely off on August 29, 1862, in Company K of the Twenty-Fourth Michigan Infantry. A few months later, on December 12, he was killed by Confederate artillery fire at First Fredericksburg.

Back home meanwhile, his oldest brother, Sapharia, had married one Lethera Brown, and they had three children; but in 1867 Lethera left Sapharia to marry this same Andrew Threadgould.

But Mary Litogot's other brother Barney fought all through the war, came safely home, and lived to become a lighthouse keeper, fathering four children—somehow steering clear of Andrew Threadgould.

In Michigan there was lots of work to be done, clearing, building, farming, and then clearing farther woods; the sun began to find broad fields all over the rich state, the wild game moving slowly north, the sawmills, the smithies, and the iron foundries dotting the streams and the crossroads, and ever the creaking wagonloads of people plodding west.

William worked, and sometime in the late 1850's met young Mary Litogot O'Hern. On September 15, 1858, he bought the southern half of his father's eighty acres for $600, while his brother Samuel bought the northern half

12.

13.

14.

15.

for the same sum: substantial money when cash was almost a curiosity.

On April 25, 1861, William Ford, thirty-five, married Mary Litogot, now twenty-one, in the house of Thomas Maybury in Detroit. They moved into a splendid new white-painted seven-room frame house that William had built to hold the O'Herns: it was big enough for all of them. Over the years four rooms were added, and in 1867 Patrick O'Hern drew up a formal deed selling the house and land to William Ford for a nominal $400, providing that Patrick retained "full use and possession, occupancy, Rents and profits, of said Land, during the life time of said Grantor."

This was the Homestead, where Henry Ford was born and raised. And there the O'Herns and the William Fords lived affectionately together until Patrick and his wife, Margaret, died, she, in 1870, and he in 1882, long after. But until he died he kept all her clothing as it had been when she was alive.

On January 29, 1862, William and Mary Litogot Ford had a son who died at birth. So the next birth was an anxious time. On a full-moon midsummer night in the next year, William Ford rode for the midwife, Grandma Holmes. They arrived at dawn of July 30, 1863—the sun rose that day at 4:50 A.M. (old time, that is, suntime).

Not long after, at 7 A.M., Henry Ford was born, well-formed and sound.

14. The Ford Homestead as it actually was, before the turn of the century, at Ford Road and Greenfield. Here Henry Ford, his three brothers, and two sisters were born; here his mother died. When he was old and rich he moved this house to the great museum-park called Greenfield Village; there it now stands, antiseptically prettied up and freshly painted. It is now open to the public, and many interested scholars get in, to find everything in place from cords of wood out back to needles and thread in the bureau drawers, reconstructed exactly from Ford's memory. This picture was almost certainly taken by Henry himself, around 1896.

15. The first picture of Henry Ford, aged two and one-half to three years, which would put this in the winter, 1865–66. Only the lace was retouched on this print, found in the basement of his home, Fair Lane.

The Homestead

16. The crib in which he slept in his mother's bedroom.

17. The organ in the parlor, where he first heard all the songs later played so often on the Ford Sunday Evening Hour. It was a footpumper, but when he restored the Homestead, Ford had the organ electrified and often spent quiet hours alone here, one-fingering his way through "Turkey in the Straw" or "Kathleen Mavourneen." The stove was a parlor feature in his time, and Ford spent much money in a long search to find an exact duplicate of the stove he grew up around.

18. The kitchen in the Homestead. Note the elevated oven, a no-stoop feature of the time. When Ford restored the house he had the earth around it carefully sifted. This turned up small shards of original broken dishes, cups, and saucers; from them manufacturers were able to make duplicates, shown here on the shelves.

19. The interior: beyond this parlor are the living room, the dining room, and the kitchen beyond that; the whole substantial house had an easy, comfortable spread. William Ford was a churchwarden who married people, a justice of the peace, a solid figure in town councils, a man who read every day not only the county paper but also a New York newspaper and who all his life never ceased to marvel that a famine-driven Irish immigrant boy could find himself the owner of honest acres in a free land.

16.

17.

19.

18.

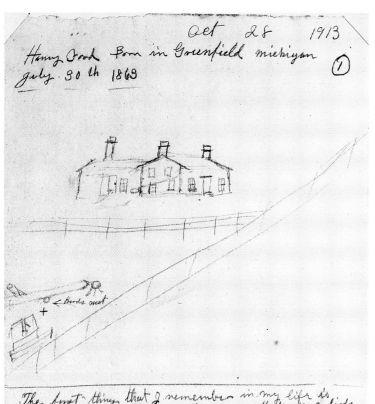

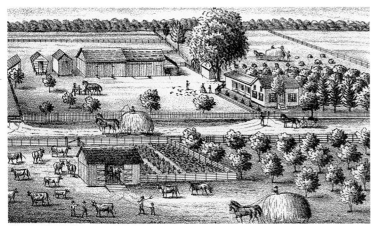

20.

21.

III. MOTHER AND McGUFFEY

The more a boy or a man knows, the more chance he has to become a leader.
—HENRY FORD

Reading the Ford handwriting is tricky enough even when he wrote things out carefully. But hundreds of the entries in his little "jotbooks" were written while he was jogging around the countryside in a Model T, and they simply defy deciphering. The notes consist of cryptic zig-zag reminders, some of them hilarious, sawed-off epigrams, shopping lists, diagrams of machinery, recipes, lists of piano rolls to buy. (In over thirty-odd years of jotting down "Tales from the Vienna Woods" he never spelled the title the same twice and never once correctly.) Some of the notes that begin most interestingly turn out to be the most impenetrable.

20. His first memory. This note, exactly transcribed, reads:

> *The first thing that I remember in my life is my Father taking my brother John and myself to see a bird's nest under a large oak log twenty rods East of our Home and my birth place, John was so young that he could not walk Father carried Him I being two years older could run along with them this must have been about the year of 1866 in June I remember the nest with 4 eggs and also the bird and hearing it sing I have always remembered the song and in later years found that it was a song sparrow, I remember the log layed in the field for a good many years this field was pasture there was a mill clost to the log where the cows used to drink now 1913 there is slight deppression where the well was and the field is a fine meadow now.*

21. Farm work and housework were hard. William Ford grew wheat and hay, tended

14

horses and sheep and cows and pigs, cut wood, pruned his apple and peach orchards, carpentered for pay, smoked his bacon, salted his pork, dug and filled his vegetable pits for the winter, tapped his maples for sugar, made and repaired his own tools, built and painted his own walls, fished, hunted, trapped, tanned skins, and went by the ancient ethics of farming that to plow a crooked furrow was a disgrace. Mary Ford cooked, washed, churned, made candles and soap, knitted, preserved, and gardened.

Young Henry loathed all this farm labor. He was sluggish on the way to a chore and light-footed on the way back. At a very early age he began to transform this normal aversion for chores into a philosophy about farm work. "My earliest recollection is that, considering the results, there was too much work on the place."

After tending chickens a few years, he reacted strongly against chickens all his life, even the eating of them. "Chicken is fit only for hawks."

After a few years of milking cows he reacted even more strongly against cows, taking out his distaste in a lifelong attack on milk. In his jot-books appears the phrase: "Milk is a mess." While he grudgingly granted that milk was full of vitamins and stuff, he searched sporadically over the years for a substitute, once jotting down a heartfelt complaint: "We MUST make milk out of something—Heaven can't."

One deep root of this intense dislike for farm work was his instinct for machinery. "This is what took me into mechanics." This became a profound belief, expressed years later: "I want to take the work off men's backs and lay it on steel and motors."

Over six decades he spent much time trying to perfect a farm tractor, and the principle of taking the hard work out of work became the base of the manufacturing system that he developed into mass production. Wherever possible, let machines do it, ran Ford's credo, and of all his achievements perhaps the greatest were the innumerable ways in which he did lift the weight from workers' backs. All these were expressions of his boyhood feeling that farm work was messy, disorganized, and brutally hard.

But in the times of Henry Ford's childhood the chores came first. Schooling, while much re-

spected, was worked in during the slack season—and things didn't slacken up much around a frontier farm until after Christmas. For after the corn and the wheat were harvested, there were still the potatoes and the fruit to be picked (Henry was known to have had an especially slow foot in getting started on the apple picking), and then the farm was cleaned up and made ready for winter; and a snowfall meant timber-cutting time, with lots of work for small boys in picking up branches and twigs. Many a farm youngster must have prayed for the school season to start, not so much because he craved learning but simply because he wanted to sit down.

Young Henry, at the age of seven and one-half, was to have started school on January 2, 1871. But the snow was too deep, the weather too cold. His mother held him back a week, and he started on January 9, at the Scotch Settlement School.

That one-room school, with the iron stove and the McGuffey Readers, of course came long before John Dewey and progressive education. Teacher and child alike would have been baffled by "the problem of the child's adjustment to society." In those times the children could hardly wait to grow up and get their hands on society and adjust *it*. No McGuffey-raised child would have understood Eliot's "trembling and afraid/ In a world I never made"; probably every man jack of them would have preferred Shakespeare's "The world is mine oyster/Which I with sword will open."

This climate of enterprise was the scene of Henry Ford's first invention, a regrettable katzenjammer type. In those days the most extreme punishment for misbehavior was to make the bad boy sit with a girl; this awful shame broke the hardiest spirit. On a day when one such sinner was being disciplined, young Henry spent a quiet recess boring two small holes in the seat of punishment; he placed a needle point upward in one hole, ran a connecting string down the other hole and under the bench to his own seat. This engineering brought gratifyingly shrill results.

Almost nothing about Henry Ford is an absolute fact, and you may as well face it now. Several sources say that a Miss Emilie Nardin was Henry's first teacher, and this seems reasonable,

22.

23.

for she roomed with the Ford family. But others say the first teacher was Margaret Stevenson, daughter of one of the first settlers. Still others say that Frank R. Ward, fife-player in the Dearborn bandwagon, was the first. Henry himself agreed with all these versions when he was reminiscing.

22. But Henry did not always agree. On the margin of this picture he once wrote: "My First Teacher," and we may as well settle for that. This is John Brainard Chapman, who kept the pupils at it from 9 A.M. until 4:30 P.M., with a half-hour recess and an hour's lunch. Chapman was massive enough to cope with husky children. This emphasis on strength rather than scholarship was a wise old American frontier custom; Abraham Lincoln's first teacher in Knob Creek, Kentucky was one Caleb Hazel, also hired for his size. One of Henry's schoolmates, John Haggerty, said: "They used to pay the teacher $45 a month. But we used to need extra discipline when Henry and I went there so they hired a cooper—his name was J. B. Chapman—and they paid him $5 a month above the scale. That man could have told Henry and me all he knew in 10 minutes. But he weighed 275 pounds and it was the weight that really counted."

But Henry loved good-humored Teacher Chapman, and when the ex-cooper later moved to the Miller School, Henry followed him.

23. Edsel Ruddiman was Henry's first seatmate in school. The two sat together, heavy with mischief, at a wooden double-desk on which they carved their initials in artistic deep relief. Behind his geography Henry tinkered on watches, with his teacher's permission; but he was not allowed to use a file—the squeaking file made too much noise. The curriculum consisted of the magnificent McGuffey Readers, filled with agonizing moral stories in which the bad boys met horrible deaths and the good boys became Presidents.

To the end of his days, Ford, like all his generation, lived in McGuffeyland. It was a wonderful land, with never a juvenile delinquent in it, because old William McGuffey's shrewdly chosen dramatic readings plunged their morals home like hot pokers, scarring the pupils all their lives with a stiff conscience, a clear knowledge of right and wrong, and an ineradicable appetite for Fourth of July oratory.

Mother and McGuffey

The McGuffey Readers taught children the love of animals and birds, duty to parents, friends, country, and God. They taught conscience, a concept that began to fade out in the 1920's—the word and the idea are almost obsolete today. They taught right and wrong, beyond the Ten Commandments, beyond the Boy Scout list of virtues, right on down to such things as punctuality, with such black-and-white clarity that a truly taught McGuffeyite would suffer terrible pangs all his life whenever he was five minutes late. And it was this kind of morality that gave Shaw and Ibsen their ready-made audience; for if tardiness were a sin, what of Hedda Gabler? Like every McGuffey-taught child, Ford could quote his Readers line for line to the end of his life. It was there, for example, in the *First Reader*, that he learned the hard fate of a bad boy:

24. *"Poor Frank was dead." A page from Mc-Guffey.*

25. *The McGuffey cabin. Not only did Henry move his first schoolhouse brick by brick to Greenfield Village, but also, in 1934, he sent crews and trucks to the hills of southwestern Pennsylvania to bring back this rugged little white-washed log house. This is the birthplace of William Holmes McGuffey, 1800–73, complete down to the clock that marked time for McGuffey as a boy.*

In addition to McGuffey, Henry's mother provided a similar influence that was just as deep and lasting. Like McGuffey, she was passionate about cleanliness, order, courage, patience, and self-discipline. But where Schoolmaster McGuffey had to operate at long distance, she was as near as the woodshed and the dinner table—and her teachings sank in.

If even a third of the things her son later wrote about her are true, she was a notably clear-headed and straight-thinking woman. Beyond all else she taught him one great lesson about living, about adjusting to people and to life, a lesson that cannot be taught out of books but can only be hammered out in the give-and-take of everyday life:

She taught us what the modern family needs to learn—the art of being happy with each other . . . that if we couldn't be happy here in this house we'd never be happy anywhere else.

Look, look, is not this Frank Brown? What can be the mat-ter with him?

The poor boy is dead. He was on his way to school, when a bad boy met him, and said:

"Come, Frank, go with me to the pond." "O no," said Frank, "I can not; I must go to school."

But the bad boy told him it was not time to go to school. So Frank went with him to the pond.

Do you see the bad boy? He stands by the side of the man.

Frank fell in-to the pond, and the bad boy could not help him out.

He cried, "Help, help!" A man heard him, and ran to the pond. But when he got there, poor Frank was dead.

What will his pa-rents do when he is ta-ken home dead?

Do not stop to play on your way to school. Do not play with bad boys. They will lead you in-to harm.

24.

25.

Father's Good Angels.

THERE are 140,000 saloons in the country, against 128,000 schools and only 54,000 churches. Manufacturers and sellers of strong drink, 560,000—twelve times the number of clergymen, four times the teachers, nearly double all the lawyers, physicians, ministers, and teachers combined. In these saloons there are 5,600,000 daily customers, one in seven of our whole population. Of these, 100,000 are annually imprisoned for crime, at an expense of $90,000,000, and 150,-000 go down to the drunkard's grave, leaving 200,000 beggared orphans.

Grasp these figures. An army of topers five abreast, one hundred miles in length. A file of men seventy-five miles long, marching steadily down to the grave; three every minute throughout the year.

26a.

26b.

Mary Ford taught her eldest son not to lie. One whole day she would not speak to him, he confessed:

> Shame cuts more deeply than a whip. For a day I was treated with contempt. There was no smiling or glossing over my shortcomings. I learned from her that wrong-doing carries its own punishment. There is no escape.

She taught him without raising her hand or her voice; particularly she taught him to work without grumbling: to do what has to be done, and get it over with cheerfully. She held him to the chores he hated, telling him "that 'I don't want to' gets a fellow nowhere." She said to him:

> Life will give you many unpleasant tasks to do; your duty will be hard and disagreeable and painful . . . but you must do it. You may have pity on others but you must not pity yourself.

A major influence in the lives of all Americans in those days was the almanac. It was the friend of the farmer—and nearly everyone was a farmer. But it was something more, much more. With an almanac in the house—and almost all homes had several almanacs—you scarcely had any need for a newspaper or a magazine. You knew when the eclipses were coming, what the weather would be all year, when to plant, and when to harvest. But you also got the benefit of the newest jokes, all sorts of household hints (how to tie the curtains back when you were sweeping the carpet with the broom), and whole collections of interesting facts about such things as the number of wives various Shahs and Pashas had.

26a, b, c. The great conditioners. Henry Ford collected almanacs, as he came to collect most American things—and these pictures may well have been among those that he pondered at night in the Homestead as a small boy. They are contemporary—and the pictures have the breath of the times, an innocence and peace that are evident in the attitudes you see here.

But the real tale of Henry's boyhood is outside both Mother and McGuffey and lies in his three passions: for mischief, for wheels, and against farm work. With a boy's instinct for combinations, he managed at times to put all three together, and those days, no doubt, were the happiest of his young life.

To his aversion to chickens and to cows, he now added horses, and this time he had a real grievance. One day he was on a frisky new colt named Jennie when a cow rose suddenly from a ditch. The frightened Jennie reared and bolted, throwing Henry—but with his foot still caught in the stirrup. He was dragged "all the way back home" until Jennie jerked free, leaving him bruised, lame, disgusted with horses, and with a new count against cows.

Ford's horseless carriage might be explained by a humorless psychologist as his classic revenge on the breed, and it is certainly true that he had very little truck with horses the rest of his life. At the time Jennie threw and dragged him, 1872, there were 8,000,000 horses in the United States. A half century later Henry wrote in one of his jotbooks a gleeful note: "The Horse is DONE."

His taste for mischief flowered among the rich opportunities open to the frontier farm boy; no modern juvenile delinquent, whose horizons go no farther than stealing from a fruit stand, can envision the dazzling vistas of imaginative mischief that lay before a boy in Henry Ford's time and place. Henry himself was a tame sort, heavily conditioned by Mother and McGuffey, but it was now that he developed a taste for practical jokes that would last until his faculties failed.

Once he was almost caught stealing watermelons; once he almost lost a finger investigating the hay-chopper; once he took home a schoolmate's handsome new pencil case, but his conscience hurt so hard all night that he arose early to take it back; once he traded his lunch sandwiches for cake, got the stomachache, and his brother John tattled on him.

He learned to skate—soon after the Civil War a national craze for ice skating spread over every American pond and stream that would freeze—and could cut a creditable figure 8.

His liking for practical jokes was reinforced from a new direction when Father William Ford employed various German immigrants as hired hands—these were refugees from the Franco-Prussian War of 1870, and they brought a hardy kind of Teutonic humor to Michigan that fitted in well. Their jokes are lost to history, except that once they gave Henry a chew of tobacco which first made him feel that he was floating and then made him very sick; but one of his revenges, complicated but thoughtful, survives.

26c.

19

from seven on i had a mechanical turn
i made water wheels and steam engines
the first was a water wheel in the ditch and then
at school where we drove a coffee grinder
and ground clay which was verry slow then
i got a ten gallon tin can made a furnace
of clay brick bats made turbine steam Engine
with tin blades and Pop gun Elder for steam
pipe and blocks of wood for Elbows and couplings
the steam gague was a lever arranged on the
bottom of the can sow that when the
preasure raised bottom sprang out indicated
the preasure on a half circle we never
got over ten lbs of steam the turbine
ran verry fast three Thousend RPM
it did not develope mutch Power about
ten of my school mates would go
to the RR and pick up Cole to burn
the boiler finally blew up and scalded
three of us and i carry a scar on my
cheek it sat the fence on fire and
raised ned in general

27.

Steam

stones

Blew a piece thru my lip, and a piece hit Robert Blake in the stomach abdomen, and put him out.

28a.

The German hired hands had filled Henry's bed with burrs. After some study, Henry struck back. He pondered over the fact that they smoked their evening pipes beneath a big willow tree near the porch of the Homestead. He bored a hole in a bucket, cut a rubber stopper to fit the hole, ran a cord from the stopper over the house and under the porch, filled the bucket with water, and set it up in the tree. In the after-dinner twilight, when the pipes were nicely aglow, Henry, sitting innocently nearby on the porch, gave a casual twitch to the cord.

Such mechanics came easily to Henry because, from the age of seven, he had wheels in his head. His thirst for mechanics and machinery was insatiable. Consider these:

He wrote: "My mother always said I was a born mechanic." "There is an immense amount to be learned simply by tinkering with things. It is not possible to learn from books how everything is made."

His sister Margaret said: "He always investigated things. If we had toys, it was always, 'Don't let Henry see them! He'll take them apart!' He liked to see what made them run."

He said: "I was always tinkering with wheels. My father used to give me Caesar."

A neighbor said: "Every clock in the Ford home shuddered when it saw him coming."

He made little sleighs and little hand wagons. He had a shop in a shed, twelve by sixteen feet, and in it he accumulated tools. He traded marbles with other boys for clock wheels. When one of the German hired hands went to Detroit he would stop at Engelbert Grimm's jewelry store to buy Henry a handful of clock wheels at ten for a penny.

His father often took him to Detroit; once in 1870 they stopped at the railroad roundhouse to see the locomotives. An engineer named Tommy Garrett explained steam to the little seven-year-old. A few days later, after a light snowfall, Henry got out his sled, borrowed two of his mother's kettles, filled one with burning coals, put the other on top filled with boiling water, and then drew the sled around the yard, playing locomotive. Seventy years later Henry Ford still remembered Engineer Garrett's name.

His love for tools was great enough to overcome even his aversion to cows and chores: once he made a whole dollar, driving cattle for a neighbor, Melvin Newton, walking a full seventeen miles. He spent this fortune on tools.

When he was seven, one of the German farmhands, Adolph Culling, let him examine a watch carefully, for the first time. Culling explained the mysteries of the escapement, the jewels, the wheels, the hands. (This very watch is in Greenfield Village, on display.) Thereafter young Henry spent his time with his nose to Grimm's jewelry shop window, watching the watchmakers work.

He studied as only a boy can study, with absolute concentration. He went to the Nicholson File Company in Detroit to see how they made files by hand and then made his own. From knitting needles he made small screwdrivers.

27. A page from Henry's notebook. A small coffee grinder was young Henry's universal machine, used in all his major boyhood experiments with steam. With two friends he built a waterwheel on the creek which ran through John Miller's farm and made a dam. Overnight the dam flooded a field of potatoes, and Farmer Miller closed the experiment out.

28a, b, c. Henry's note on a forge he and his friends made. Since John Haggerty had the only wagon, he was chosen to get the coal; he trundled along the Michigan Central Railroad tracks for three miles. The coal made a fine fire, and in an iron ladle they melted all the bits of tin and lead they could find—casting the melted mixture in molds they had made. In Henry's note on the explosive experiment he leaves out only one point: that when the boiler blew up and the schoolhouse fence caught fire, the teacher closed out these experiments.

29. Henry's note on his first watch repair. At age twelve, Henry often walked after school to Detroit and back, sometimes hooking a ride home on the train, sometimes reaching home frozen and weary as late as 3 A.M., but with his head filled with the mechanical wonders of Detroit. This note refers to a morning in 1876 at Sunday School in the old Scotch Settlement Church on Warren Avenue. After Henry "saw what was rong" in the watch he ran to the carpenter shop of another "uncle" who lived nearby. There Henry shaped a shingle nail on the grindstone into a tiny screwdriver; from his pocket he took

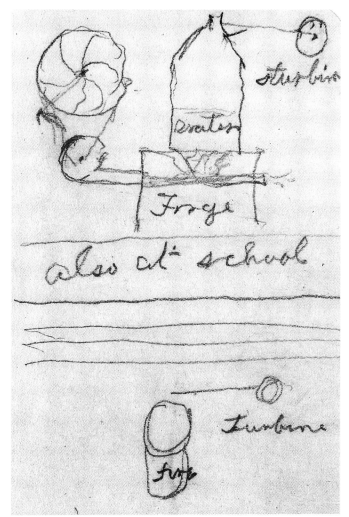

28b.

28c.

a pair of tweezers he had made from one of his mother's corset stays and with these tools he opened up the watch, unscrewing the cap which covered the balance wheel. The trouble: the escapement lever had "overbanked" because of vibration; the roller jewel was not between the horns of the escapement lever but resting against one horn. He lifted the cap over the balance wheel with the tweezers and dropped it back; the roller jewel fell into place in the notch of the escapement lever; he replaced the screw, and the watch ran. He was then thirteen years old.

Many years later, with the very same watch, he did it all over again for Ann Hood. He told her:

> I really did not know what made it overbank, but I was so pleased it ran again that I did not try to find out. Three years later I learned more. I got the watch again, took out the lever, embedded it in plaster, and put just a bit of solder on the end of this safety finger so the lever could not turn back because of vibration until this finger came into the crescent on the roller.

30. Henry's window workshop, in his bedroom in the Homestead, exactly as he restored it. His sister Margaret, who married Edsel Ruddiman's brother, James, and who at 90 was still lively as a cricket, vigorously denied that he ever had such a work shelf. But Henry vowed that this shelf was no fiction, that he worked at nights when he was supposed to be asleep, and that the whole system was quickly demountable so it could be shoved under the bed instantly at the sound of an investigative footstep. The lantern kept his feet warm on winter nights.

Henry Ford was not yet thirteen when his mother died suddenly. She was only thirty-seven. Her first child had been born dead, but thereafter she had borne Henry, John, Margaret, Jane, William, and Robert without difficulty. But something went wrong when her eighth child died at birth on March 17, 1876. Twelve days later, on March 29, she died. Henry said later, making the most powerful comparison he knew: "The house was like a watch without a mainspring."

From now on his education was in his own hands—and by his own tastes. Irresistibly, inevitably, he moved toward wheels and machines and away from the farm.

The first watch I fixed was after Sunday school Albert Hutchings came out of the Gardner House with a big watch Chain on his vest I wanted to see it it was stoped I worked in it and saw what was rong

29.

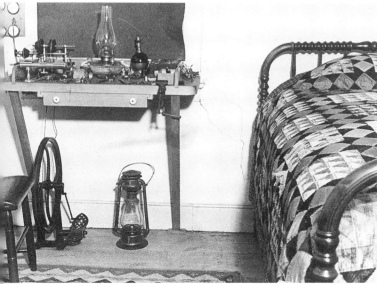

30.

22

IV. THE ENGINE THAT
RAN ON THE ROAD

*Machines are to a mechanic
what books are to a writer.*
—HENRY FORD

31.

31. The engine that ran on the road. Here it all started. If Henry Ford were still alive, he would perhaps point to this as the most important picture in this book. He kept a huge framed enlargement of it hanging in his hideout, where he could see it every day of his grown-up life. It was a profound symbol to him; it almost exactly reproduces the great single moment in his childhood, the moment that fixed his life, a moment of deep traumatic shock.

In any biography there are certain key points of interest. One is always: What made him that way? How did it all start? What was the decisive experience? Men are complex, experiences are lost or buried, biographers grapple with their jigsaw puzzles—but in Henry Ford's case it is quite simple. It is all here in this picture. It did more work than men's backs could do; it moved from place to place under its own power.

This is a road-roller, enormous, clanking, puffing steam. But the moment and the machine are almost like the moment and the machine he experienced when he was a boy. It was only a few months after his mother died; he was thirteen years old, riding toward Detroit with his father in a wagon. It was a clear, hot day in July, 1876. Suddenly the wagon came upon this astounding monster.

32a, b. One of Henry's memos on his experience written later. He also wrote about it himself forty-seven years later, in 1923:

I can remember that engine as though I had seen it only yesterday . . . I was off the wagon and talking to the engineer before my father

*In July 1876.
The first portable Engine came in our part of the Country it was owned by Mr Fred Reden, it was a 11.H.P. N.S.S. of Battle Creek Mich. that showed me that I was by instinct an Engineer.*

32a.

*Mr Reden
Let me fire and run the engine many times that and next year.
He was a good and kind man;
we have an Engine like it in the museum.*

32b.

knew what I was up to. It was simply a portable engine and boiler mounted on wheels with
a water tank and a coal cart trailing behind.

All such engines he had ever seen before had
been hauled from farm to farm by horses; "this
one had a chain that made a connection between
the engine and the rear wheels."

And consider his testimony in 1919, on another
hot July day, in the *Chicago Tribune* suit:

Q. How many turns a minute did these Nichols,
Shepard & Co. engines run?
A. I suppose about 200. [Ford had the Ameri-
can countryman's habit of using the word
"about" for "exactly."]
Q. Why do you suppose; why don't you re-
member?
A. Because I never counted them.
Q. Why do you guess 200?
A. Because I asked the man that was running
it how fast the engine ran and he told me 200
turns a minute; and I have never forgotten it.
Q. And you remember that ever since you were
a boy?
A. Yes, sir, as distinctly as anything I can re-
member yesterday.

The machine young Henry saw was not the
machine shown here; and they were in a wagon,
not a buggy. But this picture captured for him
that decisive moment of shock, clarity, and vision.

Later he discovered the faults of those steam-
engines. They did not supply enough power for
each pound of their own weight. They were huge
and heavy and yet weak and brittle. They de-
voured fuel. They were hard to start. They were
clumsy and unresponsive. They could not go
everywhere one might want to go. They were
slow.

But they were moving machines, glittering
with brass and moving parts. They were mobile
without having to run on tracks. They were the
opposite of horses and cows and farm animals.

To him the machine he saw that day was the
pure definition of machinery.

The day that the huge iron monster loomed
on the road before the farm wagon was the day
everything came together in Henry Ford's mind.
It was a day that would later change the face of
the world and the habits of men.

The year 1876 was a decisive one for him: his
mother died and the image of the moving machine became fixed in his mind. But there was
still another event to come. His father went to
the fair.

Now 1876 was a year of great churning in the
Republic, one of those years in which one brilliant, desperate, profound, comic, or tragic event
succeeded another so fast that no American could
keep pace with the news—a year in which great
events occurred beneath the surface but did not
become news until the historians put things together. It was a tremendous time to be alive: it
was the most American year yet, which was fitting, because this was the hundredth year since
the nation was born.

This was the year that Sitting Bull trapped
golden-haired George Custer in a last stand at
the Little Big Horn, with the horse Comanche
the only survivor. It was also the year that a cross-
eyed drunk named Jack McCall walked bow-
legged into a saloon in Deadwood City and blew
out Wild Bill Hickok's brains as Bill studied
a poker hand of two aces and two eights.

This was the year the National League was
formed in baseball, and a tall right-hander named
Albert G. Spalding, who had pitched every game
of the season for Boston two years before (he
won fifty-two, lost eighteen, and so did Boston),
jumped over to the Chicago White Sox, and most
of Boston went into mourning.

Intercollegiate football and track and field ath-
letics officially began that year; Hambletonian,
the great trotting stallion, died, having sired
1,331 foals; Mark Twain was advertising his
"Type-Writer"; a pale, quick, slender young man
named Alexander Graham Bell finished developing his "telephone"; and the most savage of all
American presidential campaigns saw Rutherford
B. Hayes beat out James G. Blaine for the Republican nomination and then apparently lose
the election to the Democrat, Samuel J. Tilden,
by 184 to 163 electoral votes. After weeks of national suspense and fierce argument a commission
of eight Republicans and seven Democrats voted
Hayes in as President, by a vote of eight to seven.

But of all events the greatest still was the Centennial Exposition of 1876 in Philadelphia.

There the great inventor, Thomas A. Edison,
had an exhibit, although this was three years before he would invent the light bulb and one

year before he would invent the talking machine.

There stood the enormous two-story high Corliss steam engine, the biggest ever built, generating 1,600 horsepower. There was the new invention, the band saw, with which carpenters would curlicue and festoon the American front porch for a generation of jigsaw architecture. There were the enormous cannon from the Krupp works in Germany; the great British inventions of the Maudsley lathe, the planer, and the milling machine; the actual hand and the torch from a great statue that French sculptors had not yet completed, to be called the Statue of Liberty and to be set up in New York harbor.

In Dearborn the summer went, the harvest came, and then September: and William Ford clapped on his best hat and took a trip, his first big journey in the twenty-nine years since he left County Cork.

Touring for pleasure was almost unknown, even to the very rich, for this was long before his son would make possible See-America-First and motels. Only a handful of Americans had ever traveled over twenty-five miles an hour except on a railroad train. There were no gum wrappers in the geysers of Yellowstone, no forests had burned because of a flipped cigarette, there were no secret ingredients in gasoline, no drive-in theaters, no car-hops, no eight-lane highways with cloverleafs and underpasses; and it was still impossible to drive two horses head on into each other.

In those days people would not even endure the discomfort of railroad travel unless there was a big occasion. The Exposition was the occasion: all the thirty-eight states, all the forty-five million people rumbled with the excitements on view in Philadelphia. But the eight million Americans who went to the birthplace of the Republic to celebrate American independence promptly forgot it all when they saw the new marvels of science.

The big news was not liberty but machinery.

Some men stood all day watching the vast steam-engines and hurried back at opening time the next morning to see if it were really true.

From all the land special trains rattled toward Philadelphia. In the *Michigan Farmer* appeared advertisements of a special excursion rate, Detroit to Philadelphia, $2.50, and a catalog of the dates of exhibitions and events. After some study, for this was no frivolous matter, four men of Dearborn settled on the dates of the trials of steam plows and road engines. The four were William Ford, two neighbors, Anthony Horger and William Leslie, and young George Ford, son of that "uncle" for whom our Henry was named. And George became a family joke, the kind where someone is always sure to say "Tell about the time George . . ." and everyone whoops, because he got so excited over the departure that he ran out to the wagon and climbed in—without noticing that the horses hadn't been brought up for the harnessing.

All we know about the trip is just that much. But what happened everywhere in the United States must have happened also in Dearborn: the travelers returned, loaded with catalogs, programs, and special illustrated editions, and held forth at gatherings on the marvels they had seen; and we can guess that young Henry cross-examined his father and pored over all the printed matter. He was not the only boy stimulated by that first great exposition; a whole generation was suddenly awakened, as if by blinding lightning; the two words, "science," and "invention," suddenly came to have the quick excitement of fresh meaning.

And then we lose track of the boy Henry for three years. All we know is that his education dwindled off, that he worked on the farm and didn't like it, that he had an insatiable appetite for machines, that he gradually set up a little machine shop on the farm, that he kept on tinkering with watches, and that many times he walked the eight miles to and from Detroit to see machines and buy watchmakers' tools.

V. THE APPRENTICE

*He never was a good worker, but
he was a good fellow. . . .
He had the dream.*
—FREDERICK STRAUSS

When Henry left the farm the first time, late in 1879, he no doubt had a sense of high adventure. Actually he was safe as in church. He had a place to live with a favorite aunt, Mrs. Rebecca Ford Flaherty; he had a job that paid well; and behind him, should he become discouraged or hungry, stood the security of the farm, with a loving father ready to set him up on acres of his own.

For years there were stories the two had quarreled or that Henry had run away. But all the evidence shows an old and familiar American pattern: the son who has his own bent and rejects the only life his father knows; the father who cannot quite understand but accepts the situation, though with anxiety.

There is another point. This was eighty-four years ago. Machinery was winning respectability, but farming was still the basic calling of man. Though a farmer repaired and even made his own tools, it was at the ancient and respected level of blacksmithing. William Ford must have contrasted his own broad rich acres and comfortable home with the boarding house and the grimy machine shops of Detroit where Henry wanted to go, where grease-smeared men swung rivet hammers. Yet William Ford, as "a good man with tools," must have felt some of Henry's fascination for the massive, awesome steam-engines, boiler plants, and locomotives that shook the ground and blackened the fresh sky above Detroit.

It seems important here to note what many writings about Ford gloss over or forget: that Henry came out of respectable security, and that security stood behind him. His hard times, now

and later, were self-imposed. In the early years he could have retreated at any point and lived comfortably ever after. He was always safe enough, safe if he were willing to accept defeat in everything he cared about.

33. *Where he lost his first job: The Michigan Car Company Works. It built streetcars, using a pioneer form of the assembly line. This factory had been built only seven years before, in 1872, and was one of the most vigorously booming plants in all Detroit. Henry got a fine job as an apprentice, at high pay for those days: $1.10 a day. But he was fired on the sixth day. In later times he told several different versions of why he was fired —and in one why he quit. Once he jotted: "To Carshop 6 days got into trouble babbitting a box Will Tell," but he never did tell. The soundest version seems to be that he saw where the trouble lay in some machinery that older hands were unable to fix and quickly fixed it on his own hook. This corresponds with the characteristic intuitive flashes he showed with machinery, illogical but swift; he could lay a finger on a sore spot quickly. So he was fired for being precocious. But he said: "I learned then not to tell all you know."*

William Ford came to his rescue immediately, and took young Henry over to a shop owned by their friends, the James Flower & Brothers Machine Shop, at Woodbridge and Brush streets. The Flowers sometimes visited the Ford farm to get produce.

The Flowers' foundry made brass and iron castings on one floor and finished them on another, and Henry got $2.50 for his 60-hour workweek.

The Flower Brothers shop left a mark on him —and on others who trained there and became noted manufacturers and inventors, among them David Buick. Take a look at the clanging interior of the Flower works at the time Henry was apprenticed there—the nine months from December, 1879 to August, 1880—a place where only a roar could be heard above the din. Frederick Strauss was a sweeper at the Flowers' (he was twelve and Henry sixteen), and he has given the Archives the best picture of those years. This is life among the rivet hammers in 1880:

. . . My job was roustabout in the brass shop.

Henry was working on a small milling machine, milling hexagons on brass valves.

They put Henry in with me, and he and I got chummy right away. Henry was to do the same work that I did. He didn't sweep the floor. I did that because I was more of a worker than he was. He never was a good worker, but he was a good fellow.

It was a great old shop. There were three brothers in the company, all in their sixties or more. . . . They were Scotch and believe me they could yell.

They manufactured everything in the line of brass and iron—globe and gate valves, gongs, steam-whistles, fire hydrants, and valves for water pipes. There was a great variety of work. Some of the castings of the iron bodies of the large gate valves weighed a ton or more.

They made so many different articles that they had to have all kinds of machines, large and small lathes and drill presses. Some of the large lathes stood for months without having been used, but they had to have them to take care of the different jobs.

They had more machines than workmen in that shop. The building, machinery and everything about the place was as old as the three brothers. The building was so old it was braced and shored up all over to keep it from falling down.

. . . The ceiling of the brass shop was very low and the shop was awfully hot in the summer. Across the street from the shop was a large pattern loft and downstairs it was very cool. I spent many a half hour there and I am not saying who was with me.

To young Henry Ford this must have been a fairyland- so many machines, so many operations to learn, so many mysteries. But in nine quick months he decided that he had passed all the courses, learned all there was to learn, and forthwith gave himself his own degree. At the moment all became familiar, he left.

34. Henry Ford boarded here, at 802 Franklin Street, his first home away from home. But when he was fired right away, he had to move nearer his next job, and so went to the home of Mrs. James S. Payton at 452 Baker Street. The room and board cost $3.50, and his pay was only $2.50, so he was a dollar in the hole each week.

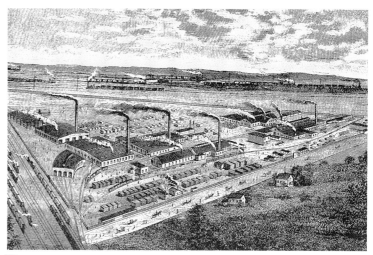

33.

34.

35.

36.

35. The jeweler, Robert Magill. To make ends meet, Henry went to the jewelry shop of his friend Robert Magill, at 390 Michigan Avenue, where Henry had often bought watch parts. He got a job at 50 cents per night, $3.00 per week for six nights of six hours each.

Henry was slight and looked even younger than his sixteen years. In order not to scare away trade, as customers would only trust their timepieces with bearded veterans, Magill had Henry slip in the side door, to work out of sight in a little back room.

After his ten-hour day in the shop, Henry ate hurriedly and went to Magill's back room. On a night when Jeweler Magill was out, Henry finished all the clocks on hand. He then started in on the watches and quickly mended a half dozen. Jeweler Magill scrutinized the work and was pleased; he merely cautioned Henry to be sure to stay in the back room.

36. The Magill shop, including bricks, gas lamps, showcases, and all, down to Mrs. Magill's fancy needlework and the turkey-red wallpaper, now stands in Greenfield Village; you can see Henry's boyhood side door on the left.

37. The Dry Docks. When Henry left Flower Brothers, he went back to the farm to eat hearty and help with the harvest. Then in the fall of 1880 he came back to work at the Detroit Dry Dock Engine Works. He is in the back row, indicated by an arrow. Somewhere in the group, but lost to history, is Henry's friend, Samuel Townsend, a brass finisher recently come from England, who had in his trunk a magazine called World of Science. *It carried an article on the invention of an internal combustion engine by a German engineer, Dr. Nicolaus A. Otto. Henry studied the article and began to read other scientific magazines of the day.*

To get his Dry Dock Company job Henry had to take a pay cut from his $2.50 a week at Flower Brothers to $2.00 a week. The 50 cents a night from Jeweler Magill added $3.00 to his weekly pay, and his board and room cost $3.50. Thus he still had $1.50 over each week.

We do not know what he did with this money, but it is fairly safe to guess he did not spend it on food. Any landlady would have made a fine profit feeding him. He was always a birdseed-type eater, who tries to please the hostess by making a brave show of cutlass work with the knife and fork, and yet somehow only slightly disturbs the food on the plate. Food just never seemed to get inside Henry. He grew up as the sort of man who always has a few peanuts or raisins in his pocket.

The only time food ever interested him came years later when he began to think of the body as a machine and the stomach as a kind of boiler that should be fed the right fuel. Those years of his experimental food theories were sheer misery to his hearty, steak-loving associates. In those years, an invitation to lunch with him was almost equivalent to an invitation from an Inquisitor to step into the Iron Maiden. A salary of several hundred thousand dollars a year was little enough when lunch consisted of what Henry blithely called "roadside greens." These were simply assorted weeds, variously prepared as salads, or lightly boiled, or even stewed—and often appearing in sandwiches. There is nothing quite like a dish of stewed burdock, followed by a sandwich of soybean bread filled with milkweeds, to set a man up for an afternoon's work. There must have been times when his guests prayed for honest spinach.

Yet this picky feeder, this food faddist, outlived hundreds of meat-and-potatoes men and had no more than a few hours of illness all his life. He was built lean as a whip, and he could hike, walk, run, chop, saw, and bicycle endlessly with easy breath; in some eighty years he wore down one generation after another, decade after decade, dancing in the evenings for hours at a time, when most of the men who started out with him were long under the sod. So perhaps there was something to his weeds and hot water and nuts.

On those far-off Sunday afternoons in 1880, Henry often dropped over to the Strausses for Sunday dinner; then he and the boy sweeper would walk down to the water to watch the yachts and sailboats—and especially the little steamboats. During the week the two often met. Strauss was at the Grand Trunk Railroad roundhouse; Henry at the Dry Dock works. The two buildings were in adjacent blocks. Across the street from the Grand Trunk was the old Detroit

37.

38.

Water Works, at the foot of Orleans Street, torn down except for a huge chimney, 150 feet high, and this chimney was a favorite loafing place for workers in both companies. There little Fred and Henry played games during their lunch hour, jumping, throwing stones.

But, as Strauss says, "Henry was always wanting to make things."

The first time I ever saw him spend any money (he usually got the other fellow to spend it) he bought a set of castings for $1.25 . . . castings of a little steam engine. . . . Henry never had any opportunity to machine any of that stuff so he brought it to me.

And thus Henry formed a habit. Many men, for another two generations, would be machining things for Henry.

Henry always had another idea. We never did get that machine finished. He always wanted to have something else. He wanted a boiler. A fellow named MacDonald made us a little galvanized boiler about eight inches in diameter, about a foot high. . . . We never finished it. . . . My mother paid the plumber $6 for the boiler.

Then we started on an eight-day clock that didn't go. . . . We never put the clock together either.

Then Henry wanted to build a boat. We had to have lumber. My mother gave us the money. We paid $2 for four boards. We never put it in the water. Every Sunday we started something and never finished it.

The Dry Dock works was the largest collection of machine shops for many miles around: nearly anything that could happen mechanically in those days happened there. We do not know how thorough Henry's apprenticeship was; he was too young for many of the more dangerous operations. But he was always an avid watcher, and he must have learned there much miscellaneous but useful information about machines.

38. Henry at the Dry Docks. He worked there through the winter, the spring, and most of the summer of 1881; returned to the farm to help his father with the harvest; returned again to the Dry Dock Company when the leaves fell. Thus he passed the three years, 1879–82; his fresh-

man course at Flower Brothers, his next two years at the Dry Docks. And he graduated himself in the late summer of 1882, believing he had learned all he could.

Henry now felt he had completed his *general* mechanical education; all his subsequent jobs were like specialized courses. He had been happy at the Dry Docks. He returned to the place again and again in later years to chat with old friends, to visit old and new machines, much like a college graduate at class reunions, for this was the campus of his youth.

He was now only nineteen; yet already he must have been as well grounded as most apprentice mechanics of his time. He lacked two things, which would come with experience: the ability to handle major mechanical repairs entirely on his own and the ability to supervise others.

Only two anecdotes have come down from his Dry Dock days, and they are truly Henry-Fordian.

39. Frank A. Kirby, who, it seems, was the great man of the Dry Dock Company. He was the construction engineer, a graduate of New York's Cooper Union Institute and a builder of shipyards as well as of boats.

One day young Henry was gaily toting a heavy Stilson wrench down some steep stairs when Kirby called to him sharply: "Don't go down that way! Take hold of the rail—or you're liable to slip and break your neck!" Henry obeyed— and remembered. Next day he was carrying a heavy chain-falls over his shoulder and did slip; if he had not been gripping the rail he might have been killed.

In 1918, when Ford himself hired Frank Kirby to help build the Eagle boats, he told Kirby that he remembered one day when he was struggling to push a heavy wheelbarrow up a steep incline into a ship. Kirby passed and called to him: "Stick in your toenails, boy, and you'll make it!" And, said Ford, "I've been sticking in my toenails ever since."

Whichever anecdote is the dominant one is unimportant—but the result was classic.

40. For when Ford built his vast Engineering Laboratory in Dearborn in the twenties, he ordered carved above the door the names of all the historically great scientists and inventors. There today, among the names Galileo, Copernicus, Edison, Newton, Faraday, and a dozen others, stands the name, carved equally tall: "KIRBY."

By March, 1882, Henry was living in a Mrs. Simms' boarding house on Jefferson Avenue. He no longer worked on watches for Jeweler Magill, who had moved across Baker Street to work alone in his own home, after selling his shop to a milliner, a Mrs. Cohen. Henry studied in the evenings, chiefly back copies of the *World of Science* and the *Scientific American.* Some evenings he worked on little mechanical problems and experiments. To do these he needed power. There was no such thing then as walking into a hardware store, buying a small motor, and plugging it in a light circuit. Detroit was only then being electrified, and there were almost no home light circuits.

To get power, Henry built a miniature turbine and attached it to a faucet in a shed behind his boarding house; the city's water pressure operated the turbine, and it developed a half horsepower, power enough to run a small lathe. This was the first practical engine he ever made.

But he would not run it on Sundays, though he wanted to. "It seemed to me that a Sunday without work at my machines was so much time gone utterly to waste. . . . But I knew perfectly well that the family with whom I boarded were Sabbatarians of the old-school rigid type . . . and never would have tolerated my lathe upon the Sabbath, which [they felt] could only be kept holy by being devoted to idleness or worship."

For Henry was not a churchgoer. "I never was especially religious. I went to Sunday School sometimes but I never thought it amounted to much. . . . I think I saved a lot of valuable time by staying away from church. . . . Man has made many gods. How do I know and how can I find out which, if any, is the genuine one? I won't try. I'll just keep busy." And he never changed much from that stand. But he always liked the singing in churches and himself built some seven chapels and contributed to others.

This was the period when he seriously debated going into the manufacture of cheap but sturdy

39.

40.

watches. He wanted to make 2,000 watches a day for thirty cents each. But after he studied the problem he shrank from the economics; to make a profit he would have to sell 600,000 watches a year, and who would buy so many?

He wrote for catalogs of machinery, he read Michael Faraday's *Treatise on the Steam Engine,* which made the "deepest impression of all"; and one day when he was at the farm he had the "enormous good luck" of learning that a locomotive had blown out a cylinder head only two or three miles away. "I hastened. . . .

I congratulated myself because I reached the locomotive before repairs were completed and I remained with the repair gang until the job was done."

His father still had hopes Henry would come back to the farm. The younger brothers had grown; John was eighteen and William, twelve; so by harvest time of 1882 Henry no longer felt any compulsion to help with the chores.

And everything dovetailed neatly to give him another date with another machine.

VI. OLD NO. 345

*The little high-speed,
quick-steaming thing
made him nervous. . . .
I was frightened myself. . . .*
—HENRY FORD

Remember that Michigan was wood country: wood was the available fuel, and coal was a costly import by rail from southern Ohio, Pennsylvania, and Kentucky. And the wonderful ancient forests of Michigan were going down at a great rate. Little portable steam-engines were beginning to go about the country threshing and sawing timber.

"The men in charge of those machines," Henry said later, "seemed to me of great importance, entrusted with vast responsibility, and fortunate to have chosen fascinating careers."

One of the good neighbors of the Fords in Dearborn was John Gleason, and one day in 1882 Farmer Gleason bought such a portable steam-engine, from Westinghouse in Schenectady, and he hired a man to run it.

Henry Ford told about that day:

I shall never forget the first time I ran that engine. . . . The man knew little of it . . . and he found himself in trouble. As a matter of fact, I have an idea he was afraid of his machine. The little high-speed, quick-steaming thing made him nervous and he did little work with it that first day. She differed from the accustomed farm engines, having many of the characteristics of a fire engine. He practically threw up his job. . . . Gleason was in a quandary.

One of the neighbors knew I knew a good deal about engines and suggested me to take the man's place.

At six o'clock the following morning this neighbor, worried that Gleason without an engineer would be unable to finish the work on his place, came to see my father. I was about as proud as I have ever been when he asked if I might run the engine while it was on his place.

My father consented reluctantly. He was afraid, I am sure, to let me have anything to do with an engine that had proved too much for a professional engineer. I was rather slight for my age. . . . He asked me if I felt certain of my ability and his tone showed that he doubted.

To tell the truth, I was frightened myself. . . . But I was unwilling to be beaten by an engine, and I solemnly assured my father and the farmer that I was sure. They finally decided to let me try.

I went to work around that little engine. It was not long before my doubts entirely disappeared, and getting a grip on the engine, so to speak, I got a grip on myself.

At the end of that first day I was as weary as I had been nervous at its beginning, but I had run the engine steadily, inducing it to stand up nicely to its work, and I forgot my griminess and weariness in the consciousness I had actually accomplished what I had started out to do. There are few more comforting feelings.

I was paid three dollars a day and had eighty-three days of steady work. I traveled from farm to farm, and I threshed our own and the neighbors' clover, hauled loads, cut corn-stalks, ground feed, sawed wood. It was hard work. I had to fire [it] myself and the fuel most generally was old fence-rails, though it would burn coal the few times coal was to be had.

I became immensely fond of that machine . . . and [its] complete and expert master. I have never been better satisfied with myself than I was when I guided it over the rough country roads of the time.

In 1913 Henry Ford began searching for that little steam-engine. All he knew was its number, 345. After a long hunt, with the help of Westinghouse, it was found on a farm in Pennsylvania, rusty with disuse. The number plate was found in the farmhouse kitchen, used as a patch on an old cookstove. The farmer wanted ten dollars for the worthless thresher. Ford paid it and gave him a new Model T as a bonus; and he

41.

threshed again with the old steam-engine in Dearborn on his sixtieth birthday.

41. And here is old No. 345, shined, fresh and well oiled, as it stands on the teak floor of the Ford Museum. By Ford's orders it must always be as ready to run as it was on that nervous morning in 1882.

And now comes a small bit of history which, more's the pity, cannot be placed exactly. Henry built himself a small "farm locomotive," that is, a tractor. As the years rolled by, he built one tractor after another, endlessly experimenting and failing, for ten, twenty, thirty, forty, fifty, sixty years, never satisfied. But the date of his first tractor would be a fine date to establish. The scholarly doctors have been over and over the ground, and all the books and documents differ, and so do Henry's stories, and it seems we will never know. Was it in 1880, or '81, or '82, or '83, or '84?

Yet we know some things about this pioneer tractor. Henry's father had an old ruin of a mowing machine, with cast-iron wheels and a wheel base of about seventy-two inches. Henry used this as the chassis for his "locomotive." He made a pattern and cast a cylinder for a steam-engine to drive it. To make such a casting is no mean trick. He heated metal until it was molten and then cast a single cylinder, three inches across and three and three-fourths inches deep. Inside the cylinder he fitted a piston which was to move by the force of the steam generated in a small old fire tube upright boiler.

He worked on this at odd moments for two winters, having trouble fastening the rig securely to the old mower. Finally he started the cordwood fire, the water came slowly to a boil, the steam pushed against the piston head, the piston went up and down, the big wheels began to move slowly.

The "locomotive" went forty feet—and stopped forever. Henry could not develop enough steam power. But he did not seem to suffer over such failures. He was a realist. He had learned a lot, in the only way a man really learns. And he had faith: if a country boy with a few tools and no resources could make a tractor that would go forty feet, someday. . . .

One of the hardest problems in the study of Ford's early life is to determine exactly *when* he first made something. But Henry Ford did not

34

keep an accurate scientist's diary of his experiments. He would fiddle around in his shop, get involved in something else, take another hack at it months later. Finally it would work *quite* well. But there was no exact dated moment, with thunder, lightning, and "Eureka." It was more like getting something to go, but with a mumbling, "Hm. Well. I'll fix the other end tomorrow."

So the sense of his innumerable failures, tries, failures, and new tries lies somewhere here: from childhood on Henry Ford had a little shop of his own wherever he went. In that shop he worked on every kind of mechanical problem. The problem that fascinated him most was how to build a machine that ran on the road. He was always working on that: how to increase the power without increasing the weight, how to link up the power with the drive, how to have more than one kind of driving speed (gears), how best to steer, how best to connect the wheels to the frame—and all the things that seem so simple today to motorists who don't even know how to lift the hoods on their cars.

But he kept bumping into two main problems. One was fuel. Steam-engines were fearful consumers of fuel. And since coal sold like gold, you had to use wood. This meant you had to carry a stack of logs around or be ready to get out and chop. Another thing about steam was that you couldn't just hop in and go; first you had to build a fire and get the water boiling and get up a head of steam. And about that time you were out of wood.

Henry began to ponder electricity and gasoline. He knew almost nothing about either. The first American oil had been struck in Pennsylvania at Drake's Well only twenty-odd years before, in 1859. Many uses had been found for crude petroleum, and kerosene was a best-selling item (people used it as a quick starter for parlor stoves and kitchen ranges, as well as in lamps), but gasoline was simply nowhere. In the next forty years, all the way to 1920, the only sure place to buy gasoline was the village store. Most storekeepers kept a gallon of gasoline out in back, but woe to the motorist who arrived after dark, when the store was shut. And the word "gas" in America meant simply illuminating gas.

Henry kept up with the catalogs and the technical magazines, reading about electricity and puzzling out the diagrams; and somewhere in these years he first saw an Otto engine at work. This was the first superior four-cycle engine, the invention of Nicolaus A. Otto, a German engineer. The one Henry saw was on Detroit's Second Avenue, at the Norris' bottling works, a stationary engine fueled by illuminating gas. The Otto engines were great curiosities in the United States, as exciting then as the first jet engines were in the 1940's; they were much exhibited at state fairs and expositions.

Henry just did not know enough. He lived far from the great mechanical, engineering, and scientific centers of his time. He was simply an apprentice mechanic, of farm background, uneducated culturally; and as to engineering . . . listen to his own review of his technical education, McGuffey period: "When I got through that district school I could find the area of circles, compute the interest on money, learn the speed of pulleys. I could compute the weight of iron, steel or water."

But the fact is that the savants, scientists, and engineers did not know much either. They were all groping. At times Henry's flashes of intuition and cut-and-try methods pulled him ahead; at other times their training, logic, and discipline proved superior. The big thing to remember is that it was all new, everything was new, and when anyone thought of a new gadget he had first to invent the tools with which to make it.

In 1882 when Henry was probably beginning to think about gasoline and electricity, he was still in love with steam, reveling in his triumphal eighty-three-day tour in Farmer Gleason's portable steam-engine, "the little high-speed, quick-steaming thing." Somewhere along this tour he met John Cheeney, a regional boss of this business and the Michigan agent for Westinghouse portables. This was a lucky stroke; both spoke steam-engine language, and the meeting was a simple case of love at first sight. Forthwith Henry signed up as Cheeney's demonstrator and repairman and put Detroit's mechanical lures out of his mind.

The next few summers Henry spent in his kind of paradise, traveling all over southern Michigan with Westinghouse engines. He became intimately aware of their defects and strengths and could make any kind of repair up to the most major.

In the winters, when the roads were snowed in, he experimented in his little farm shop, chiefly with small electric devices. He had his own forge, vises, an upright drill, a small hand lathe driven by foot-power, and a kit of various hand tools.

At age twenty, in 1883, he began to take a little more interest in husking bees, hay wagon rides, ice skating, and barn dances. He always had an eager foot and springing rhythm, and he had long since begun to notice girls.

42. McGraw Building 49 Griswold. Where the articles of incorporation of Ford Motor Company were signed in June 1903.

42.

VII. LOVE AND GASOLINE

To my Darling

> Your life I wish one
> long long Summer's
> Day
> From your own true
> love
> Henry
> —extract from letter, 1891.

As 1883 and '84 went by, Henry was the repairman for Westinghouse road engines; and then on December 1, 1884, he took another step in his own program of education. He entered a business school, Goldsmith's Bryant & Stratton Business University, located in Mechanics Hall (a name, no doubt, of notable attraction for him) at 143–153 Griswold Street, near the City Hall. He had decided he needed a business background.

42. Mechanics Hall where he studied mechanical drawing, bookkeeping and business practice, and this is the only flash of business education he ever had.

Perhaps also it incidentally equipped him to understand the business-office jests of the 1880's. In those days the office jokes centered about bookkeepers and office boys, the way they focus on girl secretaries today. One sample:

Boy: "The bookkeeper kicked me, sir."

Boss: "Well, I don't have time to attend to all these details myself."

The instructors must have spoken firmly to him about his handwriting, for it was quite legible, even a touch fancy, for most of the next ten years. Then the Goldsmith influence wore off, and his handwriting lapsed into an illegibility that almost rises to grandeur, a magnificent non-penmanship in which each simple-looking word can be construed in ten different ways.

Many years later Ford said, in an unusual bragging mood: "At the time I didn't know why I took that [bookkeeping] course, but now I know. I can understand in a minute what our financial men are discussing. I know offhand how much material, labor and money we have —in the terms of an expert accountant."

One can only gape in wonder, for the teachers at Goldsmith's must have been miracle men: Henry attended there only a few months in all.

And yet he did become an extraordinary, a supreme, businessman; he *did* know what the financial men were discussing. He was never outwitted in a business deal in his life, and this was not mere Yankee shrewdness; in moments of great financial crisis he threaded his way through the intricacies of high finance with the nimble foot of a Rothschild. In the early years of the Ford Motor Company everyone gave credit for the successful management to James Couzens, and then Ford fired Couzens in 1915 and went on to a long series of dazzling business strokes. For years he continued to fire every man with a business head. So we are driven back to reconsider the merits of McGuffey—and of Goldsmith's Bryant & Stratton. Ford must have learned somewhere, and those were the only schools he ever attended.

A big year in Henry Ford's life was 1884. One good source has it that when on July 30 he became twenty-one years old, his father, now fifty-eight and still anxious to establish him on the farm, gave Henry forty acres. Other sources say the gift came later, but no one is sure. The gift was supposedly on the condition that Henry would quit the Dry Dock Company and definitely return to the farm. Henry wrote later: "I agreed in a provisional way. . . ."

Certainly he did not return to the Dry Docks. As he said: "I was then on the farm to which I had returned, more because I wanted to experiment than because I wanted to farm, and now being an all-around machinist I had a first-class workshop to replace the toy shop of earlier days."

We must remember again the great differences between the 1880's and our times: in those days there was a very hard separation between summer and winter. When the snow came you stayed put until spring opened the roads. Today, over much of the United States, a snowfall is only a matter of irritation for a few hours;

the trains and buses and planes are a little late.

But in those days winter put a profound stop to everything. Winter meant isolation, loneliness, hibernation; all autumn the busy kitchens of the land smelled of pickles, preserves, jams; mothers laid in the supplies and fathers chopped cords of wood and battened everything down. When the first huge battleship-gray snowclouds of November stood along the horizon and the first fat fluffy snowflakes began to drift down to the hard-rutted ground, everyone nodded goodbye to the outdoor world and went inside for the winter's indoor sports.

So in the winters Henry studied bookkeeping and experimented in his shop. He measured those years by the engines he saw; these were his milestones, the way a young painter might remember his first look at the Louvre. One such thrill was his first Daimler; another came in 1884 in a call to the Kennedy Farm in Greenfield to repair a Mills engine. Ford ever after hailed Emory W. Mills, the engine's designer, as "a genius, fifty years ahead of his time. I spent all one day running that engine around the [Kennedy] farm and out Grand River and Kennedy roads. He [Mills] had in that engine many things we can't improve on today [about 1938]. Mills had the idea of a superheater long before it was thought of for railroad locomotives."

But he always regarded August 4, 1885 as a halcyon day, as his most virtuoso repair performance. On that day a ten-horsepower traction engine was delivered from New York to Farmer Christopher Rath, of the Young and Rath Farm, in Milan, Michigan. Agent Cheeney put in an emergency call for Henry, and the two traveled to Milan. Farmer Rath's threshing couldn't wait —and the machine wouldn't work. It had, said Henry, "an odd reversing mechanism and a V-belt drive." Henry found the trouble and fixed it in two hours. Henry was still proud of that repair years later; a laconic note appears scribbled in one of his jotbooks around 1930: "Engine 739 Separator 4406 Aug 4 Tuesday Young & Rath 1885." (This note appears sandwiched among these irresistible entries: "On The Wabash Banks Song On The O H I O," "Don't find fault—find a remedy," and "anybody can complain.")

Then sometime during 1885 he was called to repair **an Otto** engine at the Eagle Iron Works in Detroit. He said: "No one in town knew anything about them. There was a rumor that I did, and although I had never before been in contact with one, I undertook and carried through the job. That gave me a chance to study the new engine at first hand."

But engines were not all. His sisters Margaret and Jane had taught him to dance. And he had other social assets: a touch of city ways and his *expertise* with such delicate things as watches and such frightening things as steam engines.

Now it was natural enough, but yet exasperating, that the newspapermen who covered Henry Ford for decades could not quite see the man himself; they saw the billionaire, the auto tycoon, the eccentric whose opinions were front-page news. Many newsmen fattened on prestige and pay through their scoops from Ford; he was always good copy. But he remained a "human interest story" to them, not a human being.

Most of the reporters were interested in the news of the moment. And so they missed the great story of Ford himself, partly because they were just not *curious* enough—and that is almost the worst thing that can be said about newspapermen. One example will suffice: the Ford Museum. Not even one reporter knew Ford enough to realize that every single item in that incredible storehouse was there simply because it had a certain meaning for Henry Ford.

From the tiniest pincushion to the steam-engines and airplanes in the Museum, down to every joint of carpentry in all the restored houses in Greenfield Village, and everything within those houses: each carpet, stove, dish, andiron, porch, door, curtain, sewing-basket, table, chair, bric-a-brac—every object had a story. All that a reporter would have had to do to win Ford's confidence was to ask him about any of those objects. He loved to talk about each artifact; he had put it there, often at great expense, because it was important to *him*. In fact, a reporter could have pointed at random at almost anything west of Detroit and Henry would have been only too happy to give him names, dates, and stories enough to come out of his ears.

Every time a visitor, royal or otherwise, went on a tour of the Museum or the Village with Henry Ford he came away loaded with lore, background, stories and news, enough to make rich and happy forever any of the reporters who spent their time lounging and yawning around the Engineering Laboratory or the Administration Building at the Rouge. But to most of those reporters the Museum was a deadly bore. They were all too sophisticated to waste time there among the greatest collection of Americana ever made. And few of them realized that this would have been the way to Henry's heart.

43. But Ann Hood, a schoolgirl at the Ford School in Dearborn in the late 1930's, went right after the target. Young Ann was a reporter on the student paper and a photographer of considerable skill. Instead of writing the usual schoolgirl themes on why-I-like-school, Ann Hood began interviewing Henry Ford.

Ann Hood, not being sophisticated, simply put Henry through hours of inch-by-inch questioning. The result in the Archives is a monument of facts. It is solely due to this Dearborn schoolgirl that we can fix on a hundred important dates, destroy dozens of myths, and change around a lot of ideas about Henry Ford. Ann would point to everything in a room, and Henry, delighted, would tell her the story of each object. She gave him long lists of numbered questions, and he faithfully tried to answer each one, sometimes taking the list home to consult with Mrs. Ford.

And because of Ann Hood we have a good picture of the first meeting, and courtship, of Clara Jane Bryant and Henry Ford.

Here is Henry's description, in Ann Hood's high-school prose:

On New Year's Night (January 1) 1885, there was a big dance at the Greenfield Dancing Club. All the people, young and old, from Dearborn and Greenfield Townships were on hand. Henry came home from Detroit where he was working and attending Business College, and attended the dance with his family. As they entered the Hall the fiddler was sawing out the tunes of the old quadrille; the caller was singing out the familiar calls in his loud clear voice: "Last gentleman lead to the right, around that lady with the grapevine twist." The laughing, merry throng was a mass of marching and whirling groups. Some more daring than others "cracked the whip." . . .

43.

44a.

44b.

45.

Young Henry Ford

"Promenade to your seats," shouted the caller and little groups of friends collected about the hall.

The next dance was a circle waltz and young Henry joined in . . . dancing a few measures (with each girl) before he passed on to another. A quadrille followed, and another. Later in the evening Henry found himself with his second cousin, Annie Ford, as head couple in a quadrille. On either side was another couple, but as the dance started, Henry had eyes only for the girl opposite him. Her tiny steps, her quick and graceful actions fascinated him. He admired the sweet face, the eyes and the tilted chin.

"Why have I never met her before?" he said to himself, and then Annie introduced him. He heard the name Clara Jane Bryant, and for a few seconds talked with her. Then she was claimed by another partner. . . . Chided by Annie, he regained his senses, and escorted her to a seat. The party was nearly over, and he saw no more of Clara Jane Bryant that night. But in the next few days he found out what he could about her, and resolved to meet her again.

Henry went to many dances that winter, hoping again to meet Miss Bryant, but it was nearly a year later (winter of 1885–86) before he saw her. Then one night he went to a dance with his friend Albert Hutchings (whose watch had been the first Henry had repaired). . . . Clara Bryant was there. Albert introduced them again and Henry asked for a dance. Encouraged by this success he asked her to have supper with him, and they ate their oyster stew together. . . . But she was popular, and he found little opportunity to see her.

Late in February, 1886, the "Johnsons' Minstrels" were playing at the Whitney Opera House in Detroit, and Henry asked Clara to go with him.

A week or two later they had dinner at the Martindale House. The occasion was Henry's acquisition of a new watch, one which told both standard and sun time, steel hands for the former and brass for the latter. [Note: most biographers have written that Henry *made* this watch, but here we have his own testimony.]

40

Love and Gasoline

On April 19, 1886, they became engaged, a few days after Clara's twentieth birthday. Mrs. Bryant decided her girl was too young to be married. . . . These two years Henry spent on the farm and much of his spare time was spent going back and forth to the Bryants. Many were the long buggy rides over the country roads. . . . He got along well with her parents and especially liked Mrs. Bryant's friendly, motherly way.

44a, b. Annie and Nellie Ford, Henry's young cousins, about the time they took him to the New Year's dance where Annie introduced him to Clara Jane Bryant. Lace was almost obligatory for dress-up occasions.

45. This dance program was in the house at Fair Lane when Henry died, for he saved everything that had a meaning to him. The fact that the program was printed shows the formality of the occasion.

46. The Martindale House, where Henry first met Clara; a year later he took her to dinner there. It stood on Grand River Road at Chicago Boulevard, about five miles northeast of Henry's home and two miles southeast of Clara's. This picture was taken sometime before 1920.

47. Clara Jane Bryant, about the time Henry met her. She was the oldest girl in a family of ten children and, as they say, "had more sense than all the others put together." The other Bryant children were attractive, engaging but not harum-scarum; Clara was the steady girl, the clear-headed manager. Clara Jane was born in Greenfield on April 11, 1866, and was thus almost three years younger than Henry. Best guess is that this picture shows her at age twenty.

48. Martha Bench Bryant, Clara's mother, sometime in the years 1900–05. Martha Bench came to America in 1854, with her parents William and Mary Ann Bench, from Warwickshire, England, where she was born on March 16, 1839. In 1860 she married Melvin Bryant, a slender, mustachioed, genial farmer of Greenfield Township. They lived on Monnier Road, now Schaefer Highway, halfway between Schoolcraft and Fenkell.

41

46.

47.

48.

49.

50a.

49. *The period look: 1885. This picture had some special meaning for Henry. We can only guess. The man in the hay wagon is one of Henry's favorite "uncles," this time Sam Ford, of Redford, Michigan; perhaps he had come to town to buy the rocking chair he is standing beside. The Dickinson & Hood store sold hardware and the other things on display, from the elegant parlor stoves in the left window to step-ladders, buckets, kitchen ranges, lanterns. The boy leaning on the three graduated kegs of nails was named John (we do not know his last name), and then in order come these vanished citizens, John Toepel in beard, Wesley Smith, Andrew Tyre, and finally the distinguished proprietors, M. Wesson Dickinson and James C. Hood. Near Mr. Hood's casually cocked leg is the latest thing in washing-machines—Mother pumped the handle, which turned a paddle within the tub; this was advertised as freeing Mother forever from the hard work of wash-day. You are looking at the north side of Grand River Avenue No. 416 (now 2956) a short distance beyond Sixth Street. This was the way a store front looked the year Henry Ford met Clara Bryant.*

50a, b. *Henry Ford, age twenty-three. Photographer McMichael, of 153 Woodward Avenue (now 1059), took these photographs on November 20, 1886. First he tried Henry with the light on the right side of his face. Then he shifted the light to the left side, while Henry changed his collar to the stand-up choker, and re-tied his necktie to be less lumpy. Oddly enough, the handsome picture with the light on the right was suppressed by Henry and Clara, while that with the light on the left has been used ever since as "Henry Ford's wedding picture." (He was not married until some eighteen months later.)*

51. *The earliest preserved love letter. Apparently he had already given her the cutter in which they whirled over the snow in the sparkling frosty nights (despite the printed myths, he did not build it himself, and it was Brewster green, not red). The penmanship is of his best, or Goldsmith-business-school period, but the spelling and punctuation are supremely Henry Ford's own. It is pleasurable to read through, but for the people who do not like to read handwriting, this is what it says:*

Love and Gasoline

50b.

Springwells Feb 14th 86

Dear Clara

I again take the pleasure of writing you a few lines it seems like a year since i seen you. it don't seem mutch like cutter riding to night does it but i guess we will have some more sleighing. there is a great many sick in this neighborhood i have called on five sick persons this afternoon three in one house. it seems to bad colds our folks are about

all over it. John is going back to school tomorrow i hope you and your folks are all well. Clara Dear you did not expect me Friday night and i think as the weather is so bad you will not expect me tonight. but if the weather and roads are good you look for me. Friday or Saturday night for the Opera or Sunday night or Monday night at the party and if your Brother has got some one else let me know when you write but i guess i will see you before then. Clara Dear you can not imagine what pleasure it gives me to think that i have at last found one

so loving kind and true as you are and i hope we will always have good success. Well i shall have to Close wishing you all the joys of the year and a kind Good night.

May Flowerelts of love around you be twined

And the sunshine of peace shed its joy's over your Mind.

From one that Dearly loves you

H.

51.

43

52.

Dear Clara

I again take the pleasure of writing you a few lines. It seems like a year since i seen you. It don't seem mutch like cutter rideing to night does it but i guess we will have more sleighing. there is a great many Sick in this neighborhood i have called on five sick persons this afternoon three in one house. it seems to bad colds our folks are about all over it. John is going back to school tomorrow i hope you and your folks are all well. Clara Dear you did not expect me Friday night and i think as the weather is so bad you will not expect me tonight, but if the weather and roads are good you look for me. Friday or Saterday night for the Opera or Sunday night or Monday night at the party and if your Brother has got some one else let me know when you write but i guess i will see you before then. Clara Dear, you can not imagine what pleasure it gives me to think that i have at last found one so loveing kind and true as you are and i hope we will always have good success. Well i shall have to Close wishing you all the Joys of the year and a kind Good Night.

May Floweretts of love around you bee twined

*And the Sunshine
of peace Shed its joy's o'er your Minde
From one that Dearly loves you
H.*

52. *This note is five years later. Note the postmarks: May 4, 12:30 P.M. and May 5, 9:30 A.M. Did Henry really forget the postage?*

53. *The Bryant home, with assorted Bryants. Left is Sade, Mrs. Bryant in the rear, and the boys are Marvin, Edgar Leroy and Lloyd. Just behind Marvin, peeping over his shoulder, is sister Eva. This picture was taken by Henry Ford himself, circa 1898. It was in the deep bay window at the left that Clara and Henry were married.*

53.

VIII. THE BELIEVER TAKES A TEST

A gas engine is a mysterious sort of thing . . .

—HENRY FORD

In 1886 Henry began to clear the trees off the woodland of the nearby Moir farm. He did not farm a lick. He had no horses, no cows, no chickens, no crops, no farm tools. There is not a grain of evidence that he ever did intend to farm the land. Henry said only: "Cutting the timber gave me a chance to get married."

As always, he made a date with another machine. For $250—perhaps his own money— Henry bought a circular sawmill, rented a twelve-horsepower portable engine to run it and set himself up in business. The forty acres were mainly woodland: black oak, elm, maple, ash, beech and basswood; Henry sawed up his own trees to sell as lumber for building and as cordwood in Detroit. He took his engine around the area wherever a neighbor would pay to have his land cleared. This was profitable work.

He took Clara along, so she could ride one of the machines that fascinated him. She was wonderfully willing to listen to him talk about machines; she did not balk at riding the portable engine; she cheerfully came along to watch him pulling stumps—and all this must have convinced him that here was the girl for Henry Ford.

To add to his income, he worked two summers for the Buckeye Harvester Company, setting up and repairing their Eclipse portable farm engines. Then he worked his sawmill the rest of each year. In the winter of 1887 he worked in his home shop trying to build a four-cycle engine "just to see if I understood the principles."

. . . The little model worked well enough; it had a one-inch bore and a three-inch stroke, operated with gasoline, and while it did not develop much power, it was slightly lighter in proportion than the engines being offered commercially. I gave it away later to a young man. . . . it was eventually destroyed. That was the beginning of the work with the internal combustion engine.

The acres he cut for himself had once belonged to one George Moir, who sold them to William Ford in 1865; and as is the country custom, in 1886 it was still called "the Moir Place." A little house on the property was called "the Moir House," and there Henry prepared to settle with his bride-to-be.

Henry had set his sawmill up on Ford Road, along Emerson Road "north of the corners." Logs were usually hauled to the mill during the winters, since sleighs operating on snow were the most practical means to transport large logs. And lumbering was always winter work: farm summers are full enough of other matters.

He put up his sawmill on a small rise. The land sloped three hundred feet down to the county ditch. He stretched a pipe from the ditch up to the top of the rise, where he dug a well—really a pond hole—close to his engine, about ten feet square and seven feet deep. A small pump brought water up from the ditch to this water basin. The boiler pulled water from the basin, and Henry fired the boiler with scraps from the lumber brought in either by sleighs in snowy weather or on stone-boats in dry weather. He used a pair of oxen, as they were not frightened by the puffing thump of the steam-engine.

Henry sold his lumber to lumber yards and furniture factories, and found a particularly good market for large oak timbers in the shipyards of Detroit. He was industrious, and for five years he cut more than 200,000 feet of lumber each year. Unquestionably these years put iron into his physique.

54a, b. He had the usual small-businessman's troubles. Here we see how he attempted to get his proper pay for some wagon tongues he had cut—and how seven years later he was still after the money.

55. The Moir House, first home of the newly-weds, Henry and Clara Ford. The shed in back came later; here Henry moved his machine shop from the Homestead. Here he said he continued his experiments with gas engines, all of them made of tubing; it is easy to guess what

45

Feb 16 1889

Mr. N. Ross

will you please
pay to mr. J lawrence
as much as you can
spare and we will
settle about the tongues
after

Henry Ford

54a.

T. W. LAW,
Mngr Collection Dep't.

LAW OFFICE
....OF....

M. M. ATHERTON,

ROOM 17, BURNS BLOCK, 88 & 90 GRISWOLD STREET,

TELEPHONE,

Detroit, Mich. May 7th 1896

Mrs. Nathaniel Ross.
Dearborn, Mich.
Dear madam,— Mr. Henry Ford has
placed a claim of 17 50 against you in my
hands for collection. This is for lumber bought
of Mr. Ford some time ago by your husband and
was used on your property.
I know you do not wish to avoid paying
an honest debt, and I kindly ask you to remit
the amount to me as his agent and oblige.

Respy,
M. M. Atherton.

54b.

55.

difficulties he must have had with the timing, the stroke, the size of the piston.

When I was not cutting timber I was working on the gas engines—learning what they were and how they acted. I read everything I could find, but the greatest knowledge came from the work. A gas engine is a mysterious sort of thing—it will not always go the way it should. You can imagine how those first engines acted!

Yet later he once said laconically: "They all ran." But one definitely did not run; his main effort that winter of 1889 was his second attempt to build a road locomotive.

He got an old buggy, put threshing engine wheels on it, and tried to design a single-cylinder steam-engine that would power the locomotive. His cylinder had a two-inch bore and a two-inch stroke; he bolted it to the bottom of the buggy and connected it with the rear wheels by a belt from the engine to a shaft on which he had a sprocket wheel; a chain from the sprocket wheel drove the differential gear.

Henry simply could not raise any power, and after trying every kind of boiler he could think of—flash, fire tube and others—he had to abandon it without ever getting it to move.

Clara Ford, when she was old, tried to reconstruct that time, and vowed that she could not remember any such farm locomotive, nor any tubing gasoline engines, nor even that he had moved his machine shop there until much later. There is no way to tell whether her memory was correct.

56. The wedding invitation. The spray at the top is in silver, only a little tarnished now after seventy-five years. On the wedding day, as a wedding present, Henry's brother John helped clean the little Moir House, and sisters Margaret and Jane freshly decorated it with flowers and little surprises.

57. Clara Ford, 1888. This picture, taken the year she was married, is known as her "wedding picture," but we do not know whether it was taken before or after April 11. This was both her birthday and her wedding day. On that evening the Reverend Samuel W. Frisbie, rector of St. James Episcopal Church in Detroit—who had confirmed Clara in the church when she was fif-

teen—received a $10 fee for joining together in holy matrimony Henry Ford, twenty-four, of Springwells, and Miss Clara Bryant, twenty-two, of Greenfield, sponsored by Mr. William Ford and Mrs. Martha Bryant, at the home of Melvin Bryant in Greenfield.

58. *The wedding certificate. Henry wore a blue suit and Clara a dress she had made. They stood in the archway of the old-fashioned bay window in the Bryant home. Two of Clara's brothers served the wedding supper. One guest was Mrs. Bessie Gerecke, Clara's cousin, who recalled (in 1928): "The wedding presents were laid out on Aunt Martha's bed. I was looking at a beautiful velvet plaque which Nancy Ford, a cousin of Henry's, had given them when Henry and Clara came in to see the presents. They sat down on the edge of the bed and it fell to the floor. How we roared, as everyone came running to see the bride and groom . . . almost buried in presents!"*

Mr. & Mrs. Bryant, request your presence at the marriage ceremony of their daughter Clara, to Henry Ford, on Wednesday, April 11th, 1888, at 7.30 P. M., at their residence, Greenfield, Mich.

56.

57.

In the Name of the Father, and the Son, and the Holy Ghost, Amen.

This is to Certify

That on the Eleventh day of April
In the Year of Our Lord
One Thousand Eight Hundred and Eighty Eight
at Township of Greenfield
in the Diocese of Michigan

I joined together in Holy Matrimony

Henry Ford
and Clara Bryant

according to the Rites of the Protestant Episcopal Church in the United States of America, and in conformity with the Laws of the State of Michigan

In Witness Whereof I have hereunto put my name this
11th day of April A. D., One
Thousand Eight Hundred and Eighty Eight
William Ford
Mrs. Martha Bryant

58.

Square House

Kitchen 12 × 15'
Sitting room 14 × 14
Parlor 18 × 14
Bedroom 10 × 14

Henry the above figures are the best that I can do. But use your own judgement about it. Ask your cousin's opinion.

C.

59.

60.

59. Clara's plan for their second home. Almost as soon as they moved into the Moir House, Henry began building a better home. He followed Clara's specifications almost to the letter, and this became a lifelong habit. Clara was not a bossy woman, but neither was she fluttery or indecisive. She always knew what she wanted, in a firm, clear-headed way, with a typical feminine concession as in her note: "But use your own judgement. . . ."

Then and there they established a pattern that gave them a lifetime happiness: in all matters outside the home he was master; in all matters inside the home she was the law. This was generally true, but business and domestic matters they discussed together.

From the very first they were comfortable together. Clara believed passionately in the infallible rightness of Henry's decisions. His pet name for her was "Callie," but he treasured this name, never thus referring to her in public. In interviews he always called her "the Believer," because of her iron conviction that he was always on the right track—no matter what. And she had a rather rare human quality: the ability to be patient and sweet just when one's stock of patience is in the shortest supply, that is, at the end of a hard day.

60. The Square House. They lived in the Moir House for thirteen months, while Henry cut the trees, sawed the logs into lumber, and then designed and built the second house, thirty-one feet square, a story and a half high. For fancy-work details, such as the carving above the second-story window (upper left), and the three tiers of lathe-turned balustrades, Henry had the help of an expert carpenter whose name comes down only as Mr. Traverse. It was on the northeast corner of Emerson (now Southfield) and Ford roads.

To most tastes, the Square House is the most attractive home the Fords ever had. Henry traded lumber from his sawmill for finished furniture. Here they lived happily from about June 1889 until September 1891. Henry went on logging and stump-pulling and experimenting; he never farmed an inch.

Their home life began at once to revolve around music; both loved music. It was a "musical" time in America, with a people that took great pleasure in sounds themselves. At this time the banjo was king, both in the theater and among amateurs; one of the jokes of the day was:

"Do you play the banjo?"

"Not when other people are around."

"Why not?"

"They won't let me."

The Fords bought an organ and music for Clara to play; one of those pieces of music became famous.

On an autumn Saturday in 1891, so the story goes, Henry went to Detroit to see an engine. He came home to the Square House thoughtful. On Sunday evening Clara played the organ while he read his technical magazines. Suddenly he told her that he believed the Otto engine could be adapted as the power plant for a road vehicle, a horseless carriage. When she broke off playing, he seized a piece of the music as a scratch pad and quickly sketched out a rough plan on the back page. Henry's sister Margaret has said that he convinced Clara: "She had complete confidence that he could do it." And then Henry told her that in order to do it he had to learn about electricity; that he must work in Detroit, preferably for the Edison Illuminating Company—and this meant they must move to the city to be near his work. (In later years Henry turned out every

attic for miles around looking for that back page of music with his first sketch, but it was never found—if it ever existed. For Henry never lost any other papers of importance.)

But one fact is left out of this story: Henry already had gotten a job in Detroit, and at the Edison Company, too. Again, there was nothing of Dick Whittington in Henry; he planned carefully and moved when he was sure. And it would have been most unlike him to have sought such a job without consulting Clara. But whatever were the exact events, they did go forthwith to Detroit.

Henry's sister Margaret said of Clara's reaction: "It almost broke her heart."

Whatever Clara's feelings, this certainly was a major test for the Believer. She was comfortably settled in a good home, among the people she knew. Detroit and machines were the great unknown. But she sturdily set forth, apparently without even a grumble.

In all the later years neither Clara nor Henry ever hinted she had been unhappy about the move.

As to William Ford's views there are no facts. But he must now have known Henry would never succeed him on the farm. He had lost his son to the city and to machines.

To Henry "the timber had all been cut."

61a.

IX. GAS AND LIGHT

A good time is 2nd.
—HENRY FORD

61a, b, c. What Detroit looked like in the early nineties. Here is the Campus Martius, looking south. The Campus Martius and the Grand Circus, a half mile north, were the hubs of the city. On the left a beer wagon is driving away over the cobbles; on the right a horsecar and a long rank of hansom cabs. The corner of Michigan and Woodward, filled with awnings, open streetcars, and a scurrying small dog. The Majestic Building has still to be erected on the corner where the awnings are; it was recently demolished to make way for a new skyscraper, the Federal Savings and Loan Building; and on the left is the old City Hall, also just demolished to create a parking area. And the old Detroit Police Station, complete with a police patrol wagon.

61b.

If you look at the pictures a little, you will see why it is impossible to make a movie that recaptures another time. No matter how accurate the research, how careful the costumes, how honest the intent, there is something missing, and it is not a matter of clothes or geography. We are different because we do not think the thoughts they did, nor know the things they did, nor move the way they did. So it is all gone, with each generation, as our own grandchildren will look at our pictures and wonder.

Life in most of the United States in the 1890's was much like that in the pictures: quiet, dreamy, spacious. The land was still empty of people and things. When it is impossible to get anywhere in a hurry, no one hurries. This imparts a comfortable pace to events.

Life was no picnic, then, anymore than it ever was or ever will be; but there were no nerves, no ulcers, no psychiatrists, almost no telephones, and night-life meant being out after dinnertime.

61c.

Detroit was the fifteenth city in the United States: its population was 205,669, the U.S. population 62,622,250. The salary of the governor of Michigan had just been raised from $1,000 a year to $4,000.

In Detroit there was factory smoke in the skies, and on Friday, September 25, 1891, Henry and Clara Ford headed toward that smoke, riding in a haywagon with their furniture.

62. Transportation, the 1890's. When you wanted to go somewhere you got between the shafts of the buggy and tugged it out of the shed yourself. Then you went into the barn, harnessed the horse, backed him between the shafts, hitched him up and were ready to go. This was never any fun, and on cold days it was less than that. The man above is putting his buggy away.

63. The American road, the 1890's, in good weather: a typical country road five years before Henry Ford got his first car to run. Most U.S. roads then were typical.

In all the land there were only a few thousand miles of highway better than this; most of the good roads ended a few miles outside the cities. In the '90's the roads were actually worse than they had been two score years before, because the great railroad-building boom had put an end to the Conestoga wagons, the only long-haul road users. Road building had gone to pot; everyone took the trains. A town away from a railroad was truly isolated.

64. The American road, the 1890's, in bad weather. On a good day it was pleasant to jog along a sweet-smelling country lane behind a well-gaited horse. There were few traffic problems; two drivers steered their Dobbins to the right and saluted each other with their whips. But in a cold, soaking rain, with the horse's hooves splashing up great gouts of chocolate mud as he struggled along the ruts, travel was only for country doctors.

Notice the width of the ruts. This was one of Henry Ford's chief early-day problems. His cars were built much narrower than the wide-bottomed wagons, for reasons of design, and so for a long time motoring meant that you rode leaning to one side, as one wheel ran along the high middle of the road and the other rolled along the rut.

62.

63.

64.

65.

66.

67.

At the beginning of the 1890's, few street railways were electrified; most of them still used horses. A joke of the period:

"Move forward a little!" roared the conductor on the horsecar.

"I can't," gasped the man in front, "I don't know how to ride horseback."

65. To this house the Fords came on September 25, 1891. Here they brought their household goods in the haywagon. There must have been silences in the eight-mile ride, for the city had a different meaning to each.

After the pretty and spacious Square House, these shabby quarters must have been a comedown to Clara Ford. They took the right half of the double house, which was then residential only; the "Excellent Hand Laundry" was once their living-room. This was then 618 John R Street (now 4426), on the east side of the street between Canfield and Garfield. The house was owned by one Amos Chaffee. The rent: $10 a month. (This picture was taken in 1941.)

We do not know the thought of the Fords as they came to town, nor anything about their dim quarters except what you see here. But a piece of the flavor of those times may suggest something of what life was like then: just about the steadiest, sure-fire material for jokes in those years was the problem of which—the husband or the wife—should get up in the morning to build the fire in the stove. (Couples born to the thermostat can scarcely understand this.) One favorite was the quip: "The wife who has to get up first to light the fire makes it warm for the old man, you can bet." Another sample:

Lover: "I would die for you if necessary."

Girl: "Nonsense. Swear to me that you'll get up and make the fires and I'll consider your proposal."

66. Charles Phelps Gilbert, about 1888. This picture, which has an oddly haunting period quality, was a baffler. It was discovered in January 1952 in one of Henry Ford's old albums, and it defied identification. It was patiently compared with thousands of pictures and laid aside; when thousands more turned up, compared again. But neither the man nor the room ever appeared in any other picture. In the meantime we had learned that when Henry Ford kept anything,

52

there was a reason. This man was somehow in-volved in Henry Ford's life.

Everything in the picture said 1890. But who was he? He had dignity, a beautifully groomed mustache, small mutton-chop whiskers, a well-cut suit of rich and heavy material, and the desk looked executive. The meters and gadgetry suggested electricity: could he have been an executive of the Edison Illuminating Company? The trail went cold, for in Henry's years with Edison the executive had been Alexander Dow, and this was not Dow.

Then came a small discovery: Dow did not arrive until 1896. Could this have been his predecessor? Research finally showed that the Edison manager in Detroit before Dow was one C. P. Gilbert. But there were no pictures of Gilbert. Once again the mutton-chop picture was laid aside.

Then fresh sources established Gilbert as the man who actually hired Henry Ford. And finally, by patient police work, another cache of Ford's personal albums was traced to a filing case in a small office in the heating plant behind the Ford Museum. In the bottom drawer among hundreds of pictures, this one turned up again—this time identified on the back in Henry Ford's own writing: "Charles Phelps Gilbert, general manager from Feb. 1, 1888 to June 30, 1896, when he was succeeded by Alexander Dow. Gilbert died in Calif. Oct. 1, 1917."

The story came together. This is what happened on a September day in 1891:

Henry walked into Detroit, directly to the Edison Company. Charles Gilbert had just clapped on the hat we see hanging on the back wall and was walking out as Henry entered. He was "elderly," said Henry, who was then 28.

Said Henry: "Who's in charge here?"

"I am," said Mr. Gilbert. "What can I do for you?"

"I'm an engineer. Have you any work I can do?"

"How much do you know about the work?"

"I know as much as anyone my age." Ford, of course, knew very little about electricity, but a good deal about engines and boilers.

"Well, I do think we have a place for you. A man was killed last week down at our substation and we need some one in his place right away."

And Gilbert telephoned John R. Wilde, the substation chief. (Wilde was a friend of Henry's since the Flower Brothers machine shop days, and may have given Ford a tip on the job.) Henry was hired: the hours, 6 P.M. to 6 A.M.; the salary, $40 a month. He started on the job at midnight on September 25, 1891, the very day the Fords moved to Detroit.

67. Main Station, Edison Illuminating Company, at Washington Boulevard and State Street, Detroit, about 1891. Henry began at the substation at Woodward and Willis; he did not reach this main station until November 1, 1893.

In the substation was a machine Henry knew well, a 100-horsepower Beck steam-engine, and two that were new to him: an Arlington & Sims 150-horsepower generator and a 300-horsepower Rice dynamo. In Henry's very first month came a crisis: the Beck steam-engine broke down.

There were then three light companies in Detroit, and Edison was the aggressive youngest, only five years old at the time. The other two fought for street-lighting contracts, but the Edison Company supplied electricity chiefly to homes. It also covered all the churches, and one Sunday night the strain of supplying extra electricity for church services damaged the Beck.

When Henry examined the damage, he found a piston rod broken, a hole in the cylinder block, and a broken valve. Soon after dawn Mr. Gilbert and other dignitaries examined the damage dolefully; lengthy repairs meant a long period of lights out.

But our hero was on his home ground with a steam-engine. Henry said he could repair the damage himself. Manager Gilbert was "amazed" but agreeable, and Henry set to work. He made his own pattern for the repair to the cylinder block, and by working straight around the clock had a patch in the hole before the new parts came. Then he fixed the piston rod and the broken valve. While he was at it, he said, he devised "a slide for the crosshead" so that the accident could not happen again. A few hours before church time the next Sunday the engines were all running.

The delighted Mr. Gilbert gave Henry an immediate $5-a-month raise to $45, beginning November 1. And in December Henry's pay was raised again, to $50.

"There wasn't too much to do around the plant," Henry said later. "We had to shovel coal every few hours—hard coal because people didn't like smoke in that section. Then there was the steam-pressure gauge to watch, the engines to go over, with new parts to replace the old ones." Henry had already made a bargain with the chief electrical engineer, a man named Storey, not to tear any installation down without calling him: "I'd come any time, whether it was during my working hours or not."

68.

68. *The fourth home of the Fords, No. 7 (now No. 2032) Washington Boulevard. Early in 1892 the Fords moved to this house, living in the apartment just left of the main entrance. The house later became a hotel and was torn down soon after this picture was taken, about 1915.*

Without his own workshop, Henry was restless, so, as soon as he got a raise, later that year they moved to better quarters in a flat at 162 (now number 1318) Cass Avenue, of which no picture survives. On May 30, 1893 they went on to a sixth home, at 570 West Forest Avenue, between Vermont and Wabash. By the time Henry took a photographer backtracking over his early life the Forest Avenue place had been demolished. To Henry, who wanted a record of every high point, this must have been a sorrow, for it was at the Forest Avenue house that his only son, Edsel, was born.

69.

69. *The old YMCA Building, at the corner of Griswold and Grand River, where Henry found a workshop. In the winter of 1892–93, A. G. Studer, of the YMCA staff, hired Henry to conduct a night metal-working class, at $2.50 a night. (Henry was now on the day shift.) More important to Henry than the money was the fact he could machine metal parts in the school shop. One student who learned machine shop practice from him was Oliver E. Barthel, a young engineer and draftsman who came to be important in the early careers of two Detroit automobile pioneers: Ford and Charles B. King.*

70. *The station-house gang, 1892. Henry Ford now has a mustache, grown sometime in the four years since his marriage. He wore this modest bush for eleven years, only rarely permitting it to luxuriate toward the full handle bar, and then dropped it, perhaps by popular demand, some-*

70.

71.

72.

time in the fall of 1902. Ford is in the door on the right, in cap and overalls, with a large water-fall knot in his necktie. Not all the others can be identified, for this is long ago and many are dead and memories have faded. Seated, front row: un-known, James F. Sullivan, and three unknowns; second row: Burt Pettit, George W. Cato, John A. Ash, and three unknowns; back row: Patrick Cunningham, John Dixon (in the door) and Ford.

Henry, recalling this period to Samuel W. Crowther, said: "It was in 1890 that I began on a double-cylinder engine." (Note: the date is dubious, but this is Henry's best memory in 1921. Most of the following probably occurred after 1893.)

It was quite impractical to consider the single cylinder for transportation purposes—the fly-wheel had to be entirely too heavy. Between making the first four-cycle engine of the Otto type and the start on a double cylinder I had made a great many experimental engines out of tubing. I fairly knew my way about.

The double cylinder, I thought, could be applied to a road vehicle and my original idea was to put it on a bicycle with a direct connection to the crankshaft, and allowing for the rear wheel of the bicycle to act as the balance-wheel. The speed was going to be varied only by the throttle.

I never carried out this plan because it soon became apparent that the engine, gasoline tank and the various necessary controls would be entirely too heavy for a bicycle. The plan of the two opposed cylinders was that while one would be delivering power the other would be exhausting. This naturally would not re-quire so heavy a fly wheel to even the applica-tion of power. The work started in my shop on the farm.

There are difficulties here, but mainly in the date of 1890. Bicycles were then new and exciting things, but almost never seen or used in the coun-try, since there was nowhere smooth enough go-ing for a bicycle. It is unlikely Henry had a secondhand bicycle to experiment with, since he did not even have a firsthand one until 1893.

71. The station-house gang, March, 1893. Henry looks in prosperous fettle here, in trim coveralls, a stickpin in his tie; he may have just learned he

would be a father before the year's end. The identification is complete:
Front row: *James F. Sullivan, J. Eugene Lee, Wright B. Thompson, Frank T. Mather, John W. McNamara, George A. Crawford, Burt Pettit.*
Center row: *H. Ward Noble and George W. Cato, one of Henry's closest friends at the time and a superb mechanic.*
Rear row: *John A. Ash, Thomas J. Blackley, Walter J. Collady, little James W. Bishop, who followed Henry faithfully for the next ten years and eventually went to Dearborn to work for him, "Sandy" Sharp, Ford, John Dixon, and Patrick J. Cunningham.*

72. Henry and his bicycle, summer, 1893. Henry bought this lightweight bicycle (model 2779) on February 10, 1893 from William Clifford. (We do not know the full price, but he still owed $15.) The bicycle frame proved too light; Henry rebuilt it later. He also bought his first camera; this picture and many of those to come were taken with it.

The importance of this picture is plain if we remember that what was now happening to Henry Ford was happening to inventors all over northeastern United States: namely, the bicycle. The very first bicycle joke, apparently, was that found in most almanacs in 1882:

"How old is that boy on the bicycle?"

"Well, he's seen 15 summers and 115 falls."

But by the '90's the craze was sweeping the country furiously, and it raged like a forest fire until the motor cars chugged about. "A Bicycle Built for Two" was finally extinguished only by "In My Merry Oldsmobile."

What happened now was of enormous consequence to Americans. For the first time in two generations people suddenly had bone-shaking cause to look at their roads—and there were no roads. The railroad had dominated everything since Governor Leland Stanford of California and Vice-President T. C. Durant of the Union Pacific had taken turns missing the Golden Spike on May 10, 1869 at Promontory Point, Utah.

Cycling around town was no fun; people wanted to take picnic lunches, join cycling clubs and bike off to the virgin countryside. The sudden cry for roads was so heartfelt, so deep, so outraged, and so national that even politicians heard it. Men began scurrying about in state capitols and in Washington.

Quickly a sleepy little office in the Interior Department was dusted out, expanded, given funds it had no immediate use for, and presented to the nation as the Bureau of Public Roads.

Editorials thundered; where, oh where indeed, was the proud American eagle? Little machine shops became thriving bicycle factories. Soon tycoons of the cycle industry were buying heavier watch chains, building mansions with more iron deer on the lawns than the neighbors had, and giving cigar-flicking interviews on the state of business.

But something more happened. A new magazine, *The Horseless Age,* later estimated that around 1891 and 1892 at least three hundred American inventors began working simultaneously on designs for self-propelled road vehicles. Why? The American inventor, Hiram Percy Maxim, described it best:

> . . . I am amazed that so many of us began work so nearly at the same time and without the slightest notion that others were working on the problem.

> Why did so many different and widely separated persons have the same thoughts at the same time? In my case the idea came from looking down and contemplating the mechanism of my legs and the bicycle cranks while riding along a lonely road in the middle of the night.

> Before this . . . the bicycle had not yet directed men's minds to the possibilities of independent, long-distance travel over the ordinary highway.

The 1893 Henry, in his Panama hat, butterfly bowtie, sawed-off vest, pants clips adjusted, had a baby on the way, no workshop to experiment in, and needed more money. He had been promoted to the main Edison light station and was rising in the company's ranks. But he seemed stuck at $50 a month. So he began a campaign around the first of July 1893 to become chief engineer of the City Lighting Plant, a higher-paid position. He had no difficulty in getting favorable recommendations: three letters which survive attest to his reputation as a stationary operating engineer and a first-class machinist. One was from the mechanical superintendent of the biggest steam-engine manufacturer in Buffalo; another from the superintendent of Detroit's own Riverside Iron Works, one of the biggest in the area; a third from William C. Maybury, a politico who would soon become mayor of Detroit. But the job fell through somehow; it went to Alex Dow.

Baby or no, job or no, Henry now made a date with another machine. He had been reared on the tales of the Philadelphia Centennial of 1876; now came the Columbian Exposition of 1893 in Chicago. Henry went heading not for the famous tummy twists of "Little Egypt" but for the machinery, and he brought home a mental picture of the workings of a two-cylinder Daimler engine pumping water; it was mounted on a fire hose cart drawn by two horses.

73. Henry at work, 1893. Ford, William F. Bartels, and George W. Cato are seen in the dynamo room of the Edison Company's main station at State and Washington. Henry had cultivated his lusty taste for practical jokes; in the engine room he cured one George Flint of sloppiness. George used to leave his shoes about. So Henry nailed George's shoes to the floor with long spikes, went to the basement and turned the points of the spikes back. Friend John Wilde helped in those jokes. Once little Jim Bishop, repairing a motor with a crew in the basement, began to feel suffocated. Bishop and the crew went outside for air and found Ford and Wilde busy with a shovel loaded with hot coals. They dropped sulphur on the coals and with careful art were manipulating a bellows to blow the fumes through a knothole into the basement.

But Henry's driving energies went into other experiments besides horseplay. He had come to Detroit to learn more about gas and light, and over the next eight years he did: he was with the Edison Illuminating Company from September 25, 1891 to August 15, 1899.

He was twenty-eight when he brought Clara and their chattels to Detroit in a haywagon. At that time he had already had a long list of private failures: a steam road locomotive that ran forty feet and stopped for good, a second that never did start, innumerable clocks taken apart and never put together, engines that wouldn't run, and odds-and-ends of projects that never came off.

He had formed certain habits of mind. One of them was a cheerfulness about failure. This cheerfulness is worth a word. It was the very opposite of an oh-the-hell-with-it attitude; his contentment was based primarily on an exact understanding of why the experiment had failed. As long as he knew why and where and how and what had gone wrong, he was happy—had learned something. This contentment was based secondarily on the fact that all of these experiments were practice warm-ups for the real goal—he discovered over and over again that he needed to know more.

Another habit was now forming: let George do it. In the next few years we will see Henry steadily developing talents for salesmanship and management. He could talk other men into helping him, backing him, working for him; you will note how many times someone else was always lifting the heavy end while Henry was off talking another man into a little weight-lifting.

Henry had begun to know himself. He discovered that other men could machine things a little more smoothly, read blueprints better, follow measurements more exactly. On the other hand, he could organize better, could see the flaws in a design more quickly, could plan work ahead better. He had the combinative mind of a chess player, which is simply the ability to see both the short-term and the long-term possibilities at the same time.

All of this runs contrary to the solid old myth that Henry Ford was that typical American hero, the lone inventor, friendless, scorned, penniless, puzzling things out alone in a woodshed. In the Archives is abundant proof that, first, he was almost never alone or lonely—indeed, he did most of his inventing in the midst of a crowd of friends handing him tools, money, valves, ideas, equipment; second, he was not only not scorned but highly respected; third, he was not only not penniless but in circumstances comfortable enough to afford the theater and vaudeville and to buy music. If he ever missed a meal it was by design.

With these things in mind, the next years of Henry Ford's struggles toward his goal became easier to follow.

73.

X. THE BACKYARD AT 58 BAGLEY

It is always too soon to quit.
—HENRY FORD

Henry came home from the Fair—he must have seen the Ferris wheel there, first of its kind—and bicycled to and fro. And Clara—we know little of Clara in all those months of 1893, nor of that vanished home on Forest Avenue; in all their reminiscing they never talked about that time, perhaps because no one thought to ask.

One day in 1892 Dr. David H. O'Donnell, a young doctor fresh from medical school, met Harry Bryant, Clara's brother, in a Detroit cigar store. That night his wife had a baby safely and thereafter recommended Dr. O'Donnell.

On November 6, 1893, in the Forest Avenue house, Edsel Bryant Ford was born. Dr. O'Donnell didn't have enough money for a horse and buggy; he came on a bicycle, with his doctor's bag tied on in front.

Dr. O'Donnell said: "I didn't run into any difficulty. Mrs. Ford didn't give me any trouble at all. She never complained. Mr. Ford was in the house. He didn't get excited and he didn't bother me. Most young fathers bother the life out of a doctor. For the delivery of Edsel I got $10, and the nurse who was there twenty-four hours a day for two weeks got $4 a week." And from the early days of the Ford Motor Company until Henry Ford died, Dr. O'Donnell's cars were serviced free by the company.

Ten days after Edsel was born Henry's salary was jumped almost double, to $90 a month. Two weeks later, on December 1, Henry became chief engineer.

Two weeks and one day after that, on December 15, the Fords moved to 58 Bagley Avenue, around the corner from Grand River.

On Christmas Eve, 1893, Henry got his tubular gas engine working, at Clara's kitchen sink.

74. A gasoline bill, 1893. The "DJ" means "demi-john"; gasoline was then often sold in small jugs.

By now Henry had wangled things pretty much to his liking. As chief engineer he had the confidence of the Edison management. The new job meant he was on call around the clock, and to Henry a 24-hour day was always the most satisfactory. He had no taste for clock-punching regularity, then or ever, and, unlike most of us, was somehow able at a relatively early age to arrange his affairs so he could always duck doing anything he disliked. In later years the long procession of his secretaries quickly learned that the one safe course was to answer all correspondence with "Mr. Ford is out of town." (There are miles of such letters in the Archives.) This became a great joke within the company; to this day, whenever anything irksome comes up, men will look at each other and chant in unison: "The Ford Motor Company is out of town."

Henry kept his bicycle by the front steps of 58 Bagley Avenue day and night, installed a telephone—with an extension, naturally, to the workshop out in back—and every night, on retiring, placed his carefully unlaced high-top shoes beside his bed, so he could respond to emergencies like a fireman.

He was now freed—for life, as it turned out—from the compulsion to show up at any particular place at any particular time. He took advantage of this in a way peculiar to himself. No poolrooms saw him, no saloons got his business, and neither did the churches or any form of society or club: Henry went around to Detroit's machine shops like a scholarly browser in the bookstores of New York's lower Fourth Avenue, learning, meeting mechanics, and just pleasuring himself. These machine shops were his libraries, his clubs, his stock exchange, his laboratories, his jam-sessions. And here he met, sifting them through trial and error, many of the men who would be important in his career.

At the Wain Machine Shop, on Wayne Street, he picked up again with his boyhood playmate at Flower Brothers—Frederick Strauss. Said Strauss:

> Henry had all kinds of time and he used to come see me. He had a little shop of his own back of the Edison Company. The shop was across the alley; only one-quarter was above the sidewalk. It was a storage place. Henry used it as a hangout.

Other fellows would come sit in there. Henry had a little lathe. He had this idea of making a little gasoline engine out of scrap. We didn't work every night. We would just joke away. Sometimes we would work and sometimes not. It took us about six weeks to get this little engine built.

Saturday nights we had quite a crowd. Henry had some sort of a magnet. He could draw people to him; that was a funny thing about him.

When you are building a little engine, one thing goes after another. You bore out the cylinder, and you know you've got to make a piston, and you know you've got to have a cylinder head.

We had an awful time with the ignition. The cylinder was brass, made out of a piece of pipe, a steam pipe. . . . That one cylinder is really the first engine.

When we ran that little engine in the basement, of course, there would be quite a few people outside listening to the noise, wondering what was going on. We would run it sometimes and some nights we wouldn't.

Two of Henry's other close friends at this time were Charles Annesley, known as "Chappie," nephew of one of the wealthiest men on Detroit's elegant Woodward Avenue, and Barton L. Peck, another rich man's son. Both at first were interested in bicycles, and this interest passed quickly on to motorcars. Both were dilettantes of a new sort: the late Victorian breed who became violent *aficionados* of speed. W. E. Henley wrote poetry about this new goddess; the cult of speed worshippers that then formed about the bicycle later switched to the motorcar and still later to the motorboat, the racing car, the airplane—the three groups that exist today.

Barton Peck was the son of George Peck, one of the most prominent men in Detroit. George Peck had built up a solid fortune as a clothes merchant, and at this time was president of the Michigan National Savings Bank and—most significant—was also president of the Edison Illuminating Company of Detroit. He was Dow's boss, and therefore Henry's boss. Unquestionably his friendship with Henry gave prestige and influence to Henry's moves in this period.

There were whole social worlds between Fred

74.

Strauss, the boy roustabout mechanic, and Messrs. Peck and Annesley, the well-to-do bicycle enthusiasts. Henry's easy ability to move back and forth from the white collar to the greasy collar came about partly from the democracy of the machine shop: all men are equal before a stubborn ignition. But it also came from the fact that even then he was in the management class.

It was to Annesley that Henry would later sell his first car; it would be in Peck's tinkering shop at 81 Park Place that Henry would actually bring about the germ of his Ford Motor Company. Annesley and Peck had been college chums; they tinkered in Peck's shop with plans for a gasoline engine to drive a motorboat. Although Henry apparently met anyone in Detroit who tinkered, he may have met Barton Peck through his father's office at the Edison Company.

75. The seventh home of the Fords. This is the famous 58 Bagley Avenue—the left half of this double house; the number can be seen just above the mail-slot in the door. The landlord was William B. Wreford, and Henry paid him $25 a month rent. The Fords lived here from December 15, 1893 until July 1897. Ford himself took the photograph, and wrote on the back: "Left 1897, Taken 1898." It is interesting to speculate on why Henry came back a year later to take this photograph. Was it his sense of history operating even then?

In each picture of this home the little lawn is unkempt and littered with blown papers. The slatted lattice (on the right by the wooden steps) will show in other photos. Henry took his snapshots from a spot near his own front stoop on the left, shooting to the right toward the lattice.

It was a fine day for people interested in history when Henry took this shot, for somewhere in the later busy shuffling years of Detroit the whole house disappeared entirely—it was believed destroyed. Then Charles B. King, the gentle inventor, prowling about downtown Detroit in 1929 discovered it again. A movie theater had been erected on the Bagley Avenue site, but the old house had not been demolished; it had merely

been jacked up on rollers and given a quarter-turn to the right, so that it now faced on Grand River Avenue. Its front had been done over; 58 Bagley had become a tearoom on Grand River. The grateful Ford rushed to the scene, positively identified the building, and in 1932 sent workmen who carefully removed a number of bricks, replacing them with new ones. The old bricks were hauled to Greenfield Village and used in constructing a replica of his Bagley Avenue workshop. But what with one thing and another, the workmen had to take bricks from the wrong side of the house—the old bricks you see in the Greenfield replica actually came from the quite unhistoric 56 Bagley.

By now it should be apparent that Henry Ford was never a homebody. His heart was always in the shop. We know every detail of his many workshops down to the last tiny watch-spring, nut and bolt—the first watch he ever repaired is still on display. But we never catch a glimpse of the interiors of the many homes: we do not know what pictures hung on the wall. The only time we hear of the Bagley Avenue kitchen is when Henry does an experiment there; we only learn that they had an organ in the Square House because Henry used a piece of the music for an engine diagram.

76a, b. Henry's first gasoline engine. The first picture shows it in place in the reconstructed workshop in Greenfield Village. It is now in the Ford Museum, just about as it was when he once clamped it on Clara's kitchen sink. The second picture is the same engine in cut-out profile.

The early gas engines were, naturally enough, designed to imitate the double-acting principle of the steam-engine: you drive the piston in one direction with an explosion, then hit it with another explosion that drives it the other way. That, in rough sum, is a two-cycle engine.

But the auto pioneers ran into trouble when they tried the two-cycle principle with gasoline. The explosions came too rapidly; not enough gas was sucked in for the next explosion, and not enough burned-out gas was blown out or exhausted.

Then the pioneers hit on a new notion: suppose you give the piston such a powerful charge that the impulse carries over for *two* revolutions of the crankshaft. Then this happens: the first stroke of the piston sucks gasoline in, the second stroke compresses it (explosion), the third stroke is the power stroke, and the fourth stroke exhausts waste gas. At each stroke the crankshaft turns one-half of one revolution; the third or power stroke supplies enough power to keep the crankshaft moving around until the next power stroke. This is a crude explanation of the four-cycle engine.

Four-cycle operation depends on ignition at "deadpoint," the end of the second stroke, when gasoline has been sucked in and compressed; its sudden expansion in the explosion is what drives the crankshaft and thus the engine. The pioneers saw tremendous advantages here: sufficient gas was inhaled, and burned-out gas was completely exhaled. The problems then became matters of size and timing: the size of the piston, the size of the combustion-chamber, the length of the stroke, the right moment, exactly, at which to make the spark jump, the weight of the flywheel.

Early in December 1893 Henry went around picking up the things he needed. He got a hand-wheel from an old lathe to act as his flywheel. Next, a cylinder. Then one James Wolfenden, a boilermaker, came in to repair a boiler in the Edison engine-room; when he finished he packed his bag hurriedly, anxious to get on with his Christmas shopping. But he had a piece of tubing too long to carry. As he went to throw it on the scrap-iron pile Henry spoke for it—and a little section of that scrap pipe, almost thrown away in the Christmas rush seventy years ago, shows in the pictures as the cylinder.

Henry, no doubt with much advice, aid, and counsel from Strauss, Cato, Bishop, and others, reamed out the piece of pipe to a one-inch bore, tooled up a homemade piston fitted with rings, and attached this by a rod to the crankshaft. A two-to-one gear arrangement operated a cam, opening the exhaust valve and timing the spark. A piece of fiber with a wire through its center served as a spark plug; it made contact with a wire at the end of the piston, and when the piston moved away, this contact was broken and a spark leaped the gap, exploding the gasoline. Since this was only a test engine, he used the house current to supply the electricity—which in a car would have to come from batteries.

Henry toiled at this engine. By now, as he said, "I knew my way fairly about." Then he

75.

76a.

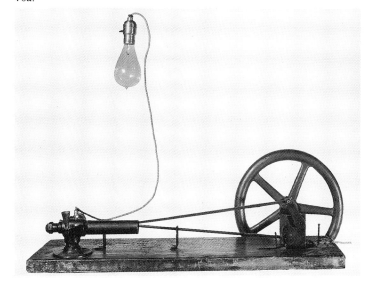

76b.

77.

78.

lugged it into Clara's kitchen on Christmas Eve with the exasperating blindness of the male animal to the real problems of life. But he had to have help; he could not do two things at once: turn the crankshaft to start it and at the same time dribble gasoline from an oilcan into the intake valve.

He clamped the mounting board to the kitchen sink and connected a wire from the kitchen light to the spark plug, grounding the engine to the sink's waterpipe. Clara was not happy. She was cooking furiously in preparation for tomorrow's Christmas dinner guests; and in the next room six-week-old Edsel was asleep.

We can almost hear Clara sighing ("Men!") and see her wiping her hands, and then listening patiently to Henry's instructions: in one hand she had to hold the oilcan filled with gasoline, and with the other hand she had to adjust a screw to let the gasoline trickle slowly or rapidly, as needed, into the intake.

Henry turned the flywheel, the air and gasoline were sucked into the cylinder, the kitchen light flickered. He made a slight adjustment, tried again, and the engine roared into action, the sink shaking with vibration, flames shooting from the exhaust.

He ran it for about half a minute, and he ran it only that one time. That was his way. He had done it.

Right after Christmas, on December 29, he began to try to build an engine powerful enough to run a horseless carriage.

We do not know whether the roar woke Edsel. No one ever thought to ask.

77. The Detroit High School. Earnest citizens fought for years with laggard politicians to get a high school building in Detroit; it was finally erected in 1876, adjoining the old Capitol building, at State and Griswold. It is shown here in all its glory of the '70's and '80's, when it graduated class after class of the men who became governors, senators, cabinet members, millionaires—and even a few poets. It was one of the most significant buildings to Detroiters, perhaps because of its association with Michigan history; it was known as the Capitol High School. And it belongs here mainly because of the next picture.

78. The fire at the school. In January 1893 the school burned down, and here is one of the pic-

tures that Henry Ford saved all his life of that important moment in Detroit history. We can be certain that nothing—the gas-engine experiments, his work at Edison Illuminating—kept Henry from that fire. Note the steamers puffing at the corners of the building.

79. Edsel's first picture. Since Henry took this picture, this is probably our only look at the interior of 58 Bagley. This is 1894, for Edsel can hold his head up; the time must be near Clara's twenty-eighth birthday, which would be April 11. Clara is crisp in bombazine with muslin sleeves; Edsel watches Daddy with his fingers crossed on his fat little right hand.

The Fords were in modest circumstances, happy enough, but without extra cash. Clara was a natural manager, capable in money matters. Clara always had enough in the budget for picnics, good clothes, a neatly kept house, and music; Henry and Clara regarded music as a necessity like food. At Bagley Avenue they splurged on a player piano.

The piano turned out to be a bit of an endurance test of the budget—or the Fords were slow payers. They bought it from the C. Whitney Marvin Piano Company in Detroit for $355—on time payments. By June 30, 1896 they had paid off all but $14 of the debt. Then the payments lagged sadly and it would be five more years and a lot of back interest before they paid it off.

A few incidents of their life are of interest. In January 1895 Clara had the parlor couch covered for $10. In May she had one of the rugs cleaned, at a price to bring strange emotions to a housewife today: 42 yards of carpet at 3¢ per yard, $1.26.

80. A dressmaker's bill, 1896.

And Henry paid a $5 coal bill—on May 28, 1895—to Detroit's up-and-coming young coal-dealer, Alex Y. Malcomson. Perhaps it was that day that Ford first met Malcomson, who was to figure later so heavily in his life during four years of stiff struggle.

81. Edsel takes a buggy-ride: probably late autumn, 1894, when Edsel was about a year old. They are out on the farm, at the Bryant homestead, and it is almost certainly a Sunday. Henry

79.

80.

Young Henry Ford

81.

82.

83.

Detroit, Mich. Oct 1st 1894

Received of Henry Ford

Twenty five Dollars

Rent for 58 Bagly ave to Nov 1st 1894

$25 00

Dean & Urban, Stationers, Detroit.

Oscar M. Springer

84.

The Backyard at 58 Bagley

was a religious man and disapproved of working on Sundays. But he himself might "tinker a little" in his shop, but this was more in the spirit of a man collecting stamps, or redding up his den. Sunday was his day for the family, for country rides, and for picnics, especially—to the end of his life picnics held for him a special glamor; he would drop everything for a chance to eat outdoors. Here are Milton Bryant and Edsel, in Homburg and frilled cap.

82. *Edsel, 1894. He was a quiet, sweet baby, not a fusser; and he grew up that way, gentle and steady. (These are professional studio poses.)*

83. *Clara at the Homestead. She seems thin. She is sitting in Father William's solid old rocker in the sun, smart in the fashionable balloon sleeves and polka-dot bowtie, a mannish straw hat perched on upswept hair. Henry took the picture.*

84. *A rent receipt, 1894.*

85. *On the stoop at 58 Bagley, probably 1895. On the steps, taking the summer air of a Sunday, is an old man, and here opinion divides bitterly. One school holds that this may be the only picture of Felix Julien, Henry's neighbor who lived at 56 Bagley; another argues it is Clara's father, Melvin Bryant. Next comes a young man who is Henry's brother John, then Clara in her best white dress, and Edsel about two years old, in his best dress. The scrubby lawn is littered as usual.*

86. *Edsel in daddy's vest. Perhaps the laughing Clara had her hair in pins, but someone had to hold Edsel while Henry photographed him in Daddy's big vest over his dress, wearing Henry's cap. The lattice at 56 Bagley shows here and in the next picture and thus locates the pictures.*

87. *Martha Bryant, now a grandmother, holds Edsel on Daddy's bicycle—this is the new bicycle—the frame that Henry had strengthened. Behind Henry's tool-kit can be seen Martha's dangling reticule. In the small widow's bonnet, made of taffeta in very dark shades (Mr. Bryant was still alive), her hair parted in the middle and combed hard and sleek to the ears, the bolero shoulder cape, and the reticule—Mrs. Bryant appeared in complete dress, de rigueur for those times for all women passing middle age.*

67

85.

86.

87.

88.

89.

88. *A Worthington pump. Henry did well at the Edison Company. On April 1, 1894 his salary was raised to $95 a month; on October 1 to $100. His career with Edison was now a sure thing. Here we see Chief Engineer Ford taking delivery in October 1895 of a massive new Worthington horizontal 14 x 20 x 15 duplex compound vacuum pump.*

On the left is Frederick B. Slocum, the Michigan representative for the pump company. Next is Henry's best friend, George W. Cato; then Henry in work-cap; in the rear an unknown. On top are two men from the Moreton Trucking Company, Patrick O'Neil and his foreman, William J. Murray. Below, in front, elegant in his Homburg hat, braided heavy wool suit and wing-collar, is the Edison manager who hired Henry: Charles P. Gilbert. Mr. Gilbert had reduced the mutton-chop effect of his side-whiskers and had begun to grow a Vandyke. This is the last we see of Mr. Gilbert, soon to retire to Los Gatos, California.

89. *At the Bryants. Edsel, still in long hair and dresses, visits Grandma Bryant. The three sisters are all in the dress-up stiff straw hats of the day: Kate at left, Eva holding onto Edsel, Martha and Clara at right. It is probably Sunday again. Edsel's rocking-horse bounced only a sedate six inches or so, and shows no trace, of course, of automotive influence.*

If it was a Sunday, they probably made music; they were all great listeners, the Bryants and the Fords; and the girls played passable piano and organ. We may hazard a guess, if they did make music, one of the tunes no doubt was Philip Wingate's hit of the time:

> I don't want to play in your yard,
> I don't like you any more;
> You'll be sorry when you see me
> Sliding down our cellar door. . . .

XI. THE BREAK-THROUGH

Mrs. Ford rode on the car the second day. . . .
—HENRY FORD

For Henry Ford, 1895 was an arduous year. By choice, he was on double duty. As chief engineer he had to maintain electric-light service twenty-four hours a day, and plant maintenance in those days was no push-button affair. Metals then were more fragile; little was known of such things as tensile strength, fatigue points, and alloys; no one had yet broken metals down to their molecular structures. Mechanical failures were common, expected, and occasionally disastrous.

The rest of Henry's twenty-four hours were committed to his obsession.

To non-mechanical people, which means most people, the natural question about his first car may be: What took him so long? Well, there was no such thing as a spark plug; it hadn't been invented. There was no such thing as a carburetor. There were no automobile wheels—only wagon wheels and buggy wheels. The front steering on wagons and buggies had to be adapted. Camshafts, crankshafts, push rods, bearings, piston rings, gears—everything had to be made from the ground up. Each tiny part was not one problem but a host of problems.

90.

90. Charles A. Strelinger, owner of the Charles A. Strelinger Company, Machinery and Tools.

Every spare dollar in the Ford finances went to buy tools and materials. Henry nursed his credit. The Strelinger hardware store allowed him a credit of only $15 a month. He drove himself hard. Even the hardware merchant, Charles Bush of Strelinger, said:

We often wondered when Henry slept, because he put in long hours working at the plant and when he went home he was always experimenting or reading.

Henry said later merely that he was in good health and slept whenever he could. And we know now that he had begun to develop his ability to be in many places at once, which simply means the technique of doing things quickly. Henry learned the art of the short call. He always seemed to be leisurely—and he always seemed to be leaving.

Clara kept a loyal watch on the budget and kept his work secret. When the Bryants and other friends came to visit, she would slip away during the evening to visit Henry out in the backyard workshop, telling her visitors only that "Henry is making something and maybe someday I'll tell you."

Every first-rate mechanic in the United States had the fever. That year—1895—the Duryea brothers were running a horseless carriage (it crashed in an accident on November 2); the Haynes-Apperson company had built a machine; inventor Charles B. King of Detroit was hard at work; a Chicago newspaper was promoting a race for motor carriages, as a stunt; Alexander Winton was making a motor wagon.

91.

91. Selden in his wagon. In Rochester, New York, a shrewd, choleric patent attorney, George B. Selden, decided the time had come to strike. He had submitted his first patent claim on a horseless carriage on May 8, 1879. Under the law he was permitted to amend this claim each year for seventeen years before finally taking out his patent; then a patent must be issued or the invention withdrawn.

Selden had carefully complied with the law, making neat little amendments in red ink on his invention, which, it should be remembered, was based on the Brayton *two-cycle* engine, and some of his amendments were as trivial as changing "the" to "a." But his timing had been perfect. Now he seemed to have a gold strike. He patented his horseless carriage in 1895, and this meant that technically he was in control of the coming automobile industry—not yet an industry but merely a rabble of inventors—for the next seventeen years, or until 1912.

Selden had little mechanical ability and a hot temper. All this made it difficult for him to raise funds. He did not even have a functioning model. Brooding, he could only bide his time. Probably not one of the scrambling American

92.

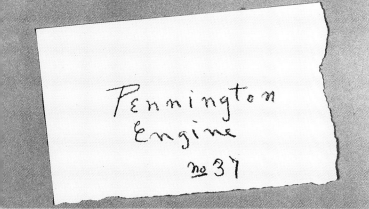

93.

inventors suspected that this unknown Rochester attorney owned them all, body, soul and horseless carriage.

The inventors were not only unaware of George Selden, they were almost unaware of each other. The magazine, *The Horseless Age,* was newly founded; reports of the motor wagons being built were as incomplete as the motor wagons themselves. Each man proceeded in his own way, and the results were marvelously different.

The matter of being first in America to build a car did not obsess them then; all that came much later. Henry himself never claimed to be first. During the Selden hearings in 1904, Ford did antedate some of his experiments with the gas engine and the first car, and this caused rare confusion for a long time. But in that year Henry and his lawyers thought that the only way to invalidate the Selden patent was to show that Ford's work had preceded Selden's.

The one man who could have dated every triumph and failure in that Bagley Avenue backyard has been dead a half-century; he kept no diary, and no one interviewed him while he lived. This was Felix Julien, who lived at 56 Bagley, in the other half of the double house, and was therefore entitled to half the woodshed.

Julien was a gentle, friendly old man, already retired. He had been a coaldealer. When he saw Henry working on his first carriage, he promptly hauled his own coal and wood out of the shed and into his house, in order to give Henry room to work. Julien's price: simply to be permitted to watch.

So in the evenings old Mr. Julien would sit until his own bedtime, watching Henry work; and as the car began to grow he became so fascinated that he would often sit alone in the shed in the daytime, waiting for Henry to come home. Children came too; around Detroit there are still a half-dozen oldsters who once skipped up the cobblestones of that alley to peek in at the door where Henry tinkered. Henry worked away in his spare time, in the Edison plant, in the basement shop behind it, and in the 58 Bagley backyard, all through 1894 and on through 1895. Strauss and King, Barthel and Cato, and Bell and Bishop and Huff and perhaps a dozen others helped him, it seems, grinding parts, joking, drilling, fitting, advising, lending tools and

pieces of scrap. They were all agreed on one thing: Henry had the dream.

One day he had a thrill—he saw Thomas Alva Edison, or almost saw him. Said Henry:

> He [Edison] was returning from his father's funeral at Port Huron and he walked past the plant, which was next door to the Hotel Cadillac where he had spent the night. I saw him with a group of men—at least, someone told me that Mr. Edison was in the group, but they passed so quickly that I am by no means sure that I saw the right man.

He took a trip to Auburn, New York, where he bought some new engines for the Edison plant, and went on to R. H. Macy & Co. in New York City, where a Benz gasoline engine was on display. And he kept touring the shops and factories.

92. John Lauer, Detroit, manufacturer of machinery. One of the best machine shops in Detroit was John Lauer's, at 112–114 St. Antoine Street. In the same building was the office of the brilliant Charles B. King. One of King's assistants was Oliver Barthel, who had studied machine-shop practice under Ford at the YMCA.

At the Lauer shop Henry saw a copy of the November 7, 1895, issue of *The American Machinist,* describing the first Kane-Pennington motor. A second article on this motor followed, on January 9, 1896.

93. The Pennington note from Ford's jotbooks, made years later. This engine gave Henry an idea for a spark breaker.

The two articles were passionately studied in bicycle shops and machine shops everywhere. The Kane-Pennington motor was light, powerful, and ingenious; its ignition system was particularly effective, since it avoided a "late spark." The article was a bit critical: "The machine work on the Pennington motors is not of a high grade; it cannot possibly rank beyond fair ordinary machine shop practice in any particular; there is nothing modern and nothing 'special' in the way of tools in the shops where these motors were built; the performance of the motor is due solely to *design,* not workmanship."

But Ford and others learned much from the

little motors designed by "Air Ship" Pennington. To digress, Pennington was called "Air Ship" in friendly ridicule because he dreamed some day of building an engine that would move a vehicle through the air. He said—and no doubt kindly people turned away to hide their snickers: "Suppose I have a cycle, screw-driven, making a mile a minute; just suppose that; then suppose I put aeroplanes on that machine, and they are well arranged and under good control, what then?" It was eight years before Pennington got the answer to his question, from the Wright Brothers at Kitty Hawk.

But none of the pioneers copied the Pennington motor. It was a tremendous stimulus; it showed how one designer had ingeniously solved problems all were pondering, and each inventor adapted those answers into his own designs.

Charles B. King was ahead of Pennington; "ahead" is relative, for he was going in a somewhat different direction. But King, and to some extent Barthel, were useful to Ford since they too were trying to design a gasoline engine.

King, then twenty-seven, five years younger than Henry, was already an engineer of national reputation. Born of a line of Americans who had successively fought in the Revolutionary War, the War of 1812, the Florida Indian Wars, the Mexican War, and the Civil War, King had been educated at Cornell as a draftsman and, in 1893, at the Columbian Exposition in Chicago, had exhibited two extraordinary inventions. One of them was a pneumatic hammer, the first of its kind, which won the Fair's highest award. The second was a steel brake beam for railroad cars, a first-class pioneer invention.

King had a long and useful career, authoring some sixty-five inventions. Some of them made powerful changes in American automotive life: he introduced the steering wheel on the left side, was the first to put the gearshift lever inside the car, and the first to extend the little mud-guards as full running-boards. But his only car, the once-famous Silent Northern, was not a financial success, and his automotive designs turned out to be peripheral rather than central, for he never built a great engine.

King and Ford were opposite in approach: King was a designer on paper whose designs were executed by others; Ford made his own rough sketches and then pretty much built the machines himself. King was at work on a four-cycle four-cylinder *en bloc* engine, probably the first of its type. Ford had come to the four-cycle principle by trial and error; King sent away for a Sintz two-cycle engine, analyzed it, was dissatisfied, and proceeded into a four-cycle design. His engine was not yet working, but he was well along, with Barthel's help.

King and Ford remained friends throughout their lives; as noted, it was King who discovered the "lost" house of 58 Bagley in 1929. Barthel did occasional, and important, work for Ford in the next few years, left him in 1901, and spent much time in later years arguing that King was the first man to drive a motor wagon over the streets of Detroit. This claim fell rather flat since Ford not only acknowledged it but volunteered that he had followed King's first trial ride on his own bicycle.

94. King's first car. On March 6, 1896, Charles B. King (right), and his mechanic, Oliver Barthel, drove the first motor wagon on the streets of Detroit. By agreement, the demonstration was held after 11 P.M. in order not to frighten horses or citizens. This picture was taken the next morning, March 7. As can be seen, King's car was really just a wagon with his own engine implanted; he had ordered a carriage, but it had not been delivered and he was anxious to go ahead. (Ford was still developing his own carriage.) This motor wagon weighed about 1,300 pounds and had a top speed of about five miles an hour. (Ford's car, ready three months later, weighed but 500 pounds and went twenty-five miles per hour.)

The press was far from excited. The *Detroit Free Press* gave the occasion a brief and cool paragraph the next morning. The *Detroit Journal* was mainly interested in the fact that "when in motion the connecting rods fly like lightning. . . ." Inventor King then made a statement that caught the tone of the soon-to-be automobile industry for years to come:

Horseless carriages are extensively used in Paris as delivery wagons, carriages, and even ambulances. I understand the Prince of Wales has ordered one. They are much in vogue among the English aristocracy, and will undoubtedly soon be here. . . . I am convinced they will in time supersede the horse.

The Break-Through

Henry Ford wanted to supersede the horse, too. But he needed one thing very badly—valves. Valves were expensive and hard to come by. And this was why it was a lucky day for him when he dropped in to the Lauer shop, met his old student Barthel, and was introduced to Charles King. For King generously gave Ford four valves (two by some accounts). These were steam valve-bodies, actually, and needed considerable conversion to function in Henry's car, but they were all-important to Ford.

95. *The first Ford in diagram. Item No. 4, the carbide lamp, was a later addition; so was the water tank under the seat. The gasoline tank held three gallons of gas.*

The car was slow in coming. Henry first set out to develop his little tubular engine into a real instrument of power. We do not know for sure whether he made more than one of these: there is conflicting testimony. But at some time soon after Clara's bread board models sink engine he began to build a true automotive engine. He had very stiff requirements for that engine; it must be light in weight, rugged, durable, powerful, simple, safe, above all, reliable. Each one of those qualities was then only an inventor's dream —and this is the hardest thing of all to realize today, when each of these qualities is taken for granted.

Since only a few people ever like to read about machinery, I will omit most of the mechanical details of Henry's long months of trial and error as he worked out his first car. But a certain sprinkling of them is necessary if the reader is to get even a glimmering of what one automobile pioneer had to go through—otherwise he might think that Henry just bolted a few odds and ends together from the diagrams in the magazines, the way a man does today with a Do-It-Yourself Kit. The point is, Henry had to *build* each part in the kit, and he didn't even know how many parts there should be, and when he put them together they wouldn't work right.

First, Henry got a piece of scrap from an old steam engine, a length of 2½-inch exhaust pipe. This he cut up to make his two cylinders, reaming out the pipe to a bore that was later measured as 2.565 inches. He made the cylinders 11 inches long and gave the piston a 6-inch stroke.

94

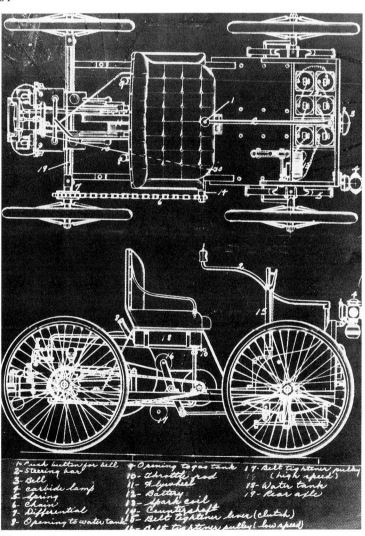

95.

73

He worked to distribute the power strokes evenly. He strove to keep the flywheel light and yet heavy enough to furnish the inertia to carry one piston through the whole compression stroke and the other piston through the whole exhaust stroke, with as little slow-down as possible.

His pistons were iron, with two rings. He went to the waterfront to the Detroit Dry Dock plant, where some old friends forged a crankshaft for him. He arranged the crankshaft to make both pistons move in the same direction at the same time, with a power stroke at every complete turn of the shaft. The valves gave him deep trouble, just as they did all the other auto pioneers, from the Duryeas to Haynes. After months of struggling, he needed luck. And that came when King gave him four valves.

Henry, or his friends, converted the steam valve bodies into poppet valves. He used two of them as automatic intake valves in the intake manifold near the cylinder. He threaded the valve stems at the end so he could put on a hexagon nut to hold a spring against the valve body. On the valve stem he fitted a loose fiber sleeve to act as a spacer which would permit the valve to open only ⅛ of an inch. He could change the pressure of the spring by screwing the nut up or down. The other two valves he used as exhaust valves in the cylinder head. They opened by a complicated but very ingenious device involving a rocker arm and a push rod.

The Kane-Pennington engine had an experimental carburetor (then called "carburetters," as so much of the early automotive language was adopted straight from the French; e.g., *chauffeur, garage,* and *automobile*). But Henry used a more practical system. He simply put the gasoline tank higher than the engine, so the gas would flow into the manifold by gravity. He placed a needle valve just above an opening in the manifold. He regulated this valve by a throttle rod at the right side of the seat; when it opened, the gas dropped into the manifold to mix with the air. He could make the mixture rich or lean by supplying it with more or less gasoline; this was the first choke, for he choked it by placing his thumb and forefinger over the air intake to shut off air.

His next big problem, through 1895 and into 1896, was the old one of ignition. He tried three different systems.

In the first, Henry attached a wire to the end of the piston, but the continual arc-ing soon burned off the end of the wire, and he dropped this system.

Next he tried a hot-tube system. (Since gasoline has a very low flash-point, the gas-air mixture can be ignited by glowing hot metal.) In this system he actually started the car by heating the tubes with a gasoline torch, and the tubes were kept hot by the burning of the mixture. This was dangerously unstable; once Henry came close to burning up his engine, the car and the shed. This must have been a hot time for old Mr. Julien.

Finally Ford came up with a third system, an improvement on the first make-and-break system. He drilled a hole in the cylinder and fitted in a spark breaker. At the farthest point of the piston's stroke a pin struck the spark breaker and opened the circuit; a spark jumped, igniting the mixture; as the piston was forced back by the explosion the spring closed the circuit.

In his first version Henry neglected to provide for cooling, and on one early trip the engine became so hot that bits of solder dropped off, "striking the ground and looking like dimes." But his final version was superior; he brazed water jackets on the cylinders and fixed a water tank under the seat with a brass pipe leading to the water jackets and back to the tank.

Laborious experiments went on and on. Then all the auto pioneers suddenly redoubled their efforts: the *Chicago Times-Herald* sponsored the first American race for horseless carriages, on November 28, 1895. The course was long—52.4 miles, from Jackson Park in Chicago to Evanston and return. The prizes were $2,000, $1,500, $1,000, and $500. Charles King, as a motoring notable, was chosen one of the umpires (his own car was not ready for entry). The Duryeas sent a car, but Frank Duryea had to crash it to avoid a frightened horse; it was shipped back to Springfield, fixed and re-entered.

On racing day snow fell; the road became a nightmare. Six competitors started but only two finished. The two electric cars were first to fail in deep snow ruts. Another car stalled. Only three were left to plow on in the drifting snow. Each car had a driver, with an umpire riding as a passenger; but in the snow these petty distinctions were lost, and umpires and drivers took equal turns in pushing. At Evanston the fourth car, an adapted Benz from Macy's in New York, dropped out; and now only two were left: the Duryea and a Benz driven by Oscar E. Mueller, carrying umpire Charles King.

Frank Duryea finished first, at 7:18 P.M. He had done the 52.4 miles in 10 hours and 23 minutes. His average speed, 6.66 miles per hour.

Far back, Driver Mueller became unconscious. Umpire King took the wheel, and supporting the half-frozen Mueller with one arm, grimly drove on through the dark down the snow-filled pike. He finished second, an hour and forty-five minutes after Duryea. King was offered half the second-prize money of $1,500 but, reverting to his amateur status as umpire, he refused it.

The news of the race spurred on the inventors. The snow excused the poor time; more, it made thoughtful men take thoughtful looks at that ancient institution, the horse. It would have been a rare horse that could have made a similar trip.

By the end of 1895 Henry had his car on wooden horses. He got most of the iron work from a firm named Barr & Dates, at the corner of Park Place and State Street. He bought tires and rims for the 28-inch wheels, drilled holes in the rims, and upset the heads on each one of the bicycle spokes, making all the little brass nipples himself. He made his own steering handle, attaching a button in the top of the tiller by a wire to the electric doorbell in front of the dashboard. (He bought the doorbell.) He bought a small buggy seat from the C. R. Wilson Carriage Works. John S. Newberry of the Detroit Steel and Spring Works made him some springs. From Strelinger's hardware, on January 2, 1896 he bought one dozen medium nuts for 12 cents, one dozen small nuts for 16 cents and a brass rod for 8 cents. With the engine solved, he knew exactly what he wanted to do with the carriage.

He used a belt to take the power from the flywheel to a countershaft, with a belt tightener to serve as a clutch. A chain transferred the power from the countershaft to the rear axle; and Henry remembered how the differential gear on a steam road engine allowed one wheel to move faster than the other around corners. The batteries he bought. The rest of the iron work he made himself—with some help from George Cato—from angle and scrap iron and steel, machined to shape in his little shop.

When Henry's belt tightener was straight up and down the car was in neutral: both belts hung loose. When he pulled the lever back the low-speed belt tightened; when he pushed it forward the high-speed belt tightened. To back up was simple enough. He merely climbed out and pushed the car backward.

There were no brakes; he stopped the car by killing the engine and letting the car run against the compression in the cylinders. The throttle was under the seat; the spark could not be adjusted unless the engine was shut off. But the car delivered slightly more than four horsepower, and it could run about twenty-five miles an hour.

Ford's first car had one tremendous advantage over many of its predecessors and contemporaries. Some parts were inferior, some only slightly superior, but the sum of the whole was truly an automobile. It was not a wagon with an engine in it. It was rugged, speedy, light in weight, durable, reliable.

96. The first car in the Bagley Avenue shed. This is the way it looked in the shop as reconstructed in Greenfield Village from Charles King's drawings and Ford's memory. It stands here on supports; the tires, pumped full of soft rubber by Firestone in the 1930's, do not touch the floor. Clara sat under the shaded bulb at the left, on a stool; old Mr. Julien sat on the doorsill to be out of the way and yet miss nothing. The door at the far left led through the backyard to the house.

97. The rear of the car, the engine, as it is now seen in the Ford Museum.

98. The first garage door. A rear view of the Bagley Avenue shed; the house is to the right, behind the fence. This picture was taken in 1911, when the shop stood much as it had in 1896.

We shall never know exactly on which wet spring night in 1896 Henry took out his little automobile for its first run; the accounts vary from April 2 to June 6. But the best judgment puts it on June 4, certainly no earlier. For example, as late as May 28 Henry bought the following order from the Indianapolis Chain and Stamping Company (they made bicycle-type chains):

96.

97.

98.

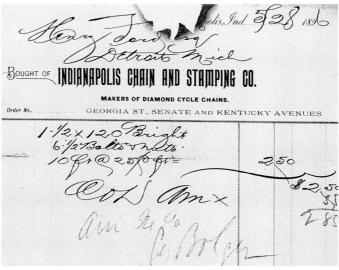

99.

76

99. An invoice from the Indianapolis Chain and Stamping Company:

1½ x 120	bright,	
6½	bolts and nuts,	
10 ft.	at 25¢ a ft.	$2.50
	C.O.D.	.35
		$2.85

Was not this the chain he used on the first car?

We do know that Henry finished the last little touches at about 2 A.M., on a June morning and that a light warm rain was falling. Clara was up to watch, a shawl over her head; faithful Jim Bishop was on hand with his bicycle. It was after Mr. Julien's bedtime. Henry had a buggy seat but had not mounted it on the car; he put a bicycle seat on top of the two tanks (for water and gasoline). And then he must have torn his hair and smitten his brow: he was in the classic dilemma of the man who builds a boat in the basement. The first Ford car was too wide to pass through the little door (then identical with the one on the left). He took up an axe and doubled the width of the opening. Then he trundled the little machine out onto the cobbles.

He turned on the current from the battery and adjusted the gasoline. He covered the air opening of the valve with his thumb and forefinger to choke it and then turned over the flywheel. The engine sputtered and roared into life.

He mounted the seat, pulled back the lever that tightened the belt, adjusted the gasoline valve, and went bumping down the alley to Bagley Avenue and around the corner into Grand River Avenue out of Clara's sight and into history. With what thoughts did he go? Like an aviator listening to an engine flutter? Like a doctor at a birth? In anxiety or triumph, chills or hope? Like Richard III or Monte Cristo? Prayerful, grateful, numb with shock?

He had done it. In a few weeks he would be thirty-three. He was "getting on," as they say, and until this very moment he had done nothing much; he had a small comfortable job with a modest future. His life work was still dormant in his head and hands; the world judges not by what is in the head or hands, but by what they have done. Now at last Henry Ford had done something.

Yet he had not gone very far, after all. He had made something. But quite a few would laugh at it, or waggle their heads. He was years away

from any kind of security. Only a few of his intimates would recognize his achievement; and most of them were helpers out of friendship rather than conviction. They thought the horseless carriage was an interesting novelty but did not feel it would ever be very important. Even Inventor King, for all his far-sighted vision, thought of the car then as a kind of expensive new toy for the very rich, with some possible other uses "for delivery . . . or even as ambulances."

And now that Henry had done it, he had no idea what to do with it. What next?

Perhaps ever since his mother's death, perhaps since the day in the Michigan Car shops when he "learned to keep my mouth shut," perhaps through the steady hours of thought over machines, whatever the causes, Henry Ford had a singular ability to keep his emotions to himself. We know he raged and wept as other men; but the course of his passions rarely flared through. His face to the world was the American countryman's face, quiet, genial, friendly, impassive, dead pan among strangers. He deliberately underplayed, was matter-of-fact in a crisis, with his real emotions kept within the four walls of the home.

Whatever he may have felt, we know his habit of mind. To him a thing done meant only that you go on to the next thing. He may not have known where he was going, but he knew he *was* going somewhere.

He did not go very far that first night. A nut came off a valve-stem; the car clanked to a humiliating halt. The faithful Bishop put aside his bicycle and helped Henry push the car over to the Edison plant. With the help of the night shift, watched by a small audience of stay-up-lates from the Cadillac Hotel next door, they put on a new nut and Henry rode home and so to bed.

There was a bright new song in the U.S. that year, written by Joseph Hayden, and perhaps Henry and Jim Bishop sang it in the night as they rolled back to the Bagley backyard in triumph, one on his bicycle, the other on his little horseless carriage:

When you hear those bells go ting-a-ling-a-ling. . . .
There'll be a hot time in the old town tonight.

Next morning Felix Julien got the big news

of the night ride. But then he and Henry began to worry about the smashed shed door. Henry hurried about and found a friendly bricklayer who started to rebuild the wall at once. The one interruption they feared was William Wreford, the butcher, and sure enough, he turned up within an hour.

William Wreford was no mere local butcher. He ran the largest and finest wholesale meat market in all Detroit. He was a man of such pride that for more than fifty years there was no sign of any kind on the clean, plain, even somber front of his shop to indicate the nature of his business. He was completely unaffected by go-getting business methods: his name never appeared on his delivery wagons; he had no business letterhead; he never advertised. Never a piece of meat, say the historians, was ever displayed in his windows or on his counters, save as it was being carved for a waiting customer. Every inch of his shop was spotlessly clean. In those days Wreford killed some 500 sheep and lambs a week, and slaughtered and dressed about 130 steers. The herds were driven through the streets of downtown Detroit to the Wreford shop, 5 Central Market, within the confines of Cadillac Square.

And little did Butcher Wreford guess, as he stood contemplating the ruin of his shed, that the automobile would ruin his business; that one day automobile traffic would become so great that the city would refuse to let his herds be driven through the streets. If he had, perhaps he would have ordered the door sealed forever.

Now he stood goggling indignantly at the wreckage made by Henry's axe. He was not at all mollified by the sight of the repairs under way. Then the news seeped through his anger: A what? A horseless carriage? Where? And so Henry showed him as persuasively as any automobile salesman of today. Suddenly Wreford was struck with a thought: It was nonsense to build the door back; how could Henry get the new car in and out? On the spot he authorized that the door be widened.

Perhaps this was the *first* true garage door in America.

On the second day Henry replaced the bicycle seat with the buggy seat and took Clara for her first ride, with two-and-one-half-year-old Edsel in her arms. The "little rig" made a brave noise,

entirely new to American ears: chucka-chucka-chucka-chuck.

100. The shed reconstructed in Greenfield Village. All is still in place, even the little tools Henry made himself in order to make parts. The shop is not open to the public. In his elderly lonely wanderings Henry, who had master keys to all the buildings, often stopped in here to tinker quietly.

101. Rear view of the first Ford: a superb picture of its actual workings, taken by Photographer Livesey in October 1896.

102. Photographer Livesey. (See frontispiece.)

103. The first car, October 1896. This was taken at the same time as the picture in the frontispiece. By this time Ford had completely boxed in the engine. Soon thereafter he sold this first machine to "Chappie" Annesley, who then sold it to a man named A. W. Hall. On April 11, 1899, Hall wrote Ford a testimonial, perhaps the first automobile testimonial. It speaks eloquently for the merits of the first Ford car:

AMERICAN MACHINE COMPANY

Manufacturers of

High Grade Bicycles

Detroit Branch,
255 Woodward Ave.

April 11, '99

Henry Ford
    City

Friend Ford:—

I am as you will see back in Detroit once more and have a desire to know how the world is treating you these days.

You will be surprised when I tell you that the little carriage is still doing its usual duty, I disposed of it this spring and the little rig was still in fair shape after all the banging around that it has had and I guess you know that was considerable; I ran it almost two years as you know and about the only trouble I had was that one tire and the springs on the sparkers working loose, but you know how they were fastened and there was nothing to prevent them from doing so, untill I put on a binding bolt and after that I never had any

100.

101.

102.

103.

more trouble with it; but I say take it all through and a rig built as you did that one just for an experiment and have it run as successfully as it has and with so little trouble, I think if you have made the one you spoke to me about last summer a year ago it ought to be a corker; you know I have the Horseless Carriage fever and consequently if you are still in it I would like to have you call around to the store and see me; if not call any way and we will talk over the past and revive some of the usual H.C. talk I want to get into the business with some good conserne that is going into this line for it is the coming thing and if you know of any thing in this line and can put in a good word for me, you know I will appreciate it, I am not a fixture with this house but they wanted me to come and sell Wheels and as I can do that as you know so theres the why that I am back in Detroit.

I was out in Chicago all last fall and looked over the few horseless rigs there and among them all I did not see one I would of rather had then that little rig for when it comes right down to simplicity they were not in it and to my mind with any experience the electrics will not be in it, for where are you on a country run if the batteries give out and where is the farm house that does not have a can of gasoline on the place, if for nothing else than cleaning up old clothes etc. etc.

Well Ford I did not intend to take up so much of your time but as I havent seen you for an age and had several things to say I kept on untill here I am besides I wanted to let you know how the little rig has behaved and it has certainly done fine and if you have the other one built you said you were going to put up with take ups on all bearings I want to see it roll it around to the store some day thats if it ever came to light, I hope she has and if so I know it certainly is O.K.

Well I trust I will see you in a day or so; I am always in of an evening so call around untill then I

remain

yours etc

(signed)   A. W. Hall

104.

XII. THE MAN AT MANHATTAN BEACH

Young fellow here has made a gas car.
—ALEX DOW

104. The Edison staff. On July 1, 1896, less than a month after Henry first chucka-chucked around town, Alex Dow left his post as manager of the city's Public Lighting plant (where Ford had vainly applied for work) and took over the management of the Edison operation in Detroit. This picture was probably taken soon after Dow came. Dow is in the center, with full droop-drawers mustache, Henry to the right in work jacket, and just behind Henry, his friend, Ward Noble. We cannot be quite sure of the others.

Dow was a straight-thinking, no-nonsense businessman, full of the general righteousness of electricity. He was a firm friend to Henry, but he took a dim view of any gas-engine experiments that Ford conducted *within the Edison plant.*

"Out," said Dow.

The impression we get—and this sounds very much like Henry—is that Ford had gradually expanded his bench-with-a-vise, for the repair of Edison machinery, to become a sort of personal shop, adjunct both to the little basement shop across the street, and to the Bagley Avenue workshop. He had everything set up so he could putter away on automotive problems wherever he was. No young man can possibly draw from Henry's career any moral lessons about being to work on time, keeping regular hours, or such nonsense—Henry was free as a bird and did his own work on the company premises and on company time.

Dow's real worry seems to have been that Henry would blow the place up, for gasoline was much feared as a mysterious and tricky fluid; for example, when little Edsel Ford once playfully took the cap off a can of gasoline, Jim Bishop

grabbed him in horror, expecting an immediate explosion.

105. Henry goes to a convention, 1896. Dow's letter is evidence of Ford's stature; the only delegates from Detroit were Dow himself, Ford, and the company attorney, Hoyt Post.

106. Hoyt Post of the firm of Wilkinson, Post and Oxtoby, Attorneys at Law.

107. Proceedings of the Convention. As can be seen, Dow was a member of the Executive Committee of the Association of Edison Illuminating Companies and gave one of the chief papers before the delegates, among whom was Thomas A. Edison himself. One other name may ring a bell, although not quite the bell of nostalgia: Samuel Insull, Edison's onetime secretary, was elected as the new president of the association—Insull, who would become a multimillionaire, a buyer of art masterpieces, a patron of the Chicago Opera; who would pyramid huge utility holding companies into the gigantic structure that collapsed in the crash of 1929; and who, fleeing the wrath of stockholders and government, would die in plush exile in France in 1938. Another great man also present (as we shall see) but not listed here, was Charles P. Steinmetz, a hunchback, already on his pain-wracked way as an even greater genius in electricity than Edison.

The list of the Detroit delegation appears seven lines from the bottom.

108. The Oriental Hotel at Manhattan Beach, New York City. This picture gives a lively sense of the time: summer 1896. The monster spread of the building, the enormous sweep of the veranda stretching infinitely, the turrets, the acres of striped awnings, the whole Chinese birds'-nest effect, the captain's walks atop it all—this is late Victorian America on the eastern sea coast.

Note particularly the style and shape of the lamp-posts: they were a clue in identifying the following pictures. When these first prints were carefully made in the Archives they were studied with equal parts of excitement and bafflement: here was Henry, here was Thomas Edison, on the same roll of film. But the pictures did not check out with the much-photographed meetings between the two, from around 1911 on through

81

THE EDISON ILLUMINATING COMPANY,
OF DETROIT.

GEO. PECK, President.   E. W. VOIGT, Vice-Pres.   ALEX DOW, Gen'l Mngr.   GEO. WIL...& Treas.   HOYT POST, Attorney.

Incandescent Electric Light, Arc Light, and Electric Power.

OFFICE, COR. STATE ST. AND WASHINGTON AVE...

Detroit, August 8...

W. S. Barstow, Esq.

        858 Pearl Street, Brooklyn, N...

Dear Sir,

        This will introduce to you Mr Henry Ford, the Chief Engineer
of this Company's plant. He goes east to attend the Convention; and
wishes on the 10th to visit some of the stations under your charge for
the purpose of getting such information as he may, regarding your steam
practice. I beg that you will give him such assistance as may appear
proper to you.

        I am likely to be detained by some busi... ...ich will
prevent me reaching the Oriental till Monday night, ...ssibly Tuesday
morning; but intend to be present at opening time.

                Yours truly,

                Alex Dow

                Genl Manager, E. I. Co., of Detroit.

105.

106.

108.

Convention of the Association of Edison Illuminating Companies.

The seventeenth convention of the above-named association was held at the Oriental Hotel, Manhattan Beach, Brooklyn, on Aug. 11, 12 and 13.

President C. L. Edgar called the meeting to order at 11 o'clock, Aug. 11, and the session was devoted to the reading of reports of committees on Welsbach light, storage battery, etc. At 1 o'clock an adjournment was taken until the afternoon.

At the second session, which was called to order at 2.30 p. m., a paper was read by Mr. C. E. Pattison, of Boston, on "The Storage Battery in Actual Operation in the Boston Edison Stations." The experience of the Boston Edison Company since the installation of its first storage battery several years ago was fully described and discussed.

The next paper was one by W. I. Donshea and H. A. Campbell, entitled, "The Storage Battery in New York Edison Stations."

The third session was called to order Aug. 12 at 10 o'clock, by President Edgar, and the first business was the reading of a paper by Alexander Dow on "The Selection of Alternating-Current Apparatus for Central-Lighting Stations." This paper was immediately followed by one of the same character by Mr. W. S. Barstow, of Brooklyn, entitled "The Alternating Current System as a Pioneer." Both papers were discussed and many of the representatives of Edison companies gave their experiences with alternating systems used in combination with the Edison system.

At the fourth session, in the afternoon, Mr. R. S. Hale, of Boston, read a paper on "The Wright-Demand System of Charging for Current." An interesting discussion followed the reading of this paper as to the results met with in the system of discounts as outlined in a paper read at the last convention. The Chicago, New York, Cincinnati, Brooklyn and several other companies gave their experience in the new system of charging for incandescent light.

A paper was then read by John Wolff, of Brooklyn, on "A Self-Cooling Condenser in the Second District Brooklyn Edison Station."

The last paper of the convention was one by Mr. W. S. Andrews, of Schenectady, on "Some Recent Developments and Modifications of the Edison Underground System and the Use of Cables as Auxiliaries Thereto." An animated discussion as to the merits of the several underground systems and the use of different makes of cables followed the reading of this paper.

The very satisfactory financial condition of the association and the good work of the treasurer, as shown by the report, elicited much favorable comment.

The Committee on Nominations then made its report of the officers for the ensuing year, and they were elected as follows : President, Samuel Insull, Chicago; vice-president, R. R. Bowker, New York; secretary, W. S. Barstow, Brooklyn; treasurer, J. W. Lieb, Jr., New York. Executive Committee: C. L. Edgar, chairman; Alexander Dow, George R. Stetson, A. W. Field, J. H. Vail; ex-officio members, Samuel Insull, R. R. Bowker, W. S. Barstow and J. W. Lieb, Jr.

The visiting ladies were entertained by the Brooklyn Edison Company. The following is a list of those who attended the convention:

Thomas A. Edison, Llewellyn Park, Orange, N. J.; W. E. Gilmore, Edison Laboratory, Orange, N. J.

General Electric Company.—S. D. Greene, general manager lighting department; E. W. Rice, Jr., third vice-president; W. S. Andrews, manager central station sales; A. D. Page, manager lamp sales (incandescent lamp department); J. R. Lovejoy, manager supply department; J. W. Howell, engineer (lamp works); W. S. Clark, wire and cable department; John Kruesi, mechanical engineer; Caryl D. Haskins, motor department.

Illuminating Companies.—H. T. Edgar, Jas. G. Rossman, Atlanta, Ga.; C. L. Edgar, C. R. Pattison, R. S. Hale, Boston, Mass.; W. S. Barstow, W. F. Wells, John Wolff, Theo. Quillauneu, C. V. Driggs, Brooklyn, N. Y.; Samuel Insull, Joseph Insull, Luther Stieringer, Chicago, Ill.; A. L. Smith, Appleton, Wis.; E. A. Armstrong, J. J. Burleigh, Camden, N. J.; John I. Beggs, Cincinnati, O.; Samuel Scovil, Robert Lindsay, Cleveland, O.; A. W. Field, Columbus, O.; J. S. Crider, Cumberland, Md.; J. A. Colby, Des Moines, Ia.; Alexander Dow, Hoyt Post, Henry Ford, Detroit, Mich.; Christopher Wustenfeld, Elgin, Ill.; G. R. Stetson, C. R. Price, New Bedford, Mass. R. R. Bowker, J. W. Lieb, Jr., W. I. Donshea, W. H. Lawrence, G. N. Moore, J. Van Vleck, Arthur Williams, E. A. Leslie, New York City; W. H. Johnson, J. H. Vail, Philadelphia, Pa.; G. A. Redman, Rochester, N. Y.; Reginald Van Trump, Wilmington, Del.; A. E. Kennelly.

107.

82

the 1920's; the scenery was obviously non-Michigan; the film itself and the costumes in the pictures were clearly nineteenth century.

It looks as if Henry had taken his little camera along on his trip to the Edison convention in 1896.

109. A shot from the veranda. This picture was the prime clue. Here was the Oriental Hotel type of lamp-post; beyond it the miles of benches, the ocean. Then everything fell into place. Henry shot pictures everywhere on that trip, and some of them follow here.

110. Brooklyn Bridge, 1896, as Henry photographed it. The bridge had been opened thirteen years before, on May 24, 1883, but it was still one of the wonders of the world.

Besides such shots as this, Henry took many pictures of machinery and steam-engines, naturally. These are photographically excellent, considering that he was shooting interiors with natural light, long before the flash bulb, but they would only interest collectors of period machinery. He shot the Palisades along the Hudson River from his train, people at the beach, and assorted other people that he may have known but we never shall.

111. Brooklyn 1896. Or is it Manhattan? The picture repays study: the row of identical hansoms with glittering brass lamps, their heavy wheels shod with hard rubber. Was this a funeral procession? (The second driver is not in black.) The open-side trolley says "POST OFFICE." Or is it a horse car? Awnings then were as universal as air-conditioners are today. And the man who quickly crossed before Henry's camera, with umbrella and panama: a doctor hurrying to a case on foot?

What was New York like in 1896, when Henry Ford saw it? William Dean Howells wrote in that year:

South of Central Park the whole island is dense with life and business; it is pretty solidly built up on either side; but to the northward the blocks of houses are no longer of a compact succession; they struggle up, at irregular intervals, from open fields, and sink again, on the streets pushed beyond them, into simple country, where even a suburban character is lost.

83

109.

110.

111.

Of late, a good many streets and several avenues have been asphalted, and the din of wheels on the rough pavement no longer torments the ear so cruelly; but there is still the sharp clatter of the horses' shoes everywhere; and their pulverized manure, which forms so great a part of the city's dust . . . seems to blow about more freely on the asphalt than on the old-fashioned pavements.

Not long before, Colonel Waring had started the first city street-cleaning department, but his famous "White Wings" were far from ubiquitous.

The hotels all carried signs: "Do Not Blow Out the Gas," in an effort to educate the rustics who were more used to oil-lamps. The Miss Daisy Miller skirt, known as "the Rainy Daisy," was the Dior-like sensation of the day: it exposed the shoe-top to ogling eyes.

The cigarette was used only by fops, weaklings and sinister women; a real man stayed with cigars or "eatin'" tobacco. Most cigar stores carried a little sign:

Cigarette smoke,
Like lighted punk,
Hath a fetid stink,
Like a lively skunk.

The first real commercial invasion of upper Fifth Avenue was the opening of a women's specialty shop by Franklin Simon on 38th Street—almost in the heart of the lower residential section. But the consternation of the elite was steadily succeeded by capitulation.

Many Americans were astonished to learn that the Prince of Wales—later King Edward VII—*never* used a tooth-pick, either during meals or after them. Hoop-skirt factories were being converted to other products. The main patent medicines were soothing syrup, pain-killer, horse liniment and vegetable compounds: all contained a high percentage of alcohol.

One became aware of unemployment in the city on any midnight by watching the line-up outside the bakeries, when a dole of the night's first hot bread was issued.

A fine set of custom-made single harness cost $50; double harness ran about $150, and this might include silver mountings instead of brass and perhaps your monogram on the blinkers. According to Edwin V. Mitchell, the proper shape

for blinkers on driving harness was "square, or with only slightly rounded corners. D-shaped, horseshoe-shaped, and round blinders were seen only on cab, grocery and cart horses."

In a few decades, the sale of buggy whips would crash from scores of thousands a year to nothing.

The vaudeville houses played twice a day; a sturdy customer got five full hours of entertainment for his fifty cents: a "kalatechnoscope"; a banjo act; an acrobatic act; some equilibrists; twin sisters; refined singers and dancers; "The Singing Lesson" (a playlet about a jealous husband); a pastoral playlet, about a little girl waif and a grumpy codger with a heart of gold and a carpetbag full of money; monologs and songs by a real Afro-American; seals and sea lions; and a trick cyclist.

The girls that year wore foulard tissues; sometimes crisp white blouses with great leg-o'-mutton sleeves. On a quiet night the tinkle of the horse-car bells on the 42nd Street car-line could be heard for several miles.

112. Charles P. Steinmetz. Henry unwittingly made history with this picture; there are very few photographs extant of the great wizard, and most of them show him as a much older man, kneeling painfully on a stool in his laboratory. Here he walks with the other convention notables; they are probably at the Pearl Street Station of the New York Edison Illuminating Company on an inspection tour. In the center, head bowed, is Thomas A. Edison; this is his rumpled, vest-open cigar-ash-strewn look, but his face is in shadow.

Pearl Street was the first commercial electric plant installation in the world and one of the great engineering jobs in history. To build it Edison had to invent, design and custom-make every single item, including the switches, fixtures, pipes, junction-boxes, conduits, meters, sockets, circuits, conductors, pressure-gauges and wires. Here he established 110 volts as the standard. Here electricity came out of the laboratory and became commercially practical, efficient, economical, and safe to use all the way from the generator to the light bulb and back.

113. Edison telling a story. At the convention, Henry probably had no more than a reception-

line handshake with the great man. But he kept circling him with his camera; this picture is the first on the Edison-Manhattan Beach rolls in the Archives.

114. Headline: "NEVER TO BED" from the Plainfield Press, *Plainfield, New Jersey, October 23, 1914.*

"Never to Bed" may have been Edison's slogan, but he seems to have made up for this by napping all day. He could sleep on a bookshelf, with a pair of books as a pillow; in any kind of chair, large or small; on any kind of ground except perhaps swampland, as you will see. And the more one sees pictures of the grand old inventor catching up on his "sacktime," the more difficult it becomes to retain the illusion in which two American generations were reared: that Edison worked so furiously around the clock that he simply never slept.

115. Edison napping at the Oriental Hotel. One of several pictures that Henry took of the great man asleep on the hotel veranda. The other man is in stylish summer best, with heavy vest; in the rear you can see a child of the period, bored and proper, sitting in Buster Brown hat and sailor suit.

116. At dinner, August 12, 1896, the second night of the convention. This painting, by Irving R. Bacon, is stiff, amateurish, photographic; but it is an accurate enough reconstruction, made under Henry's direction, on his recollections, of a decisive scene in his life. Left to right: Hoyt Post, John Van Vleck, Charles L. Edgar, Henry Ford, Thomas A. Edison, Samuel Insull, John W. Lieb, John I. Beggs, Alex Dow. (It must be noted that Dow seems to have grown a heavy beard in the past six weeks.)

At one session the convention discussed a new field of revenue: the charging of storage batteries for electric vehicles. Since they were all electricity minded, one guesses that they all assumed automatically that the horseless carriage of the future would be an electric vehicle.

Into the discussion Alex Dow dropped a small conversational bomb. Said he: "This young fellow here has made a gas car."

Perhaps Dow did this deliberately, hoping the electric-carriage men would wipe the floor

112.

113.

"NEVER TO BED," EDISON'S SLOGAN

Future Man Will Sleep Less, Declares Inventor.

AND FINALLY NOT AT ALL.

It May Be a Million Years Before This New "Advance In Civilization," He Admits, but Believes Time Will Come and Also That Humanity Will Live In Double Shifts.

Humanity will have to live in double shifts by and by because the world will be so crowded that it will have to sleep less.

By sleeping less it will enormously increase its productive power, for sleep is an absurdity—a bad habit.

Nothing in the world is more dangerous to the efficiency of humanity than too much sleep, except, perhaps, stimulation.

Calls Sleep a Bad Habit.

"I think this matter of sleeping is one of the serious things which humanity must begin to study. I never yet have come across the case of a man who had been hurt by want of sleep.

"There really is no reason why men should go to bed at all, and the man of the future will spend far less time in bed than the man of the present does, just as the man of the present spends far less time in bed than the man of the past did.

114.

Young Henry Ford

115.

116.

with Henry and thus end his experiments, for Dow had high hopes for Henry if only he would quit his gasoline car nonsense. Yet perhaps Dow said it merely as a matter of news.

Dow went on to tell how he had heard something pop-pop-popping beneath his window; on looking out he saw Mrs. Ford and a little boy sitting in a little carriage without horses, and then Henry coming out of the plant, climbing in, and the carriage went pop-pop-popping off.

Someone asked Ford how he made his carriage go. He started to explain, "speaking fairly loudly" (everyone knew Edison was deaf). "Mr. Lieb saw Mr. Edison trying to hear," said Henry later, "and motioned to me to pull up a chair from another table and sit beside Mr. Edison and speak up so that all of them could hear. I got up but just then Mr. Edgar offered to change places with me, putting me next to Mr. Edison. He began to ask me questions which showed that he had already made a study of the gas engine. "Is it a four-cycle engine?" he asked.

I told him that it was and he nodded approval. Then he wanted to know if I exploded the gas in the cylinder by electricity and whether I did it by a spark or by a contact. . . .

I told him that it was a make-and-break contact that was bumped apart by the piston, and I drew a diagram for him of the whole contact arrangement which I had on my first car, the one that Mr. Dow had seen. But I said that on my second car, on which I was then working, I had made what we today would call a "spark plug"; it was really an insulating plug with a make-and-break mechanism, using washers of mica. I drew that too.

. . . He asked me no end of details and I sketched everything for him, for I have always found I could convey an idea quicker by sketching than by just describing it. When I had finished he brought his fist down on the table with a bang and said:

"Young man, that's the thing; you have it. Keep at it! Electric cars must keep near to power stations. The storage battery is too heavy. Steam cars won't do either, for they have to carry a boiler and fire. Your car is self-contained

—it carries its own power-plant—no fire, no boiler, no smoke, no steam. You have the thing. Keep at it."

That bang on the table was worth worlds to me. *No man up to then had given me any encouragement.* [Author's italics.]

I had hoped I was right, sometimes I knew I was, sometimes I only wondered if I was, but here . . . out of a clear sky the greatest inventive genius in the world had given me a complete approval.

117. Back at the plant. This picture, at the end of the Edison-Manhattan Beach rolls—taken by a fellow worker?—shows Henry immediately on his return. He is in the plant with a man identified as John Ford; one of the two bicycles in the rear is probably Henry's. He is in his early physical prime, before age shrank him from a bit more than five feet eight inches; he is huskier here than he ever was again. Note his hands, big and long fingered.

When he arrived at the plant, he found a letter from Clara, who had taken Edsel to stay with the Bryants in their Greenfield home while Henry was in the big city. The letter, dated August 13, 1896:

Darling Henry

. . . I suppose there is a letter from you waiting for me but Pa is going to the city tomorrow and I will get it. And I will be so glad. I never was so anxious to hear from you. . . . The heat was so great we could hardly stand it . . . and then the dreadful storms. I thought surly we would have a Cyclone one day.

. . . It is 5 P.M. now and the baby is having a glorious time on the lawn. . . . I asked him if he would like to send Papa a kiss and he said yes paper him over one. Just like one of his speeches. . . .

I suppose you have seen great sights. . . . I hope things will be all right at the Station so that you can come out. For I want you awful bad. . . .

Dearest husband
Good bye
Clara.

117.

118.

119.

{ XIII. COMMITMENT }

He did want me very badly to go. . . .
He said, "Dave, Dave, you'll go
with the business."
I said, "What business?"

—David M. Bell

118. Trip to the Homestead, 1896 or 1897. William Ford, on the right, is older and stooping; Henry's big, jovial sisters Jane and Margaret tower over her; Edsel is still in curls. The white picket fence of the old home shows in the rear.

119. Edsel at the Homestead a little later. Fortunately he has lost his curls and has become a boy.

William Ford told a neighbor a year or so earlier: "John and William are all right but Henry worries me. He doesn't seem to settle down and I don't know what's going to become of him."

When Dearborn farmers—William's neighbors —went to town they often dropped in to the Edison Main Station to see the worrisome son, where he worked and tinkered. He, like as not, was nowhere to be found in the steam plant but was outside in the street with his contraption, perhaps taking people for a ride. One neighbor reported those days: "At the noise of its starting, Old Man Renaud, who knew all the family, would stand up on his cane and say, 'There goes that Ford fool again, fooling with that machine!'"

Ford's friend Charles B. King once wrote a story about William's reaction to Henry and his car that was long accepted as the true picture of the Fords' relationship:

Ford talked much with me about a test run of nine miles out to the old farm at Dearborn, and the "great hit" it would make with the "old man" and the neighbors. He wanted me to go along. I consented, the day was set, and we started.

Ford drove the machine alone and I followed on a bicycle as his sole escort. Much tinkering was done on the way out, the ignition requiring the most attention.

Considerable water was put in the tank. A number of frightened horses were passed until we finally reached the farm. I opened the big gate and Ford drove in—and around to the kitchen.

The door opened and there was the tall form of his father, William Ford, Justice of the Peace, Church Warden, and Farmer. He stood there, said nothing. He was certainly lacking in enthusiasm. The neighbors were coming across the fields. I can see it as yesterday, because such things make deep impressions. About a dozen had arrived and their whole expression was one of sympathy for the Senior Ford, rather than praise for Henry. In other words, it was a "frost."

Ford sensed it, exactly as I did when that back door was opened. His picture had been shattered. He looked at me and said, "Let's get out of here."

I opened the big gate and we tinkered our way home, reaching the big city in the dark of the evening. . . .

The only trouble with this story is that it is not true. But perhaps it will suffice to say that the whole weight of the facts and testimony in the Archives shows a much more reasonable state of affairs.

The facts are that William constantly jogged in to Detroit, usually every other week, to see what his son was up to; and he followed the progress of the car with the keenest interest. William would have a drink in Jimmie Burns' saloon—he was not as abstemious as his son—then a sirloin steak, and then track Henry down at one or another of his numerous workshops.

There is not a jot of evidence that he disapproved of Henry's car, although he may have.

Thus part of the Ford myth is dispelled: that of the lonely inventor, the icy father, the disapproving neighbors, the mocking crowds shouting "Crazy Ford!"

The plain fact is that it takes a very great deal to stir people up. Most people don't even notice what is before their faces; and when it is pointed out they merely nod perfunctorily and pass on, intent on what's for dinner. Put it this way: it is probable that when one of the first cars chugged through the streets there was one American boy who shouted mockingly: "Get a horse!"; there

were probably ten who were anxious to learn how it ran and a hundred who never noticed it at all. One of the finest evidences ever discovered of this ancient human obliviousness is shown here, fresh from the Ford Archives:

120. Street scene, Detroit, probably 1899, Campus Martius and Cadillac Square. Going off to the far left along the street, just below two delivery wagons, you can make out a small horseless carriage.

121. Close-up, from the same scene. Now if you examine this carefully you will see that only one man has bothered to turn his head to notice the only horseless carriage in sight, in a world and in a time of horses.

Now we cannot prove by magnifying glasses or otherwise that this is Ford's horseless carriage, Henry himself pop-popping through the streets. But the temptation is great; the carriage looks exactly like Henry's first car as we see it on pages 76 and 79; no other horseless carriage of the time was built in this style; there were almost no other automobiles in Detroit then. It is not King's wagon, it is not an Oldsmobile nor a Duryea. If it is Henry's car it is his first—and this would date the picture definitely before 1897, for he sold the car that year. But still we cannot be sure.

The superb luck of the photograph is that the photographer was simply trying for an ordinary street scene in Detroit when this little motorcar flashed past; he may not even have noticed it as he exposed his plate.

And the moral of the picture is plain enough: the little vehicle attracts almost no attention.

In fact, Henry actually had to go out of his way to provoke comments. He would drive to Belle Isle, chain the car to a bench or a tree, and then hide in the bushes to listen to the comments from the strollers and bicyclers. The one he heard most often, he said, was "What kind of a nut is he?"

The word "nut," however, was not often applied to Ford in Detroit's higher business circles. We have seen the early evidences of the respect in which Ford was held. His father was well known and held in high regard. His father had been married in the home of Thomas C. Maybury, a community leader. Maybury's son William was Henry's friend and now became mayor of

120.

121.

122.

Detroit. When Henry had applied for the job in the city light plant in 1893 he had been able to drum up recommendations from leading citizens. Dow, prominent in the city, had a high esteem for Ford. Somehow, other city fathers, lawyers and bankers came to know him. The only conclusion we can draw is that in his wanderings about Detroit Henry must have visited white-collar places as well as machine shops.

And a prime factor, certainly, was Henry's relationship with George Peck, not only president of the Edison Illuminating Company but also a bank president, and with Peck's son Barton, who was puttering with a motorcar in his own shop at 81 Park Place.

It seems quite clear that Henry felt he had a great affair by the tail, and that soon after he had finished his first car he began to move steadily toward getting financial backing in order to manufacture it.

So Henry knocked on the doors of bankers and merchants and lawyers; and they came to knock on his door. There was no mad rush to back Henry, but neither did Henry rush madly about soliciting backers. He drove around, answered queries, and set to work to build another horseless carriage.

Henry's was a policy of gradualness. He was nowhere near manufacture; his first car had been merely a pilot model, and we can easily see how dissatisfied he was with it by noting the radical changes in each successive model. In the meantime he went about building up his public relations, getting the confidence of businessmen, and generally conducting himself with a shrewdness and care that was, at the least, unexpected in a young uneducated Detroit mechanic.

We can see the fruits of this gradual approach if we set Ford's movements against those of the other auto pioneers. Most of them plunged immediately into a manufacture that quickly proved abortive; they floundered on through enthusiasm into mismanagement and bankruptcy.

122. Ransom E. Olds, President and General Manager, Olds Motor Works.

Only the Duryeas had made a real automobile, and they were already bumping over a road of rocky financing in their first manufacture. Winton's car would soon come along fast, and in a year or two Ransom E. Olds would begin the

90

first important auto manufacturing in the nation, with his "merry" Oldsmobile. King could not attract capital, and in 1898 left to fight as a naval lieutenant in the Spanish-American War, where he was decorated for heroism. Even on his return King could never find proper financing. In Rochester, from 1877 on, George Selden could never interest serious money. And so the large picture of these times is one of numerous inventors in little shops, tinkering with carriages, certain that the horse was doomed, but generally unable to finance or manage a steady manufacture. Each found it easy to sell his first car to a rich man as a toy; then each had to start all over again and handmake a second car.

By the arithmetic of dates Ford was behind other pioneers; but his first car was far ahead of most of the motor wagons that lumbered about. Winton's car weighed 2,000 pounds, whereas even after Henry added tanks, water jackets and other equipment, his first car weighed less than 700 pounds. Ford's rig was faster perhaps than any except that of Frank Duryea. And perhaps because of its superior combustion, Ford's car was reputed to have less smell; most of the other cars, clanking slowly about, issued vast odorous clouds of half-burned smoke.

Each early ride must have been a small adventure. Little Jim Bishop often rode ahead on his bicycle as an advance man, even entering saloons and stores to warn people to hold their horses.

On one such ride Henry and Clara had the first recorded *auto accident with a pedestrian* (Duryea's crash into a pole before the Chicago race in 1895 was the first automobile accident). In turning a corner their automobile ran down a slow-moving Detroiter; prostrate on the street, he was wedged between the front and rear wheels. Henry and Clara leaned over from the seat and discussed the problem with their victim: Should they run forward over him? After some parley, they got out, and Henry and a bystander lifted the car off the man, unhurt, though doubtless dusty.

Mayor Maybury came around to Bagley Avenue, rode in the car, gave Henry a driving license (oral), and left to spread among his friends a serious view of Henry's carriage.

123. William C. Maybury, 1848–1909. This pic-

ture was taken in 1900. (See also the discussion of Maybury in Chapter XIV.)

124. Maybury helps, January 9, 1897. There is a friendly fib in this letter from the mayor: the statement that Ford would take this borrowed lathe "to his home." Actually the lathe went either to a new place, 151 Shelby Street, or to Henry's little workshop behind the Edison plant. Above Maybury's name on the letterhead is that of E. A. Leonard, financial secretary of the insurance company. Leonard and Maybury were among Henry's first backers.

The basement room of the Edison Company was in the Tolsma Building, right across the alley from the main station. The Tolsmas were an old Detroit family, owning considerable property along State Street; S. F. Tolsma, head of the family, knew Henry well and had offered him this basement rent free. Henry refused, and they compromised; Henry paid seventy-five cents rent per month and everyone was happy.

125. Receipt from Henry, Jan. 11, 1897. The borrowed lathe turned out to be quite a bit of equipment, as listed here.

An unsigned letter found in the Archives tells how some of the gay blades of the time, roistering about Detroit, found Henry at work. "At three or four or five o'clock in the morning we would roll around to State Street and very often find Uncle Henry ready to kid us a little. He was serious about his work and we were frivolous about ours." (This shows Henry at work around the clock; on his return from the Edison meeting he had told Clara: "You won't be seeing much of me for the next year.")

The letter gives a touch of those days. The roisterers would sail the Detroit River and at Walkerville (Ontario) buy "a ten-gallon cask of Walker whiskey for which we paid ten dollars, catch fish and take them where a fine French lady cooked them free if we would buy her beer for ten cents a bottle."

[We] sported around with the muskrat Frenchmen seeking furs and froglegs, shooting ducks and catching fish which we cooked on the spot. . . . In the morning I had to swim across the Detroit River to Cicottes for my cup of coffee and a bit of bread. . . . The Cicottes were famous river folk. . . .

123.

CASH CAPITAL $200,000.00.
$200,000 Deposited with the State Treasurer of Michigan for the Security of Policy Holders.

GEO. H. HOPKINS, 2nd Vice-Pres.
M. W. O'BRIEN, Treasurer.

D. A. PERRY, President.
C. C. BOWEN, Vice-President.

E. A. LEONARD, Financial Sec'y.
W. C. MAYBURY, Managing Director.

THE STANDARD
Life and Accident Insurance Company,
OF DETROIT, MICH.

Address All Business Communications to the Company.

MOFFAT BLOCK.

DETROIT, MICH. Jany.9/97

Mr. A.A.Robinson,

City.

Dear Sir:-

This will be handed to you by Mr. Ford.   He is doing some
work for me at his home, and needs the use of a small lathe for a short
time.   Will you kindly loan him one on my account, take his receipt
for it, and I will see that it is returned as good as when taken,after
Mr. Ford has completed the work he is doing.   I am anxious to have
his work completed before Feby. 1st, and will be obliged if you will let
him have the lathe at once, and he will take it to his home with my responsibility for its return.

Yours very truly,

W.C.Maybury

Henry Ford

124.

CREDIT MEMORANDUM.

FROM

DETROIT, MICH. _____ 189__

THE DETROIT MOTOR CO.

1343-1355 CASS AVENUE.

TO

We have this day credited your account as follows:

1 Lathe
1 Motor & Box ——— *Returned*
1 Counter Shaft
1 Lathe Chuck
1 Drill Chuck
1 Gear Wheel
1 Lathe Dog
2 Chuck Wrench   *Received same Jan 11 1897*

Henry Ford

125.

If you had to remain all night you slept on a board. . . . I saw Ford for a little visit; we had left State Street together some 40 years ago . . . the look out of the bright eyes just as he used to look when expressing mild disapproval of our gallivanting around instead of sleeping.

Eddie Cicotte, of this family, became a baseball pitcher, a member of the famous Chicago Black Sox of 1919. The Cicottes were prominent Democrats in Wayne County and leaders in the Democratic conventions which were held for years at old "Coon" Ten Eyck's tavern in Dearborn.

126. Jim Bishop and a friend, in the Edison plant, about 1897–98; picture by Ford. Jim was one of the first members of the first Ford team that Henry put together. Over the years there would be many teams—one array after another of the most glittering abilities in Detroit.

Bishop and George W. Cato, of the Main Station, stayed on with Edison, Cato rising to management posts and finally retiring in California. Bishop finally left Edison to work for Ford in December, 1929.

127. Ed Huff (perhaps). (This is almost certainly Edward S. Huff, but I cannot prove it; however, Henry took this picture.) We know nothing of Ed Huff's origins save that he came from Kentucky. Huff, an Edison mechanic, was quietly spectacular. He was an electrical wizard, not Steinmetzian, but in exactly the way Henry needed electrical wizardry, at the straight level of application in a car.

Huff was consistently inventive; over the years he refined and simplified the electrical system of Henry's cars so brilliantly and consistently that he should be given major credit. He designed and invented the magneto, which in one bound made Henry's early cars superior to even the most expensive.

Huff was usually on the loose: by 1904 he had held more than a dozen jobs, usually at good pay, but in a month or two he would simply drift out of town.

Huff was soft-spoken, quiet, sensitive. To Ford, Huff could do no wrong. Over the years, when-

126.

127.

128.

ever he had an attack of temperament, or drank, or got involved in a new marriage (he was married seven times), or simply ran away to Kentucky, Henry would pay the bills, take care of him, nurse him, and generally smooth things over.

Huff chewed tobacco, and Henry abominated tobacco chewing. Ford was the first American industrialist to banish the spittoon as a standard article of office furniture. (This came about a few years later when Ford found a negro worker busily cleaning a long row of spittoons. "That's no work for a man," roared Ford. He ordered trucks to the offices; all spittoons were hauled off to the scrap pile, and boxes of chewing gum were placed conspicuously on all desks.) Nevertheless, Huff, who often chauffeured Ford around the plants, installed a built-in cuspidor below the dash of his Model T and their happy rattles about the countryside were punctuated with the occasional whang! of Huff "ringing the bell." Long-suffering Henry, whose trousers may have been splattered with tobacco juice, never said a word; anything Huff did was all right.

One bond, perhaps, was that their feet hurt as they grew older. Ford came to wear especially soft light shoes, and for years Huff wore tennis sneakers everywhere, indeed, to the day of his death.

128. David Bell, on his wedding day, 1888. The fourth man of that early team was David M. Bell, still alive in 1955, aged ninety-one, with a memory fresh as lilacs in early May. No picture exists of him of about 1900.

But listen to the simple music of his description of the little shop in the Tolsma Building and the way things were in Detroit in those days:

The highest building where visitors and everybody went first was the City Hall [five stories high and now demolished] . . . up to the tower where the clock is . . . to take a look around.

It was a very small town. Nothing, only two-story places.

You've no conception of what the place looked like now, you know. It was all hand work. The town was a sleepy little town. There were cedar-block paved streets. That was the town then.

Some friends [in Ontario] had got me to join the Odd Fellows in St. Thomas. They always told me, "If you go to a strange city, the first place you go is to an Odd Fellows Hall and you'll find friends right away."

I came to Detroit. What I did, I left my suitcase at the depot and I hunted up the Odd Fellows Hall. I went to the meeting in the afternoon. After the business of the meeting was over, they followed the custom and asked if the stranger (me) had anything to say. I said I wanted a job.

They got me a job, on a dredge in the river. But I was a carriage blacksmith. One Friday afternoon I was on an open streetcar on Jefferson Avenue and a man on the sidewalk kept waving at me.

"Get off the car!" He was an Odd Fellow.

He told me they wanted a man at this powerhouse.

I went there on the 13th of July, 1896, to see a man named Ford, who was an engineer there, at the corner of Washington Boulevard and State Street.

I went there and saw this Mr. Ford. I told him I heard they wanted a blacksmith and he said, "What kind of a blacksmith are you?"

Then he said, "Oh, a carriage blacksmith. You come to work!"

How long I was there I can't recall when Mr. Ford took me to see a small new buggy body. [This was Ford's first car.] There were no metal parts on it. It was resting on two wooden stands. It was in the basement of the next building, the first door back of the alley, downstairs. That wasn't the property of the Edison Company. It was a private place.

I made the crank for the engine and front wheel parts. The hardest to make were the parts for the front wheel to run on and connecting parts to steer them. He had never seen one, only the pictures, and I had quite a job.

Different men around there, whoever happened to be handy, used to swing a sledge for me. He had a little forge built under the sidewalk on the State Street side, in line with the boiler. A small part of it was reserved for a shop. They built a little forge there with wooden sides around it and filled all around with ashes [for safety]. You could use it for a blacksmith's fire, and they got the wind from a compressor in the building instead of bellows.

I made a small device to form the spokes for the four wheels. . . . I also made the radius rod from a piece of pipe.

I made many other things which were not used—because Mr. Ford had some other thought in mind that might work better. He was still experimenting. And the hand-rails on the seat.

Several times I saw Mr. Bishop and Mr. Cato trying to help him install a steering post on the thing. I never did anything on the car, only make things for it.

It was all understood that he had the dream. Oh, he'd talk just like a friend, you know, talk it over.

Well, Henry was strictly a citizen, he didn't interfere with anybody. He was really interested in one thing, just one thing, this dream of his, and he was a clean living man. The men liked him.

Henry Ford, he was a memory to a lot of men that are now all dead. . . . He deserved everything. He had to go through a lot by other men that wanted to take the thing over. . . . He had lots of trouble. I wouldn't have wanted to go through his troubles. . . .

Mrs. Ford and Edsel, the small boy, used to come there quite often. Mr. Ford's father used to come from the country.

We [William Ford and Bell] used to look out the [Edison] window on Washington Boulevard and chat about something that would happen to pass.

There was never anything only a man on a bicycle, or a little delivery wagon passing by. That's all we could see those days.

It was the summertime [when] Mr. Ford's father used to come in. He was an old gentleman.

Now Dow was riding a bicycle up and down looking for trade. Dow was as honest a man as was ever born. He wanted no man to tell him any cock-and-bull stories, no lies, to get around anything. . . . He had to know the truth whether the Company lost money by it or not. He had to know what happened. Not to censure anybody, but he just wanted to know.

None of the men went with Mr. Ford when he went from there. . . .

He did want me very badly to go. He was riding a bicycle and so was I. He was always riding a bicycle. He said, "Dave, Dave, you'll go with the business."

I said, "What business?"

Before he went away [from the Edison Company], he said, "You know, Dave," and he shook me, he said, "Dave, I like you."

He said, "You know, at no time I was ever out with you, Dave, did you ever ask me to go into a saloon, and I like you, Dave."

"Well," I said, "Henry, I wouldn't have gone if you asked me." I told him, "Henry, I've got a wife and a family and I can't take the chance."

He said he couldn't pay me wages, but he would keep a record. He'd give me paper for it.

It would have made me rich.

A number of things show up here. One is that Henry, by sheer magnetism, was somehow able to prevail on these Edison workers to spend many hard hours helping him: "different men used to swing a sledge." Another, his endless experimentation: "some other thought that might work better." A third, that not one of the men had enough faith in the car to leave their jobs; they would do anything for Henry but nothing for the automobile. A fourth, the general understanding that Henry was possessed: "he had the dream."

129.

129. The eighth home. Sometime before July 1897 faithful Jim Bishop and a moving man, Mr. Leonard of Leonard Bros. Storage, helped Henry and Clara move their goods from 58 Bagley to this house. We do not know why they moved. This is 72 East Alexandrine Avenue, on the south side of the street, between John R and Brush streets. (The house disappeared long ago; its location is now No. 230.) Henry took the picture.

Clara sits on the porch steps, and the little child must be Edsel, although he was now 3½ years old, which seems a bit mature for the dress and the curls. Note the wooden sidewalk.

The lawn is shaggy, so this picture may have been taken as they moved in, for a bill exists in the Archives from William Ellis, LAWN MOWING AND ROLLING NEATLY DONE. Ellis clipped this bit of sward for the entire season, spring to October 1, for the total sum of $1.50.

The Fords stayed in this house through 1897, 1898, and 1899. We know nothing of its interior and little about their life here, but we know almost every shackle-bolt that Henry bought. The Archives contain—one insight—bills from Grocer George Forsyth for $8.10 worth of groceries in July and $5.46 worth in August. Bread was then five cents a loaf, a quart of tomatoes five cents, a 5½-pound lamb roast was eighty-eight cents and a chicken forty-eight cents.

130. The second car: first version. This is the only contemporary picture of the second car. Ford probably began it in the fall of 1896, after Edison had encouraged him. We do not know when he finished it, as shown here, but it was probably late in 1897, perhaps early 1898. Although the details cannot be seen, this car differs radically from the first car in almost every respect, from the ignition to the oiling. Each man who helped Henry gave the same testimony: Ford was endlessly chopping and changing. He was a natural experimenter. "Try this," "Try that," "Throw this out," "Let's see what would happen if. . . ." These were his words. He would try any man's idea or modify his own, for he was not hampered by that most ruinous quality, the stubborn pride of authorship.

This flexibility made progress slow. Speed in making things can begin only after the design is frozen, as the Armed Forces learned again and again in World War II. In this early period Henry was totally opposed to freezing any single item, from the very nuts and bolts up. He was ready in a moment to discard ruthlessly the polished, carefully tooled work of months. In his own mind he had certain goals of simplicity, strength, reliability, lightness; to these he imperiously sacrificed any refinement, no matter how attractive, that might not stand up.

Some day a work of great interest to engineers will be done when some caliper-minded writer makes a careful study of the actual engineering progress made by Ford in these years; it will show above all else his thoroughness. He was not always right, but he was never slapdash. And in the end his very slowness turned out to be the fastest way to proceed: the tortoise passed the hare.

97

130.

131.

132.

131. The second car: final version. Ford revised this car sharply again and again. Note that the car seen here (as preserved in Greenfield Village) has a different fender line; the front wheels are now smaller than the rear wheels; throttle and spark have been moved to the driver's right hand just below the seat, and so on.

During the spring of 1897, R. W. Hanington, an engineer from Denver, spent several months working with Charles Duryea at Carteret, New Jersey. He found the operations of Duryea "a total failure." Before returning to Denver he deliberately traveled about the United States, trying "to see every motor wagon that was being attempted." Mr. Hanington wrote Ford in 1939:

> The last stop was in Detroit where, through a Mr. Maybury, who I believe was then Mayor, I had the pleasure of an hour's interview with you in the engine room of a large electric light plant, where as I recall it, you were Chief Engineer. You were working on an ingenious device for feeding gasoline into the cylinder; a sliding carrier, like the bobbin of a sewing machine, that would pick up the proper measure of fuel from the tank and transfer it into the combustion chamber.

Without Ford's knowledge, in 1898 Hanington made (for a friend) a very thorough analysis of Ford's second car. Here are excerpts from the analysis:

> The wheels . . . represent the type which has been most successful. . . .
>
> No compensating gear is shown on the rear axle. This device has been found absolutely essential. . . . The Whitney steam wagon provides for the vertical oscillation of the front axle in a similar manner. This is a feature the Duryeas neglected. . . .
>
> The design of the motor is excellent . . . similar to that of the Springfield Duryea's (J. Frank Duryea, Charles' brother) wagon. The sparker is better however. . . .
>
> The cooling tanks show ingenuity and thought. The idea is not original . . . but has not been carried out in such detail. The Duryea wagons have no device for cooling, nor has Max Hertel. . . .
>
> The carburetor is good. The measuring device is complete and ingenious. . . . The design of

the gearing is compact and well-balanced. I cannot see anything particularly novel or valuable in Ford's arrangement over Duryea's except compactness. . . .

> The whole design strikes me as being very complete, and worked out in every detail, and . . . the carriage should equal any that has been built in this country.
>
> The success of a motor-wagon seems to rest on its ability to keep in order and run over all kinds of roads without breakdowns or hitches, and *the first wagon to do this will be the successful one.* [Author's italics.]
>
> In general, the engine is good, the transmission mechanism is good. . . . It is apparently a first-class carriage, well thought out and well constructed, but embodying no *novel* feature of great importance. Novelty, rather than good design, has been the idea of most of the carriage builders.
>
> Simplicity, strength and common sense seem to be embodied in Mr. Ford's carriage, and I believe that these ideals are the essential ones for a successful vehicle. (Denver, December 28, 1898.)

This private analysis, of course, would have delighted and encouraged Henry Ford in 1898; it probably would have been worth many hours and dollars to him in helping to convince his first nervous backers.

132. The second car: the engine from the rear. This picture should be compared with the picture of the workings of the first car, on p. 79. The batteries on the right are modern and should be ignored: in Ford's day this box held primitive glass-jar batteries.

The picture shows brilliantly how Henry had progressed. In every detail this is obviously both more complex and more sophisticated. Henry's first car had a new basic simplicity; now he is proceeding through complexity toward a true simplicity again, best seen in the completely functional, stripped-down workings of the 1903 Model A (p. 185).

Steadily, consistently, and persistently Ford was *graduating* himself from his contemporaries. Little by little the farm boy had passed his apprenticeship and moved toward a career. He had risen until now he was among the top half dozen automobile men in the nation.

Commitment

He had moved beyond his farm friends, his machine shop friends, his steam-engine-days friends; now he was about to graduate from his colleagues at the Edison plant.

His virtues were already known: he had a profound common sense that occasionally reached genius; he had a quick sympathetic instinct for human beings that would make men of talent happy to work for him and make it easy for humbler men to work with him; he had a bred-in-the-bone belief in the general worth of the American competitive system; he did not know how to brag; he had so little temper that hardly a man ever saw him angry; he was temperate, sober, industrious. His weaknesses were almost entirely those of a lack of higher education, and this lack would be serious in later years.

133. The clinch. One can almost hear Henry telling son Edsel: "Now kiss her!" Edsel is obliging but unemotional. Beneath his huge fancy tam Clara has wound a band of cloth to keep his ears warm.

134. Fauntleroy in lace. Edsel was about four when this was taken, about mid 1897. Clara has obviously taken great pains with him for the studio; his hair has a wave on top and every curl is in place; his lace shirt has been ironed to the last millimeter of ruffle; and though almost invisible here, he is wearing buckles on his shoes, like Bobby Shaftoe in the ballad. This was the end of the curls; from now on we see Edsel in manly haircut.

135. Haywagon ride, 1898. Henry shot several pictures of this scene, but this is one of the few in which he appears. The man standing up is his brother Will; he is holding a handsaw as he pretends to cut off a Dearborn head. Beside him, derby hat tipped jauntily askew, is Henry, also mustached. At the front, in cap, is Edsel; Clara, in Tyrolean hat, holds him; Kate is second to the left of Clara in the sailor hat.

136. Tricycle, 1898. Henry kept Edsel well supplied with toys. This was a late model tricycle in 1898, with wide wooden seat. Edsel is immaculate in spanking new sailor suit; the little double clips of his garters show just above his kneecaps.

137. Henry in 1898, age thirty-five. He handed the camera to Clara for this shot in the unkempt

99

133.

134.

135.

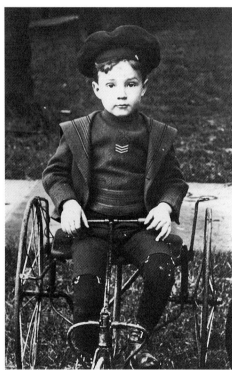

136.

137.

backyard on Alexandrine Avenue. He is in boiled shirt and sawed-off vest; his coat was a five-button model.

138a, b. The sheet on the fence. No doubt dissatisfied with the fence as a background in previous pictures, Henry hung one of Clara's sheets on it, and then he and Clara took turns making portraits. In the one shot the sheet has been shifted to a clothesline—perhaps the following Sunday, for the sheet is now wrinkled. Edsel's face is a study in small-boy expressions: the pout and the monkey-face smile.

Now we are spang into a tricky period, perhaps the most mysterious part of Henry Ford's life. The four years, 1898, 1899, 1900, 1901, and the first part of 1902 are the despair of biographers.

In this period Henry is a real slippery creature. He is elusive, baffling, protean; submerged, he slides along for a month or two and then pops up in a dozen places at once, like a whole school of dolphin. There is no lack of material, new and old; the trouble is that his life simply will not flatten out and lie down in an organized pattern.

There is, of course, the clue. The only pattern to his life is that he lived it. No other pattern can be imposed on it. A biographer, no matter how careful or honest, tends unconsciously to impose a pattern of his own on his subject's life. Ford's life is a salutary lesson because he led so many lives that his story rejects all patterns except his own.

It all actually happened; but it wasn't the careful program of a man studying to be a bank vice-president or rising notch by notch in the civil service—this was Henry Ford as he began to go down twenty railroad tracks at the same time.

He had a workbench in the Edison plant; a little basement shop across the alley; a little workshop at home; he had helped his old Flower Brothers playmate, Fred Strauss, set up a machine shop at 151 Shelby Street. He would drop in at Nageborn's, Lauer's, Wolfertz's, the Fred Kahl foundry, Barr & Dates, Strelinger's, the Eagle works, the Dry Docks, Barton Peck's shop at 81 Park Place, and perhaps a dozen other places. Everywhere in Detroit a man was working at something for Henry, making a part in his spare time, helping design something, casting something, tooling or grinding or fitting. He must have wangled and coaxed and talked his way through a thousand problems and situations.

At Fred Strauss', it turns out, Henry was making gasoline engines for boats. Strauss tells how Henry helped for two months and gave him two orders for gasoline engines: one for a neighboring farmer in Dearborn, the second for one Will Hurlbut, who wanted it for his boat. Strauss also helped Henry make a crankshaft, with no idea it would turn out to be the crankshaft for a later automobile engine. Strauss never once even saw Ford in either his first or second car.

Strauss was ashamed of the little engine that he and Henry built for the Dearborn farmer. Strauss could never get the engine to kick over. It just wouldn't start. Here is his account:

> The farmer used to come in every two weeks to see how we were doing, how the engine was getting along. There was quite a hill down Wayne Street, and as the farmer would come down the hill, the boy I had in the shop would tip me off, "Here comes the farmer!"
>
> I was ashamed I couldn't make the engine turn over. So I would sneak out of the shop. I didn't want to meet the farmer. One day when the boy said, "Here comes the farmer," I sneaked out and the farmer came in, picked up the engine and took it away. I was tickled to death.
>
> A week or two passed and all at once the kid called out, "Here comes the farmer down the hill!" I got out of the shop again.
>
> The farmer came in and said, "Boy, that's a beautiful engine—and how it runs!"
>
> The farmer had gotten the thing to run somehow. He said, "Gee, I've got that thing running like a son-of-a-gun. It runs to beat the band."
>
> I was so glad to get rid of it I didn't care.

That was the first engine Ford and Strauss made in the shop. To help design the second engine, the perpetually mobile Henry found a young draftsman, Billie Boyer, who had lots of spare time—apparently, any Detroiter with spare time spent it working for him. The second engine was for Will Hurlbut's yacht, and while somewhat superior to the first, was still no bargain. The exhaust pipe turned red-hot; its glass-jar batteries wore out after ten to fifteen minutes' use; the boat stalled on the river. Hurlbut refused to

138a.

138b.

pay for the engine, and so Ford and Strauss went down to Griswold Street and found a lawyer.

The lawyer got the partners a settlement from Hurlbut and lived to bless the day Henry saw his shingle. For the lawyer was Horace Rackham, of the firm of Anderson and Rackham; the $5,000 that Horace Rackham later invested in the Ford Motor Company made him a millionaire.

Strauss himself illustrates a number of things about Ford seldom brought exactly into focus. One is Henry's charm, though that is a doughy word: from the time Fred was the boy roustabout at Flower Brothers, Henry could always talk him into or out of a job; again and again Strauss meets Henry, becomes helpless, works furiously for Henry, finally strikes out for himself, meets Henry again, is again enthralled, and so on, the cycle repeating itself. As Strauss said eight years ago, "He had the magnet."

A second thing is that while Strauss never became a millionaire, neither was he a victim—few of the people that Henry magnetized into working for him or investing in him, even in the companies that failed, ever got hurt financially.

Strauss actually came as close as anyone to the final jackpot. A piece of paper dated 1902 and signed by Henry promised him a share in the business—just before the true Ford Motor Company came into being. And it was just then that Strauss finally broke away from Henry for good and all. Like so many, he was anxious for the security of a better, steadier job than Ford could then offer, and the piece of paper didn't look like much. So Strauss went on to a solid and comfortable life, and he and Henry remained friends down through the years.

A third thing about Strauss, a much bigger thing, takes us right back to 1897, and to a facet of Ford's character that reveals the true iron of the man. This is a point already made in passing: *Strauss did not see Henry in the first car; he did not even know Henry had made an automobile and was now making another.*

Yet they were as intimate as partners. Strauss had come to Detroit in December 1896; had met Henry on the street; had talked of setting up his own machine shop; Henry had picked out the location at 151 Shelby Street and had put up some of the money for equipment, and had paid the rent for the two months of January and February 1897. Henry had found another partner

for him, Frank Dimmer. Strauss and Ford had built two gasoline engines together, neither of which worked well. Yet not once had Henry mentioned his first car nor the plans for the second; not once did he show Strauss a new carburetor invention on which he would file a patent application on April 7. Even more, Strauss worked on a crankshaft with Dimmer and only discovered two years later that it was for an automobile. And finally, it was not until the spring of 1899 that Strauss discovered with surprise that Henry was going into the automobile business!

We know that Henry had learned to keep his plans to himself, but this is certainly an extraordinary example of a man who keeps his own counsel, who plays his cards close to his chest. This is the real Henry Ford, operating coolly and separately with many different men, with each according to his capacity. All over Detroit there were now Ford friends in machine shops, banks, and law offices; each thought he knew the real Henry Ford. Yet Henry had a different relationship, a different piece of business to do, with each of them.

But an even bigger point about Ford, beyond his reticence about his own plans, lies in the fact that he could sell his first car within a few months from the time he completed it and never think about it until he needed it years later as an exhibit in the Selden patent suit.

You have to stop and think about this. If you had spent upwards of three years in building a horseless carriage—from December 1893 until June 1896—and the mere ownership of such a miraculous vehicle made some people admire or shake their heads, and if it set you apart and gave you a local mixture of fame and notoriety, would you sell it almost immediately, knowing it would be another two years before you could build another?

But Henry not only could but did. He drove his first car for a few months and then sold it to "Chappie" Annesley for "about $200" (once he said "for $160"), who sold it to A. W. Hall, of Cleveland, probably in the spring of 1897.

Henry had this quality—whatever it is—in supreme measure. He did not look back. He spent many months building his first little tubular gas engine; the moment it worked, on Clara's sink, he put it away and never ran it again until he was an old old man. The moment he had achieved something he was indifferent to it. His mind was always on the next thing, and each height led to another, the way a climbed mountain shows a higher mountain beyond. He never spent any time standing around admiring his own handiwork; he walked away from it.

This gave other, more normal, people great trouble all of Henry's life. He would work with day-and-night intensity and fascination on some problem, working intimately with some expert, some friend, some worker; the moment the problem was solved Henry would walk away, and the man he had worked with so closely might not see him for many weeks, months, years, sometimes never again.

These are the qualities to keep in mind as we watch Ford lift himself step by step out of the ruck of the scores of American mechanics working on horseless carriages, these and his imperviousness to criticism, to delays, to pressures, to deadlines, as he patiently discarded, rejected, chopped and changed, seeking something nearer perfection.

Only thus can we make the bridge between 1898 and 1903, for at the beginning of this time Ford is a stationary engineer in an electric light plant and at the end of it he is the managing partner of an enterprise that quickly became the biggest American automobile company.

So he sold his first car and began the second. The date of its beginning is in doubt. Henry said that he began it right after he returned from the inspiration of the meeting with Edison, which would be August 1896. Another time he said he began it "late in 1896," and this seems likelier, at least to me.

The date of its finishing is even more in doubt. Once he said it took a year and a half to finish, and this would put it somewhere in the first half of 1898. But there are three pieces of evidence that he was still "jiggering" it around in August 1898. Soon after that, however, he was again taking prospects for rides.

On July 18, 1898, J. W. Duntley, president of the big and long-established Chicago Pneumatic Tool Company (with offices in New York) wrote Henry to ask about the progress of his latest "Motor Carriage," adding, "When will you be in a position to take this matter up with me in regard to foreign business?" This letter indicates

the spreading favorable knowledge of Ford's activities; it also indicates the changing climate about horseless carriages.

The automobile was growing up swiftly. Great impetus came from the East: New York society had made a high-fashion fad of the motor carriage. Women shopped in their little electrics (most gasoline cars were odorous); Newport society paraded at fetes in cars decked and filled with flowers; Alexander Winton had driven all the way from Cleveland to New York, and had set a speed record for a mile. In eighteen months, by 1900, more than a dozen companies would be making motor cars. In 1901 the little one-cylinder, curved-dash Olds, the "merry Oldsmobile," would be manufactured in the staggering quantity of 425 cars in one year.

Men of finance in Detroit watched the boom with a thoughtful eye on Henry Ford's car. On August 1, 1898, Ellery I. Garfield, of the Fort Wayne Electric Corporation (with branches in fourteen cities), wrote a serious letter to Mayor Maybury, full of confidence in Ford.

A little later that year Garfield, Maybury and two other men came together to ponder backing Ford. The other two were the aforementioned E. A. Leonard of the Standard Life and Accident Insurance Company and a Detroiter, Benjamin R. Hoyt. They drew up a memorandum of agreement, which is too lengthy to reproduce, but which records certain significant points.

139. Dr. Benjamin Rush Hoyt.

First, it was to supplant a previous "oral agreement."

It notes that "the second parties have collectively advanced money to meet expenses," thus explaining how Ford was able to afford men and materials and "to pay for patents on devices invented by the first party." Ford had applied for his first patent on April 7, 1897, and he assigned that patent on August 30, 1898 to Maybury. On December 8 he would apply for his second, a reach-rod construction covering the steering.

All patents thereafter were to be shared, one-third to Ford, two-thirds to the others; and the same proportion was to apply to all motor wagons built. Each of the four was to put up $500. If a corporation was formed after this trial period, Ford was to be employed "on fair compensation" by this company.

139.

During 1898 and 1899 Henry spent much time in selling William H. Murphy, a well-to-do lumber merchant whom Ford had met at his sawmill in Dearborn. And Murphy meant the bigger kind of backing that made Mayor Maybury's little group feel more comfortable.

Duntley of Chicago kept writing Ford for dates to see the carriage, through 1898 and into the spring of 1899; apparently Henry was "out of town."

Actually Henry was working very hard on car No. 3. It was a delivery truck, an almost unheard-of novelty in that day. Sometime in the spring of 1899 Mayor Maybury took Ford and Fred Strauss —Henry had captured Strauss again, after two years' absence—to an empty factory building at 1343 Cass Avenue (old number), a block or two north of the Edsel Ford Expressway. The building was ideal, more working space than either had ever had. Here they broke the news to Strauss that Ford was going into the automobile business.

That building belongs in the history of the automobile, not only because Henry Ford struggled there; out of it came the Cadillac Automobile Company; out of it also came the Fisher Brothers, who made car bodies a symbol of elegance.

By summer Henry and his backers felt ready. They formed the Detroit Automobile Company in July and made it official on August 5, 1899.

Only then, on August 15, did Henry Ford resign from the Edison Company. As usual, before leaving a job, Henry had lined up the next one.

Alex Dow wanted Henry to stay with Edison as general superintendent in Detroit. But Henry would have to drop his automobile nonsense. Said Dow:

"I simply wanted Henry to know what we were planning so that he could make his plans accordingly, but there was no threat to discharge him nor any time limit set before he must decide. The talk was entirely friendly. Henry at this time had the dream of an American automobile to be in common use."

Henry said: "I had to choose between my job and my automobile. I chose the automobile. . . ."

XIV. THE DETROIT AUTOMOBILE COMPANY

You'd be surprised at the amount of detail about an automobile.
—FRANK R. ALDERMAN

140. *The first news story was on Henry Ford's second car. The caption beneath the engraving (middle, right) is in error, of course; the drawing actually was made from the photograph on page 97. The ride the reporter describes began at the Ford home at 72 East Alexandrine Avenue.*

Notice the newspaper's date: July 29, 1899. Henry's timetable worked like this:

On July 24 the Detroit Automobile Company was organized, capitalized at $150,000, with only $15,000 actual cash paid in.

On July 29 this news story appeared, rousing interest in Ford's movements—*and yet this story is on a car that is at least a year old* and in which he had been driving about Detroit for some time.

On August 5 the papers for the new Detroit Automobile Company were officially filed.

On August 15 Henry officially quit his post at Edison.

Thus we watch Henry leap from security to security. The new job is well in hand before he quits the old; everything is carefully set, with artillery preparation laid on, before he moves.

Now, finally, Henry had bet his whole life on his main idea. He was now totally committed. There is no record, no hint, no implication anywhere that he had anything less than the serenest confidence.

141. *The first Ford company, the third Ford car. This building is 1343–1355 Cass Avenue. Here is the scene of Ford's main struggles from the spring of 1899 until late in 1901. Here he first encountered the problems of making more than one car at a time. Here he first learned all the things that stand behind the businessman's phrase of criticism of the intellectual: "He never met a*

THE DETROIT JOURNAL, SATURDAY, JULY 29 1899

FORD'S AUTOMOBILE HAS NEW FEATURES AND IS A NOVEL MACHINE

THE FRENCH AUTOMOBILE, WHICH IS TO RACE WITH THE WINTON MACHINE.

WINTON'S AMERICAN MACHINE.

FIRST FORD MACHINE, COMPLETED, MADE IN DETROIT.

WORKING GEAR OF THE FORD MACHINE, MADE IN DETROIT.

140.

105

141.

142.

payroll"—the employees that are sick, or drunk, or incompetent, or eager beavers; the materials that come in too late, the wrong size, or defective; the drains that stop up; the motor that burns out; the accidents; the weather; the salesmen from other companies that interrupt you in crises; your own salesmen who never seem to get an order.

Here he failed again. Ford worked like a madman. He was in his prime, whipcord, whalebone and clear blue eyes. He had determination, backing, the nucleus of a team of professional motor mechanics, a fine factory to work in. But he failed, flounder-flat.

One reason is simple: he built a wretched car. The delivery truck you see was slow and heavy, hard to make and easy to break. It was as fragile as a child's cast-iron toy. The fading memories of the few old men now left who once worked on that model can scarcely recall a time when this truck even ran successfully around the block. And yet, you will see that it did run at least once, and most beautifully, too, giving birth to one of the greatest of all Ford headlines: "SWIFTER THAN A RACE HORSE IT FLEW OVER THE ICY STREETS."

The first car (1896) weighed 500 pounds when first built, and then about 675 pounds after cylinder-jackets, water-tanks and other things were added. The second car (1898) weighed 875 pounds, as Henry added complexities. This third car (1899) weighed about 1,200 pounds. Henry was losing his battle to make a car rugged, fast, reliable—but above all light in weight.

142. The truck itself. The gentlemen in the droop-drawer mustaches are the same as those in the shot of the truck outside the factory: left, Henry Ford, right, Frank R. Alderman, treasurer of the Detroit Automobile Company, and a first-water optimist. This picture was taken inside the plant.

The mayor, William C. Maybury, Henry's friend and booster, had been using the 1343 Cass Avenue building for a modest enterprise of his own, the Detroit Motor Company, trying to cash in on the rising demand for gasoline engines for all purposes, particularly to propel boats. The business died quietly.

Fred Strauss recalls taking the Woodward Avenue streetcar with Henry Ford to the Cass plant in April 1899:

When we got in there it opened our eyes. It was just perfect for our shop. The place was empty. There wasn't a thing in there except an engine and a boiler and a main line of shaft.

Then Henry told us we were going to make an automobile. We did find out at that time. That is the first I knew I was going to work on an automobile.

The first thing I did was start to get the boiler and engine ready.

Strauss may not have known until that moment that he was going into the automobile business. But Ford did.

And so did about two dozen men of Detroit, the men who joined in July of 1899 to back Henry Ford with $15,000. By the time they gave up, in the fall of 1900, the venture had cost them $86,000. Who were these men who, at the turn of the century, had such faith in Ford? The men who put up the money for the Detroit Automobile Company are usually dismissed as a little group of speculators.

Exactly who were Ford's first backers?

We have to go back into Detroit history a bit, into a success story so fabulous as almost to seem preposterous, a story little known and long forgotten.

143a, b. James and Hugh McMillan, capitalists. For the present generation, I should point out that in those days there was no opprobrium attached to this simple description of one's life work; on the contrary, it was considered just about the ideal occupation: you put up your capital to help other men start out in business. A Scots immigrant named William McMillan settled in Hamilton, Ontario in the early 1800's. Frugal and industrious, he worked his way up to become one of the men who helped establish the Great Western Railway. Two of his sons were James, born 1838, and Hugh, born 1845.

James at fourteen became a hardware clerk, at eighteen moved to Detroit to work in the wholesale hardware store of Buhl and Ducharme, and by the time he was twenty was purchasing agent for the Detroit and Milwaukee Railroad. Then came the Civil War, great expansion of the

143a.

143b.

railroads, and the usual great wartime pressures for quick deliveries. James left the railroad and prospered mightily as a free agent who could satisfy contractors.

In 1864 James McMillan and his friend John S. Newberry joined with two others to set up the Michigan Car Company. They made railroad cars. As you may remember, it was at the Michigan Car works that Henry got his first job and was fired six days later: even then (1879) it was the largest manufactory in Michigan and one of the biggest in America.

Hugh McMillan, seven years younger, joined James in 1872. The brothers moved fast. To supply the Michigan Car works they set up the Detroit Car Wheel Company. To make parts, they set up the Baugh Steam Forge Company. To handle the iron ore, they set up the Detroit Furnace Company. Then they spread out and really went to work.

They built and owned car works in London (Ontario) and St. Louis. They organized and owned the major share of the Duluth, South Shore and Atlantic Railway. Before 1880 the brothers were splitting more than $5,000,000 a year, and this was long, long before there was any income tax of any kind.

They built, bought and expanded numerous other railways, but perhaps their best railroad operation was the formation of the Detroit, Marquette and Mackinac. Hugh was a director and secretary and treasurer; James, a major stockholder. Hugh joined with financiers from New York and Chicago to add 200 miles to the Marquette, extending it to join with the Northern Pacific at Duluth and eastern railroads at Sault Ste. Marie. Then he sold it to his own group for $3,000,000.

The McMillans always went to the source. They owned iron mines. They bought up most of the big Great Lakes boat lines to bring in their iron. Then they formed a railroad elevator company to store things they shipped and then moved the rest of the way on their own railways, haulage and other transportation companies. They owned electrical works, docks, foundries, pipe companies; and they owned entirely the Detroit Dry Dock Company, the scene of Henry's third job. They even owned the Union Depot in Detroit.

When they needed places to put their money, they formed banks right and left.

They needed fire, marine and life insurance companies, so they set them up or bought into them. Paint companies, power and light companies, lumber companies, even the Michigan Telephone Company became theirs.

They were careful politically. Although Republicans, they made sure that many key Democrats were their friends; in their two dozen corporations and companies and interests they set certain Democrats in high directorates. For a generation they surrounded Republican governors with their men and held the Michigan legislature in light but firm control; but no top Democrat was left in want.

The Board of Trade, the Detroit Chamber of Commerce, all the key trusteeships from universities to art institutes to hospitals to charities down to the very memberships of the top clubs, all these and many more came under the benevolent control of the McMillans.

They made many men rich and some rich men much, much richer. To be a friend of the McMillans was to succeed in life.

144.

144. Dexter Mason Ferry, whose concentrated energies made a success of the great seed firm, D. M. Ferry & Co., which by 1900 was doing a business of about $1,500,000 a year. The McMillans interested him in a broader view of life and soon he was heading up a number of McMillan enterprises and banks.

The full story of the interlocking enterprises of the McMillans and their friends does not belong here, but it bears on the story of Henry Ford at a number of points. Although in my notes I have traced the McMillan relationships in detail, I can only sketch cursorily what would in itself fill a massive volume. Let me indicate where and how the McMillan empire entered Ford's life.

The Larneds, Sylvester and his father, were inveterate doers of good, and Thomas W. Palmer came to know them well, along with William Austin Moore, a prominent attorney who did much legal work for the McMillans and was on many of their boards, and Dexter M. Ferry, who also was a doer of good. (Moore and Ferry carried their temperance notions too far at one

145.

point;' they opposed the sale of beer on Belle Isle Park, and the outraged citizens of Detroit quickly retired both of them from public life forever.)

145. Thomas Witherell Palmer, 1830–1913. Senator Palmer was born to lumber (the town of St. Clair was originally named Palmer); he married into a great lumber fortune and soon devoted himself to good works and public service.

Palmer was truly a kind man, gentle and steady, literally without enemies; he represented Michigan with honor in the Senate for three terms. He had "an elegant house with extensive grounds" in Detroit, "a palatial establishment" in Washington, but his especial pride was "a log house that cost many thousands of dollars [to build], located a few miles outside of [Detroit] in Greenfield [Township]. This farm, about a mile square, contained 657 acres of rich land, on which he raised Percheron horses and Jersey cows." It was the Senator's pastoral retreat.

The Senator and Ferry were directors of leading McMillan banks, both had holdings in their security and safe deposit company, the directorships of both crisscrossed through various other McMillan holdings, such as in the big lake boats, iron works, furnaces, foundries, iron mines, timber lands, railways, transportation companies, and insurance companies.

Late in life the Senator married as his second wife a young sister of William C. McMillan's mother. Ripe with honors and wealth, he prized most three achievements: the Soldiers' and Sailors' Monument in Detroit, the Grand Boulevard around Detroit, and the establishment of a girls' reform school. Before the time we are considering, 1899 and 1900, Senator Palmer had retired from the Senate.

The Republican boss of the state, of course, was none other than James McMillan. McMillan, after years of advancing the political as well as the monetary fortunes of such friends as John S. Newberry, now wanted to go to the Senate himself.

Then the legislatures (until 1913) elected United States senators, which was one reason the Senate differed only a little in atmosphere from most rich men's clubs. Yet it was no small tribute to James McMillan's power that the

Michigan legislature elected him *unanimously*, no member from the remotest part of the state dissenting.

In the 1890's and the 1900's, the big business of Detroit was done in the Moffat Block, the Campau Building, the Union Trust Building, and a few financial offices on Griswold Street. (McMillan's mother was a Moffat; so was Senator Palmer's second wife.) The McMillans and the Murphys, father and son, owned a great deal of Detroit's downtown real estate. But most of the McMillan holdings centered in their own building, the Union Trust, where they operated from the eighth and ninth floors.

146. William C. McMillan. This was the man who worked at 804 Union Trust Building, vigorous youngish William C. McMillan. He was keeper of the moneybags of both his father and his uncle. He served as secretary and treasurer to:

Detroit Iron Mining Company
Detroit Iron Furnace Company
Detroit Railroad Elevator Company
Detroit Transportation Company
Newberry Furnace Company
Michigan Peninsular Car Company
Duluth & Atlantic Transportation Company
Fulton Iron & Engine Works
Railway Car Loan & Rolling Stock Company
Star Dockage & Warehouse, Ltd.

He was a director of the First National Bank of Detroit (D. M. Ferry was president), vice-president of the Buffalo & Duluth Transportation Company, a director of the Iron Star Company (Truman H. Newberry was treasurer), first vice-president of the Union Trust Company (of which Ferry was president).

And he was one of the backers—perhaps the key backer—of Henry Ford in the Detroit Automobile Company. He held one hundred shares.

Now let us take a look at the management of D. M. Ferry & Co. Ferry was president and general manager, James McMillan, the vice-president. Charles C. Bowen, one of the big four who started Ferry in the seed business, was the secretary, and his son, Lem Bowen, the treasurer. Albert E. F. White was the auditor.

147. Lem Bowen spent his college summers selling seeds and for the rest of his life spent

his summers in Europe buying seeds. By 1901 he had become general manager of the Ferry Seed Company and on Ferry's death in 1907 became president. Besides his father's close ties with the McMillans, Lem himself was a director of two banks and a hospital trustee, sitting on boards with other McMillan men.

He was closely associated with the lumber and real estate king, William H. Murphy, through their mutual love of music. Murphy founded the Detroit Orchestra Association that brought about the famed Detroit Symphony, and Bowen was its faithful backer. Both had magnificent pipe organs in their homes. Murphy, one of the first to back Ford, stuck stoutly for three years of failure, paying a great many of the bills personally.

With McMillan money backing Ford, with Murphy supporting Ford, no doubt Lem Bowen felt more than safe. But he had a further reason: Bowen was also a director of the Edison Illuminating Company and thus had first-hand contact with both Alex Dow, the general manager who had been Ford's immediate boss, and with George Peck, the president of the Illuminating Company. We know Dow's confidence in Henry and his efforts to keep him at Edison.

Lem Bowen stayed on with Henry as a backer to the last point of disgust, and then went with the rest into the revival of the Detroit Automobile Company as the Cadillac Automobile Company. Bowen was president of Cadillac until 1909, when William Crapo Durant bought Cadillac to integrate it into his new General Motors Corporation. Until his death in 1925, Bowen remained grumpy about Henry Ford: on a seed-buying trip outside Paris in 1924 he arrived back at his hotel, tired, hot and furious. His car had broken down, and after several hours of waiting, he had finally been forced to take a Ford taxicab, thus breaking a lifetime vow never to ride in a Ford.

148. George Peck, 1834–1913. Peck, as a dry-goods merchant on Woodward Avenue, had survived fantastic vicissitudes: the panic of 1857, the bank failures of 1861 with the disappearance of gold and silver, a great robbery of all his silks in 1864—to come out wealthy and respected. In 1877 he quit drygoods to take several directorships on McMillan boards, became president of

111

146.

147.

148.

149.

150.

151.

the Michigan Savings Bank and president of the Edison Illuminating Company.

Peck's connection with Henry Ford was something more than that of a president to his chief engineer. Peck's youngest son, Barton, was a speed buff who began with bicycles and then went enthusiastically into automobiles. He is supposed to have made a very poor car, at the same time that Henry was making his first car, but although it fell apart his enthusiasm remained high. He was on allowance from his wealthy father, who set him up in the shop at 81 Park Place. Gradually Henry took over the right half of that shop with young Peck in the left half. George Peck may have asked Henry to help Barton along. At least he was completely and favorably aware of Ford's activities.

Barton had a curious career, too. After Ford left his shop, Peck converted it to the manufacture of wholesale electrical furnace supplies, and it was in one of his furnaces that the porcelain for the first porcelain spark plug was baked, the invention of Dr. E. W. Sanborn, the dentist to King's helper, Oliver Barthel. Then somehow Peck shifted to making hair restorer. This business died while he was still on allowance from his father. Still a speed buff, he bought the first Curtiss flying-boat and then moved to Florida. To have room to fly he bought up great sections of flat land for flying fields and at the height of the Florida land boom sold them out for a fortune far greater than all his father's industry had ever brought in. Peck then retired to Arizona to die a leading citizen.

149. Albert E. F. White, 1844–1924, was a school teacher who liked to travel. He once taught school in Springfield, Illinois, for a year because his train stopped there when he was down to his last dollar. He came to Detroit to visit his brother, Henry Kirke White, one of the big four who started D. M. Ferry in business. Henry had become wealthy, spending the best part of each summer at Siasconset, Nantucket Island, Massachusetts, where he owned fourteen cottages, renting thirteen of them. Albert became a seedman, too, and stayed with the Ferry Company continuously for sixty years. At this time he was auditor for Ferry. As a McMillan man he became a director of numerous corporations and several banks.

112

The Detroit Automobile Company

150. *Colonel Frank J. Hecker, 1846–1927, capitalist, was a Civil War veteran, had become a well-known railroad superintendent by the '70's, had helped the McMillans organize the Peninsular Car Company, and was a colonel of volunteers in the Spanish-American War.*

151. *Mark Hopkins. I found little data available on another of Henry's backers, Mark Hopkins, another capitalist, the key Republican watchdog for the McMillan interests. He was related to the main Hopkins family in America—I don't exactly know how—but came to own a hotel in St. Clair, Senator Palmer's old town. He served two governors as private secretary and was the executor of the fortune of Governor Bagley.*

152. *Frank R. Alderman. The only contemporary view we have of Frank R. Alderman, the first and last treasurer of the Detroit Automobile Company, is the picture of him seated in the truck with Henry. Alderman was an ebullient life insurance salesman, representing a Philadelphia firm—we do not know how he came into Henry's orbit.*

But his experience with Ford somehow must have taken the snap out of his garters, for Alderman quit insurance, tried to sell stocks and bonds, became the "treasurer" for a small local mineral bath sanitarium, and then drifted to Chicago and out of Ford history.

153. *Frank Woodman Eddy, 1851–1914. Eddy came to Detroit as a wholesale hardware salesman and settled down with a firm of ship chandlers who also handled belting and mill supplies, thus inevitably doing business with the McMillans. Soon he graduated to a number of their boards.*

At Williams College Eddy had been an athlete—baseball, weight-throwing, rowing. To his dismay he found that Detroit in 1876 was no sporting town, the only sport being cricket. Eddy changed all that. He became president of the Excelsior Boat Club and developed some champion oarsmen; he took over the cricket grounds for baseball, built a clubhouse, became the first president of the Detroit Athletic Club in 1887, and saw to it that the first national meeting of the newly organized Amateur Athletic Union was held on the club's grounds, September, 1888.

113

152.

153.

154.

155.

156.

157.

Young Henry Ford

He was already a notable figure in the city, known everywhere as the father of the D.A.C., when he and the other McMillan men decided to back Henry Ford.

154. Safford S. DeLano. Another backer was Safford S. DeLano, a young man at the turn of the century and the son of another notable Mc-Millanite: Alexander DeLano of Oneida County, New York State. The father, a Civil War veteran, went to work for James McMillan in Detroit in 1868. By 1878 he was wealthy enough to join with John S. Newberry in organizing the Detroit Car Spring Company, and then the Detroit Steel Works, consolidating the two in 1883, DeLano as president and general manager. Safford had the run of his father's finances.

155. Frederick S. Osborne, 18??–1908? Osborne was a well-dressed young man who headed one of Detroit's leading brokerage firms, Cameron, Currie & Company, members of the New York Stock Exchange.

156. Everett A. Leonard, 1855–1918. Leonard handled the financial affairs of the Standard Life and Accident Insurance Company.

And this brings us to the man who did more for Henry Ford in all these years than anyone else, a man who has never had proper credit for his enormous influence on Ford's career. William C. Maybury, the general manager of the Standard Life and Accident, unquestionably was not only Ford's first backer and first influential friend but probably the one who introduced Henry and his car to the McMillans and their friends. (See the photograph of and references to Maybury in Chapter XIII.)

The first thing to keep in mind about Maybury's relations with Henry Ford is that the two families were from the same community in Ireland; they settled down only a few miles apart in Michigan, and they maintained the closest friendly contact.

The three Ford "uncles" had migrated in 1832; two years later three Maybury brothers of the same age followed them to Michigan. One Maybury went to Jackson, Michigan; two built their houses on Lafayette Boulevard in Detroit. In one, that of Thomas C. Maybury, William Cotter Maybury was born on November 21, 1848. And in that house William Ford married Mary Litogot

114

on April 25, 1861. Young William Maybury, age thirteen, may have been at the wedding.

Maybury may have helped William Ford get Henry his first few jobs: the Michigan Car Works, Flower Brothers, the Detroit Dry Docks; we cannot be sure. But the genial young politician was known everywhere in the city: he had the natural gift of the glad hand, the graceful speech; he was always in demand for a few remarks to brighten an occasion. And no doubt William Ford had a sense of security about young Henry's early working days, with William C. Maybury always at hand to help out.

Henry probably turned to Maybury for advice often. And for more than advice. A hop and a step from the Bagley Avenue backyard where Henry built his first car was the carriage and blacksmith shop of the Gray Brothers. The Grays often did the rough blacksmithing for Ford as he built his second car; but stern J. Allen Gray, perhaps because Ford was slow in payment, would never do a stroke of work until William C. Maybury's check had been received. The checks came every Saturday. Thus Maybury, even in 1897, was helping Henry with hard cash.

And it was Maybury who wrote the letter asking for the "loan of a lathe" to Ford; Maybury who gave him his first auto license (an oral one, in 1897) when people complained of the chuckety-chuck noise made by Ford's car. It was Maybury who built the first oral agreements into the undated (and perhaps unsigned) agreement of 1898 into a pledge of real financial support for Ford, and no doubt it was Maybury's solid political prestige that swayed the McMillanites into backing Ford in 1899 and again in 1901.

Maybury was a Democrat and the kind of dedicated politician who never marries. Even in grade school he was distinguished for his gift of ready speech, and by the time he graduated from the University of Michigan, aged twenty-two, he knew his career. He was taken into an old law firm, of the two Conely brothers, but soon was elected and re-elected city attorney of Detroit. He got an M.A. from Michigan in 1880, was professor of jurisprudence at the Michigan College of Medicine and then went to Washington as a member of Congress for two terms.

Although Michigan was a solidly Republican state, Maybury's personal popularity brought

him into office over great odds. He became mayor of Detroit in 1897, and it was during the next five years that his prestige was at its peak—exactly during the years when Henry Ford most needed help from on high. As mayor, Maybury gave real grace to the rough-and-ready factory town; for the first time, Detroit became a city for conventions. Maybury put through a long series of improvements, parks, monuments—but most typically, he hung a huge sign "Welcome" over the entrance to the City Hall—and meant it.

Maybury actually came just short of the impossible—he almost won the governorship of Michigan in 1900, despite the Republican sweep for McKinley, when the solid Michiganders feared all Democrats as tools of William Jennings Bryan.

Maybury had another connection with the Fords: he was a close friend of Republican Senator Thomas W. Palmer. Maybury was in the House for Michigan while Palmer was in the Senate.

And now let us look back over a list of Detroit Automobile Company stockholders:

W. C. McMillan, son of the most powerful man in Michigan, and secretary and treasurer of most of his interests; Mark Hopkins, capitalist; Safford DeLano, capitalist; Albert E. F. White, director of many Ferry and McMillan corporations and banks; Lem W. Bowen, the key man in D. M. Ferry and Company; Frank R. Alderman, insurance salesman; Col. Frank J. Hecker, capitalist; William C. Maybury, mayor of Detroit.

Besides these and others there were William H. Lake, of whom we know nothing; Everett A. Leonard; Ellery I. Garfield, the electrical manufacturer from Fort Wayne, Indiana, who had been trying to invest in Ford for two years; Dr. Benjamin R. Hoyt, a close friend to Mayor Maybury; Frank W. Eddy; a wealthy lumberman named Patrick A. Ducey; and an even wealthier lumber magnate named William H. Murphy.

157. William Herbert Murphy, 1855–1929. If any of the stockholders felt faint of heart despite the fact that the McMillan interests were so thoroughly represented, their spirits must have been restored by the thought that William H. Murphy was backing Henry Ford.

William's father, Simon Jones Murphy, was a well-to-do lumberman from Maine, where the source of the family fortunes had been the timber along the Penobscot River. (In the Abenaki Indian language, "Penobscot" means "the whitening of the sky before dawn," and Simon never forgot it, as you shall see.) When the timber thinned out along the Penobscot, Simon Murphy brought his family to Detroit, in 1866, and started lumbering on the St. Clair River near Port Huron and to the northwest in the Thumb area.

Simon was a stern man. When William was in his teens, he was sent logging with his father's crews, spending the winters skidding the logs from the woods to lake ice. One spring he was at Gooden Creek, watching the ice break up, the huge logs beginning to float toward Saginaw Bay. A giant sunken tree snagged the logs; they started to pile up, threatening to break the dam that was Simon's pride.

Simon Murphy roared, "Break her loose!"

A foreman and young William, each with a peavy in hand, leaped out onto the jam, levering the logs with their peavies. The key log began to move. The foreman leaped to safety, but young William stuck it out: he was caught on the pile as it broke loose. As his father watched, William fell from a spinning log into the water and disappeared. Finally, dodging the swirling logs, he bobbed up and swam heavily through the icy lake waters to shore. Simon dragged him out. Then he said: "You'll never make a good lumberman. You lost the peavy."

That night William, grieving over the lost peavy, told the foreman that he still wanted to be a good lumberman. The foreman told his father. Said Simon Murphy: "Bless his heart. Now that he has explored the water both above and below, I have decided to call it Will Murphy Lake in his honor." It is still known as Murphy Lake.

William Murphy was educated at the University of Michigan, and then went to Boston to be treated for deafness. His deafness was tragic to him. He was so passionate about music that even as a child he rose at 7 A.M. to practice his violin before school. In Boston he listened to all the music he could, memorizing the sounds.

Then he came back and threw his energies into the lumber business.

The Murphys lumbered the forests of Michigan swiftly and then moved operations to Wisconsin. But even there the woods thinned out too fast. They moved on all the way to California, attracted by the giant redwood forests.

In the meantime both Murphys had operated around Detroit with the kind of happy energy the McMillans had shown. But whereas the McMillans concentrated on transportation—on anything that moved, the Murphys focused on real estate—on anything that held still.

The McMillans and the Murphys owned most of downtown Detroit, and the rest was held mainly by such friends as the Buhls, the Algers, the Ferrys, the Joys.

There was the Murphy Power Company, the Murphy Oil Company, the Murphy Lumber Company, the Pacific Lumber Company, and at the top, the Simon J. Murphy Company.

Simon bought up the Moffat Building, where many of the McMillanites held offices, and put up next to it a skyscraper, the first section of the Penobscot Building (13 stories), so named from his boyhood days in Maine. In the week before he was to move into his new offices, he died (1905). His son William put up the second section of the Penobscot, even taller (47 stories); and in the week before it opened, he died (1929).

William Murphy, despite his almost total deafness, was one of the best friends of music Detroit ever had. He organized the Detroit Orchestra Association and brought in Ossip Gabrilowitsch, who made the Detroit Symphony a first-class orchestra. For years William Murphy paid the annual deficits and never heard a note, it was said, until in 1925 the new invention, radio, was linked to his box, and for the last three years of his life he heard the concerts through stepped-up earphones.

Murphy had first become interested in horseless carriages in 1883, when he read in the newspaper that Philadelphia had a horseless fire wagon, propelled by steam. He made a quick trip, and bought it for the Detroit Fire Department. His interest in the department was transmitted to his son, C. Hayward Murphy, among whose passions not the least was that of attending all major fires.

In Detroit the horseless fire wagon created

116

more consternation than acclaim. It had such a furious exhaust that it shot sparks far out on both sides as it rumbled off to fires. Said Murphy: "It set more fires with its sparks than its great speed permitted it to extinguish." Citizens' complaints poured in so vehemently that the City Council doused the fires in its pioneer horseless carriage, tacked a pole to it, and let horses pull it ignobly off to the blazes that Murphy loved to watch.

When Henry Ford, perhaps with Maybury's aid, convinced William Murphy the real sale was made. And perhaps not the least of the advantages to Murphy was that the factory Ford moved into, Maybury's old Detroit Motor Company plant, was at 1343 Cass Avenue, and thus hard by the old Cass Fire Engine House.

158. Clarence A. Black, 1853–1924. At the head of their new company, the stockholders put Clarence A. Black, a wholesale hardware merchant who had quit business for politics. Nothing better illustrates the sweet reasonableness of the McMillan-Murphy controls than the fact that Clarence Black and William Maybury could happily join hands in a commercial enterprise. Black, a Republican, had helped put Maybury's foe, Hazen S. Pingree, into office as mayor and had been rewarded with the job of city controller. Twice he had posters out proclaiming his candidacy for mayor. He also invested in the Cadillac Motor Car Company; when Durant bought Cadillac, Black took his proceeds and went west to Seattle, where his brother Frank was mayor, to enter the hardware business again.

159. The Detroit Automobile Company's handsome brochure. There are the names of the officers and directors; behind them stands the whole tapestry of money, power and prestige represented by the stockholders described above.

Now all of these facts, freshly brought together, suggest that a square look may never have been taken at the Detroit Automobile Company, despite the fact that it was Ford's first venture into the automobile business.

What do these facts add up to?

First, a new perspective on Ford that is a lethal blow to the old American success myth of rags to riches.

To repeat, Henry Ford was not poor; he was

158.

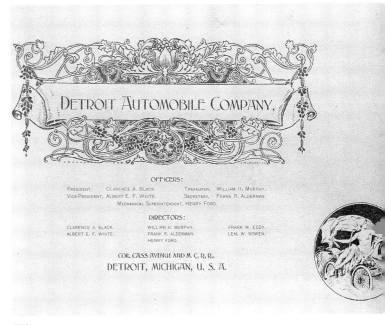

159.

never hungry, except by his own will; he never lacked comfortable shelter. He was never lonely, never friendless; indeed, his friends were in such legions that it is almost impossible to reconstruct the original scene in the Bagley Avenue shop, Henry working alone at nights on his first car, Clara quietly knitting beside the workbench. So many men have turned up who loaned Henry the valves, made the parts for him, gave him pieces of pipe, did blacksmithing, finishing, lathe work, sledge work, that there is hardly room left in the Bagley shed for Henry, let alone Clara.

Nor was he mocked as a crazy inventor, except perhaps by a few owners of startled horses: it is clear that his mere ownership of his first car gave him prestige, a distinction immediately enhanced when people learned he had built it himself.

Nor could he have had to struggle very hard for his first backing—well, perhaps he did have to argue, persuade and sell, but it is clear he was not spurned or kicked out of offices. Doors did not slam on him; they were opened to him. With W. C. Maybury, W. C. McMillan, and W. H. Murphy interested financially, Ford's first automobile enterprise rolled off to a racing start.

This brings us to another fresh point: actually, no other pioneer automobile company began with backers of such stature, such influence, and so much cash in ready reserve. Against this beginning, most other companies of the time look like small bicycle shops.

160. The horse vs. the auto. The horse, crying into his towel, probably pleased Henry Ford. As the figures show, it would cost $816 more to support a horse and buggy over a five-year period. In the automobile figures, note that it was deemed necessary to paint the car anew each year, at a cost of $25; this was the usual practice in the upkeep of wagons and buggies in those days, and it would be years before the automobile industry could seriously improve the finish on cars.

161. Unhappy subject, probably in the winter of 1899–1900. Several pictures show that Edsel did not want to play outdoors in the cold and snow; in one of them, rather blurred, Clara is obviously waving at him from a curtained window to stay out and let Daddy take your picture! Here Grandmother Bryant had come to visit them in their ninth home since marriage; for this is as close as

we can come to a picture of 1292 Second Boulevard (now numbered 5842), where they moved in the autumn of 1899 not long after the Detroit Automobile Company began.

162. Henry's handwriting, December 4, 1899 (facsimile). His endorsement on the back of one of four checks he endorsed in one year. Like anyone else's handwriting, his signatures show slight changes. These four checks and the Cadillac car, which has undergone a few changes since, are all that survive of the old Detroit Automobile Company, Henry Ford, mechanical superintendent.

The Detroit Automobile Company radiated optimism at the start. It took a three-year lease on the Cass Avenue building. Secretary Frank R. Alderman said, "We expect to have 100 to 150 men employed before the year is past." He hailed the delivery wagon as good for fifteen years of service, and said that seven other models were in progress. That was on October 1, 1899 when the wagon was well along.

163. Headline of February 4, 1900, The Detroit News-Tribune:

SWIFTER THAN A RACE-HORSE
IT FLEW OVER THE ICY STREETS!
Thrilling Trip on the First Detroit-Made Automobile When Mercury Hovered About Zero.

This is the narrative accompanying the headline:

"She's ready," said Ford.
"But you didn't touch a match to something or other."
Ford smiled.
"No necessity. The ignition is by electricity. Didn't you see me touch the switch up there? . . ."
By and by a man opened a factory door and with incomparable swiftness the machine picked up its speed and glided into the snowy, wind-blown street.
"First we'll try her on the rough country road," said Ford, as he veered around an unexpected corner.
The puffing of the machine assumed a higher key. She was flying along about eight miles an hour. The ruts in the road were deep, but the machine certainly went with dream-like

161.

Comparative Cost.

The cost of an Automobile, and expense of running for five years as compared with a horse and vehicle for the same period :

Automobile.

Original cost,	$1,000 00
Cost of operating, ¼ cent per mile, 25 miles per day,	114 00
New tires,	100 00
Repairs,	50 00
Painting, four times,	100 00
	$1,364 00

Horse and Vehicle.

Original cost, horse, harness and vehicle,	$ 500 00
Cost of keeping horse five years,	1,200 00
Shoeing horse,	180 00
Repairs on vehicle, including rubber tires,	150 00
Repairs on harness, $10.00 per year,	50 00
Painting vehicle four times,	100 00
	$2,180 00

Effecting a saving of $816.00 in five years, in favor of the Automobile. At the end of five years the motor vehicle should be in good condition, owing to its careful and solid construction, while the value of the horse and carriage would be doubtful. There is always the possibility that the horse may die during the five years, while the Automobile can always be repaired at a nominal cost. Then too, the Automobile will do the work of three horses.

160.

162.

SWIFTER THAN A RACE-HORSE IT FLEW OVER THE ICY STREETS

Thrilling Trip on the First Detroit-Made Automobile, When Mercury Hovered About Zero.

SHOWING HOW EASILY AN AUTOMOBILE MAY BE STEERED OUT OF DANGER.

163.

smoothness. There was none of the bumping common even to a street car.

"Hold on tight," said Ford. "When we strike the asphalt we will have a run."

"How fast?"

"Twenty-five miles an hour."

"Hold on! I get out."

Bang, bang, went the warning bell underneath the seat. A milk wagon was coming ahead. The horse shivered as though about to run away.

"Ever frighten horses?" I asked Ford.

"Depends on the horse," he replied.

By this time the Boulevard had been reached, and the automobileer, letting a lever fall a trifle, let her out.

Whiz! She picked up speed with infinite rapidity. As she ran on, there was a clattering behind—the new noise of the automobile.

There has always been, at each decisive period of the world's history, some voice, some note, that represented for the time being the prevailing power.

There was a time when the supreme cry of authority was the lion's roar.

After that it was the crackle of fire.

By and by it was the hammering of the stone-ax.

Then it was the slapping of the oars in the Roman galleys.

Next it was the voice of the wind against sails.

It came at last to speak with a loud report, such as announced the reign of gunpowder.

The roar of dynamite was a long time later.

The shriek of the steam whistle for several generations has been the compelling power of civilization.

And now, finally, there was heard in the streets of Detroit the murmur of this newest and most perfect of forces, the automobile, rushing along at the rate of 25 miles an hour.

What kind of a noise is it?

That is difficult to set down on paper. It was not like any other sound ever heard in this world. It is not like the puff, puff of the exhaust of gasoline in a river launch; neither is it like the cry of a working steam engine; but a long, quick, mellow, gurgling sound, not harsh, not unmusical, not distressing, a note that falls with pleasure on the ear. It must be

heard to be appreciated. And the sooner you hear its newest chuck, chuck, the sooner will you be in touch with civilization's newest lisp, its newest voice.

Down an asphalted street, Ford rushed her. People came to the windows and looked out with apparent curiosity. Pedestrians stopped to see her pass. She picked up speed as she traveled; and excepting that new noise, the run was smooth as it might have been in a dream.

"Look out," cried Ford.

Before an answer could be given, the danger was past. With a simple twist of the wrist, the big machine turned gracefully to the right just sufficiently to allow a loaded brewery wagon to lumber on its way.

I began to have a creepy feeling and told Ford I wanted to get out.

"Nonsense," he replied. "No danger. All you have to do is to keep a sharp look-out ahead. It's like a bicycle, you see. . . ."

"But that man at the crossing, right ahead."

"Gone," came the broken answer as another block of houses vanished in thin air as the automobile's speed developed. Block after block.

"Now you see how quick we stop her," said Ford. "I'll wager that a race horse going a mile in 1:40 can not be hauled up in less than one-sixteenth of a mile; we'll do it in six feet."

With that, the automobileer pushed something, and with the suddenness of a complete collapse, the auto's speed died instantly away, and the big machine came almost to an immediate standstill.

"Whew!" was all I could say.

Slowly Ford re-applied the power and the big machine picked up speed and flew again up the street, like some frightened ghost.

"How long would it take to learn to run her?" I asked.

"Oh, that depends," replied Ford. "Have you any sense about machinery?"

"Little."

"Well, in a few days, maybe a few hours—there's little to learn. Ride a bicycle? It's the same thing. If you don't look out ahead you may get into trouble. That is the secret of it. When you are running fast, you must keep your eyes open. Then you are perfectly safe. I have a speed-regulator under my foot. If I lift my foot, it stops her instantly. What more could you ask? She simply can not run away."

"But that puffing. Isn't she liable to blow up?"

"Nothing to blow up."

"But we are sitting on three gallons of gasoline."

"That's nothing," said Ford. "It's perfectly safe. There is no fire around here and then, we are in the open air."

Ford pointed to one side of the street and said: "See that harness-maker's shop? His trade is doomed."

By this time, the automobileer had turned into the thick of Woodward Avenue, as far south as Montcalm Street, and was whizzing along through the crowd of vehicles. The speed was about eight miles an hour, but there was not the slightest danger.

"There is prejudice against the automobile?" I asked.

"Oh, not much," Ford replied. "A number of truckmen have been to see me to have motors attached to their trucks, thinking that it would cheapen their work. But you can't attach the motor to an ordinary wagon. You need special construction."

A loaded truck lumbered slowly into sight. As the auto approached, the irate truckman glared fiercely and then shook his fist. The passengers on the auto saw his lips move, as if he were framing a curse, but not a sound came, for whiz, the auto flew past like a flash of light.

The clanging of street car gongs mingled with the sound of the auto bell, adding a new noise to the alarms of daily life. But she slid over the earth with infinite ease, and careened in and out among trucks, delivery wagons, carriages and bicycles; and everywhere, people had a welcoming smile and an expression of delight. The new chuck, chuck, the newest voice of civilization, sounded like rare music in their ears—a music as yet involved with the delight of absolute novelty.

"The horse is doomed," I said to Ford.

At that moment, the auto whizzed past a poor team attached to a big truck.

"That's the kind," said Ford. "Those horses will be driven from the land. Their troubles soon will be over."

And the chuck, chuck of the new voice

sounded for the first time in the strange horses' ears.

Meantime, the auto had slipped like a sunbeam around the corner.

But a little later in February, Secretary Frank Alderman made a telltale remark to a reporter: "You would be surprised at the amount of detail about an automobile." The Detroit Automobile Company had run up hard against one of the facts of manufacturing life: for want of a nail, the battle was lost.

One main factor operated against success. This was Ford's perfectionism, his stubborn insistence on making the kind of car he felt would be most successful. This would take time, money, patience. Most of the stockholders were not of his mind; they were used to making the most possible money quickly.

About the time that William Murphy signed the last check to Ford, the Detroit Automobile Company was dead. And there is no doubt that the fault was with Henry Ford. He had not made a good car, and he had made the model too slowly.

Two views of Edsel, 1899–1900:

164. Young fisherman, 1899. Clara loved this picture: her inscription around the rim reads: "Edsel, age 5½ years. After having caught his first string of fish, Orion Lake, Sept. 1899."

165. Wild West scene, 1900. The movies were yet to be, but Clara holds her pistol with the aplomb of a modern cattle queen, while Edsel makes his very best stupid face for Daddy's camera; in the back are the Homestead barns.

166. Interior, Detroit Automobile Company, 1900. Here is the only view of what the best-financed automobile company of that time looked like: one big bare room, thirteen of Henry Ford's team of workers.

At the right, on wooden horses, is a truck like the one we saw; above is the center shaft from the main control motor that ran machine shops in those times; you can see the belts crossing below the beams to wheels above the workers, whence other belts take the power down to individual lathes and presses. One of Edison's greatest inventions was the development of individual small motors that could be placed to operate in-

164.

165.

166.

dividual machines; this permitted Ford and other factory planners to "bring the work closer together" for more efficiency.

In this very room, Henry Ford began to learn the process of manufacture. When he had learned it all, he would change the world.

Among those thirteen workers were W. W. Pring, George Wetterich, Louis Doerr, George Abbott, Joseph Roerich, Arvy Wilson. We do not know which is which; the eyesight of the few workers left today is as dim as the memory of 1900.

Ed Huff did not work at the Detroit Automobile Company; it is always hard to keep track of him. But he came back soon, for Henry needed him.

The flywheel in the car was too heavy; Henry kept disguising it in the design. The bodies were built by the C. R. Wilson Body Works, which moved into another part of the Cass Avenue building. The bodies were as elaborately built, designed, painted and finished as are pianos. Their manufacture by hand was desperately uneconomic. Parts of the motor came in haphazard and lay on benches while Henry struggled to make other parts work.

What was needed, as always in a new venture, was a strong management proceeding along a strong program with a strong design and a clear set of objectives. What actually happened was that Henry pieced things out as he went; he would go off in the nearby woods with Billie Boyer, a draftsman for a patent attorney, and doodle up the design for the next piece, while everything else waited. He worked hard, indeed furiously, but he made more misses than hits. Pretty soon the stockholders were more than grumbling.

Said Fred Strauss:

> The directors weren't satisfied. . . . We did get one of the engines to run, but we had an awful time doing it. . . . There were a lot of hotheads in the Detroit Automobile Company. Colonel Hecker wanted to throw in the sponge. He said everything was going too slow. Alderman wasn't very well satisfied; it was going fast enough for him. But Hopkins and Murphy were for the company.
>
> They had a directors' meeting, and Henry said he wasn't going to do any more on these cars until they gave him a better settlement.
>
> Henry had told me they were going to have that meeting. He said, "If they ask for me, tell them that I had to go out of town."
>
> Alderman came out and asked me, "Where is Mr. Ford?"
>
> I said, "Mr. Ford isn't here; he had to go out of town."
>
> So they had their directors' meeting but I guess it wasn't very successful.
>
> The next morning Alderman came out to me and said they were going to give up this big shop and I should move out into the front of the shop in a smaller space. He told me to lay off the men except for a few I wanted for the little experimental shop.
>
> Then he said, "Now call the junk man and get rid of all this stuff on the bench."
>
> Mark Hopkins was the hard one. Some directors wanted to keep some of the stuff but he said, "No, start all over. Throw all that stuff out, burn it, get rid of it."
>
> We were to destroy these four [truck] bodies. We put them in the boiler room. Charlie Mitchell, our blacksmith, and I took sledge hammers and busted all these beautiful bodies. Then we burned them under the engine-room boiler.
>
> All at once Henry came in one morning and came into the experimental shop. Huff came in. He was very smart and studying all the time. He and Henry were always monkeying with something. Wills came in, part time. He was the draftsman.
>
> They started to make a little car.

167. The fourth car, reconstructed. This is the "little car." As Strauss said, "It ran pretty good" and "They were very well pleased with this little car."

Henry tinkered away, this little car ran better, but as the months fled by the stockholders began dropping out. By the late fall Mayor Maybury—in the middle of his election campaign for the governorship—had picked up some 450 shares to add to his own original 50, loyally sticking by Henry. Murphy stuck, too, continuing to fork out solid cash; it is likely that he paid out the bulk of the $86,000 that Henry ran through without ever getting a car into production.

A further exasperation must have been the fact that the little one-cylinder Olds, the "merry" Oldsmobile with the curved dash, was producing and selling great guns, 425 cars during 1900. Henry's car seemed better throughout, more powerful, more reliable, stronger, but he just couldn't or wouldn't get it into production.

One worker, W. W. Pring said: "The stockholders wanted to force Ford to say, 'This is it. We'll go ahead and make it.'" But Ford would not freeze his design until he was satisfied.

In 1900 nearly every motorcar maker of the time seemed to be getting ahead of Henry Ford, despite his gilt-edge backing, his superb opportunity.

He may have been right, he may have been wrong. He never explained or complained about this period except for a few dry remarks about speculators who were more interested in making money than in making a good car. The fact is, as we have come to know him, he was no more interested in his failures than his successes—no more and no less. The stockholders, shall we say, did not share this view. And so the Detroit Automobile Company sagged, drooped, withered and died.

167.

[XV. THE GREAT RACE]

Well, of all things to win,
a cut glass punch bowl!
Where will we ever put it?
                                        —CLARA FORD

The century has turned. This is 1900.

Ahead of mankind, say the editorials, lie such vistas of peace and progress and prosperity as have never been dreamed.

Science, they say, has become the handmaiden of the arts of living.

War, at last, will be abolished; although it must be admitted the Chinese are being more than troublesome, the Russians and Japanese are looking hard at each other in Korea, President Roosevelt has his big stick out over Venezuela, Kaiser Wilhelm II has been rattling his sword, and the Boers are giving the British a steady beating.

In Paris Dr. Roentgen has been perfecting his mysterious ray which will actually photograph *through flesh:* a picture in *Leslie's Weekly* has plainly shown the bones of a human hand, and the editors insist the picture has not been retouched. (The ray had no name at first, and, in a sense, it never did get a name, coming down as simply "X-ray.")

News about the possibilities of flight in "aeroplanes" is occasionally noted, but comment about this activity is usually handled facetiously by lightweight editors. One such editor seriously suggested that aeroplanes would mean the end of war, because they could carry bombs and no army general in the rear would risk being bombed himself.

Horseless carriages are much in the news, although the term "automobile" is in favor because of its elegant French sound. Automobile news has many phases: It is the highest of society news, since the great of Newport and Tuxedo and Fifth Avenue—the Vanderbilts, Whitneys, Belmonts—have made the automobile very distinguished. It is business news, because

of the rush to get aboard—fifty-seven automobile companies are announcing brave plans. And it is the most exciting sports news, because fresh auto speed records are being set almost weekly for every distance from the half-mile to twenty-five miles.

The great racers of the day are Henri Fournier, a mustachioed French daredevil in a French-built Mors racer; William K. Vanderbilt, who buys cars the way other millionaires buy caviar—he is discarding his Daimler now for a Mors racer; it cost him $15,000 plus $7,000 customs duty, but he calls it the "Red Devil," and wins with it; and the genial, steel-nerved Alexander Winton, a youngish Scots immigrant who has pioneered his own powerful cars out of a Cleveland bicycle shop.

All three are trying hard to be the first man in history to go a mile in a minute. The record is creeping lower, toward one minute and ten seconds.

In Detroit Henry Ford seems a bit out of the automotive main stream, which is clearly racing. He has been defeated in his first venture at manufacturing automobiles.

But Henry still had the confidence of some of his original backers. Black, Bowen, Hopkins, White and the patient Murphy yet believed Ford was on the right track. Sometime in the late fall of 1900 they dumped the Detroit Automobile Company, filing formal notice of dissolution in January 1901, with this to take effect on February 7, 1901. This little group purchased the assets at a receivers sale and immediately engaged Henry to carry on in reduced quarters at the same address: 1343 Cass Avenue. His assignment was to continue working in the experimental shop until he announced he was finally ready.

Henry must have reasoned that part of his failure was due to his inability to assemble a really first-grade team, from designers to assemblers. It must be remembered that there were no proper automobile men in those days; they were even scarcer than working parts.

Henry's first act was to bring in Ed Huff. Then he got the part-time services of a new friend, a commercial artist named Childe Harold Wills, who had also been an apprentice toolmaker, and a draftsman for the Detroit Lubricator Com-

168.

pany. Henry could not afford to match Wills' salary, although it could not have been much; so Wills worked half time as a draftsman and half for Henry. Sure enough, Henry's half time soon extended far into the night.

168. The first Ford giant. This stiff, tall, proud brilliant young man is Childe Harold Wills, then twenty-two years old. (Wills was not as fond of Byron as had been his parents; all his life he went as C. Harold, or C. H., Wills.)

Ford, who probably met Wills in December 1900, liked him instantly. The two had many common interests and a common passion for work.

Wills was studying engineering, chemistry and metallurgy at night, but was anxious to graduate to real design problems. Their part-time bargain worked out brilliantly, since each thought nothing of a two-shift life.

The gifts of Wills complemented those of Ford. Both were totally fascinated by machines. Ford had supreme intuition: he could spot flaws in design and weaknesses in structure; and he had considerable inventive ability. But his great asset was to approach each problem as if it were naked new. He had no compulsion to revere things as they were, and would ruthlessly strike out weeks and months of his own work if he suddenly saw a new way to do something. Wills was a superb craftsman-draftsman, who could create advantages and strike out disadvantages right on the drawing-board: he could "see on paper" as well as Henry could see in the round.

Wills was to go on to become one of the giants of the early automobile industry; he was the first of the long line of automotive great men who trained under Ford.

Ford could get men like Wills to work for him and men like Murphy to back him, only because he had a great deal of personal charm. As Strauss said: "He had the magnet."

Charm is not a quality associated with Henry Ford for many years, but it was there, although some people may rebel at the thought. But those who actually knew him, before he was too old —even those who quarrelled with him, quit him, or were fired by him—always regarded him with a kind of tenderness. They all groped fantastically, hopelessly to explain exactly what it was about him that they liked so much.

126

One example: the very first "Profile" in the first issue of the *New Yorker* magazine was of Henry Ford, written by Niven Busch, the novelist and script-writer; one can see Editor Harold Ross in 1925 rubbing his hands at the thought of picking the biggest, most vulnerable target in all the United States. Yet the piece is tender, kindly, sensitive, for Busch had talked to Ford. (It is almost as tender as E. B. White's later, famous "Farewell to Model T.") Busch saw in the millionaire something that many men have tried to describe but none has quite put a tongue to—a kind of personal magnetism, a bird-like sensitivity.

Once a worker at Chevrolet, who had been unfairly fired from the Ford company, was asked why he still liked Henry Ford personally. He boxed around with the question for a while and then finally blurted: "That guy has a bird in his head." It is just that difficult to explain.

Whatever Ford's peculiar personal quality was, he had a certain something as engaging as the candor of a child, yet strong as steel. He seemed to have no layers of manners, attitudes, politenesses, sophistications, social graces. But when you talked to Henry Ford you talked directly to the best in him, and he obviously assumed he was talking to the best in you. He had a blue-eyed directness, a naked-child simplicity; he was basically shy, and yet he was cool, clear, hard and quick, as ruthless as Peter Pan's childlike but frightening ruthlessness.

This unnameable quality was his greatest single power, greater than his inventive ability, greater than his native shrewdness, deeper than his foresight. This was what enabled him to handle men and engage their enthusiasm to do miracles. He had it down through the decades to the time when a frail, bony, faded, aged hawk of a man yet had enough spark left to inspire men to create Willow Run out of scrub woodland.

But he had no gift of gab. He preached to Americans for a generation: the counsels of virtue, McGuffey, motherhood, industrialism, free enterprise, pacifism, Republicanism—and never made a convert.

But when he *did* something, people noticed. He was a prime demonstrator. What he did became a symbol everyone could understand: the Model T, the $5 day, "Out of the Trenches by Christmas," and "Will It Run?"

These were the qualities that gave men confidence in Ford.

So while Ford was in his experimental shop on Cass Avenue, the whole automotive world was passing him by. Auto companies were already splitting into two classes: bigger cars, with more horsepower, more elegance; and cheaper, smaller, lighter cars. The trend to bigness was almost irresistible: fashion, racing and high prices made the car the rich man's toy. By 1903 most automobile companies would be making cars to sell at $3,000 and $4,000, and by 1906 the trend would seem fixed.

But Henry now was quietly making a new critical decision, one that would apparently set him back even farther. Instead of freezing his newer design he decided to build a racing car.

Walter Lippmann says that every critical situation offers a choice between a hard and an easy solution. The hard solution, he says, is almost always right, the easy one almost always wrong. "In general, the softer and easier side reflects what we desire and the harder reflects what is needed to satisfy the desire."

Without benefit of Lippmann, Henry nevertheless chose the hard way—to go into racing. Now this was the hard way because to make passenger cars was the certain way to make more money more quickly. Ransom Olds and others were making real money by producing cars. Whereas the rewards of racing were truly precarious.

But racing unquestionably had an attraction for Henry Ford: the building of racing cars, like the breeding of thoroughbred racehorses, was the best way to improve the automobile.

This was not widely understood then. Certainly Ford's backers did not understand it. But Ford, with his mechanic's instinct, probably saw that if he solved the problem of speed, the hardest possible automotive problem of the time, all the other problems would become easier. To get speed would mean the attainment of more perfect performance in every mechanical respect: speed would drag all other solutions in its train. A racing car meant perfect ignition, combustion, steering, endurance, cooling, power, and more endurance and reliability in all parts,

127

all tested under the excruciating conditions of all out speed.

Ford saw that if he could conquer speed and then transfer his findings to his passenger car he would be in the position of a pianist who masters Mozart and then only has to play "Chopsticks."

In automobile history, this pioneer racing period is crucial. The "breeding" of high-powered racing cars quickly forwarded automotive engines out of the ricky-ticky-ticky class. Today's engines are the result of innumerable slight refinements in design—infinitesimally delicate changes of the curves in combustion chambers, and the like. Those advances became possible when Henry Ford and other experimenters began to pour power into their little alarm-clock engines.

The demand for speed brought a demand for better fuel. Improvement in fuel permitted higher compression ratios, and in turn, increased power, increased engine speeds. Greater engine speeds required changes in combustion-chamber design, resulting in a more even burning of the fuel in the cylinder. Most particularly, as engine speeds increased, the timing of valves became more critical. High operating speeds required that the valves be held open for longer periods to allow sufficient time for the fuel charge to be inhaled and the burned gas to be exhaled.

So Henry Ford went into racing: there might be money in it; it was the craze of the day; and it was a way to make better cars.

169. Papa writes Edsel. During May 1900 Clara had taken Edsel for a brief visit to Louisville, where one of Clara's brothers, Milton Bryant, was a drummer for a drug firm. The two corresponded steadily, for Clara was Big Sister to all the Bryants, and Milton was anxious to leave the not-so-gay life of a traveling salesman. Henry printed this letter to Edsel in capital letters to make sure his six-and-one-half-year-old son could read it easily, but he had a little trouble with the "J" in "Jugs" and with some of the capital "N's." The family was then still living at 1292 Second Boulevard (later numbered 5842), their ninth home: it was the north half of a double, two-story brick house, at the southeast corner of Amsterdam, now taken by the Edsel Ford Expressway.

William Ford, Henry's father, was seventy-four and had relaxed his iron grip on the farm. In 1899 we saw him jogging into Detroit for a glass and a steak and a seat in the Edison plant window with Davey Bell, to watch whatever might go by. In 1900 he took his first real vacation train-trip since the Centennial of 1876, going all the way to California to see one of the "uncles," another Henry. William wrote Clara about it on July 22, 1900:

. . . We have a very pleasant and good time of it. We got here on the 4th of July. . . . I am glad the work is going on very favourable. . . . We have drove around a great deal to see the mountains the mines and the sawmills; in one mine we went two miles under ground in the tunnel, we could see the gold very plenty in the rock and . . . they were blasting with the same kind of cartridge that Henry blew up the stumps. . . . It was very warm about 95 in the shade and about two minutes walk you could have a good snowbaling. . . .

During all these years, Henry's sister Margaret had kept house for their father, but now in the autumn of 1900 she married James Ruddiman, brother to Edsel Ruddiman, Henry's first seatmate at school, for whom little Edsel had been named. William did not feel up to wintering in the Homestead, so he and Henry's second sister, Jane, came to live in the winter of 1900–01 with Henry and Clara. But 1292 Second Avenue was too cramped, so the Fords moved to their tenth home.

170. The tenth home, 582 West Grand Boulevard, on the east side of the street between Dix Road and Toledo Avenue. Sometime after Margaret's marriage in the fall of 1900, William and Jane moved in here. We believe they lived upstairs, but cannot be sure.

On January 7, 1901, Clara records in a diary: "Commenced to pack up to move." On January 8 she wrote: ". . . Then moved down to Grandpa Fords got there just as men got there with furniture." They all settled in here, and William probably paid the rent.

Now it could be that the two families moved together for reasons of economy. Certainly Henry was officially out of a job; we have no physical

CLARENCE A. BLACK, PRESIDENT.
ALBERT E. F. WHITE, VICE-PRESIDENT.

Henry Ford

FRANK R. ALDERMAN, SECRETARY.
WILLIAM H. MURPHY, TREASURER.

DETROIT AUTOMOBILE COMPANY.

COR. CASS AVENUE AND M. C. R. R.

DETROIT, MICH., *May 21 1900*

My DEAR LITTLE SON

I AM WELL AND HOPE YOU
ARE ALL OK. SAY DO THEY CARRY WHISKEY
JUGS AND BANDWAGONS IN THEIR BLOUSE IN KY.
I HOPE YOU ARE HAVING A GOOD TIME AND WILL BE
BACK SOON FOR I AM LONESOME

FROM YOUR LOVING

PaPa

169.

170.

129

records of monies paid to him at this time; we cannot prove that Maybury, Murphy, and others were still backing him. These months are clouded with hypotheses, thick with interesting facts, but barren of the one thing we really need to know: where was Henry getting his income? If there was no income, was he spending his own savings? If so, when and how had he saved money?

My own construction of the next four months cannot be proven, but seems reasonable enough. William had steadily been turning his land over to his sons, for such pleasures of farm life as arising before dawn on frosty mornings to milk cows had begun to lose their attractions.

It seems likely he felt he would be lonely in the Homestead with Margaret newly gone; and that Jane might want to marry too. What better than to take a warm city apartment for the winter months, play with his only grandchild, and peek in on the fascinating things Henry was doing?

A further point: Clara was soon to leave for Jasper, Michigan, to help her sister Kate through childbirth for some three weeks. Even more: Henry had announced he was going to spend many nights on a cot at Cass Avenue near his newest automotive creation. So there would be ample room.

And as to Henry's finances: he could not have been too tightly pinched, for on February 11 he loaned his brother John $200 to help meet a bank loan that would not fall due until March 1.

He must have had financial support, for even though Huff and Wills may have worked for nothing, the materials and tools and electricity and all the rest cost money. Ford was long past the point where he could say "made all the parts myself." He was now working in much more sophisticated fashion, and sophistication costs more in machinery than anywhere else.

Clara's diary gives the routine of their lives. The Fords' love of music shows; night after night Clara mentions, "We had a little music. . . ." Some excerpts:

January 9, 1901   Worked all day getting settled. Very tired tonight. Edsel found lots of his playthings that he had not seen for some time. Decorated [his] rocking horse with Xmas-tree trimmings.

January 11   Snowed all day. Edsel got soaking wet. He and Grandpa played checkers. Edsel cheated awful and beat every game. Went to bed so full of laughs he could not say his prayers.

Sat. January 12   Went downtown, got Edsel shoes and leggings. Went into Sheaffer's store to hear the music. After supper we tried to learn Grandpa to play cards. *Henry got patents of entire machine.*

Sun. January 13   Edsel and I went to S. School. . . . Came home, had dinner, then Henry fixed Edsel's old sleigh to take him coasting, but Edsel would not go, said sleigh was no good. He was sent up stairs for punishment for his pride. He was sorry.

January 15   Edsel started lessons for first time this morning.

January 16   Pa making ice. [This means Mr. Bryant, out in Greenfield.] Henry came in while we were eating (downtown) also met him on streetcar while coming home.

January 19   Henry bought Edsel new coaster.

January 20   Henry and Edsel went coasting on the boulevard. After dinner went out to Maggie's [Margaret Ford Ruddiman]. Maggie brought to the car.

Far, far away, on January 22, at Osborne House, in East Cowes on the Isle of Wight, Her Majesty, Queen Victoria, Empress of India, died at 6:30 P.M. She was eighty-two years old and in the sixty-fourth year of her reign, the longest in British history. It was a cold, drizzling, dark night; all the day had been dark.

In London, at 6:58 a footman posted a bulletin:

Osborne House, January 22, 6:45 P.M. My beloved Mother has just passed away, surrounded by her children and grandchildren.
ALBERT EDWARD.

Then the bells of London began to toll, and the sound of the bells clanged from tower to tower throughout England.

The inhabitants of Cowes, said a reporter, "walked as if in a dream through the streets, but they did not hesitate to stop to drink the health of the new monarch."

The last person the Queen recognized was her grand-nephew, Kaiser Wilhelm II of Germany, who had hurried from Berlin, and he was the first to address his uncle as the new King, Edward VII.

The funeral was to be perhaps the most magnificent gathering of royalty in all Christian times, a dozen or more kings and emperors, and a mile of grand dukes and earls, the lords of the earth. Jackboots and plumed helmets and steel cuirasses glittering, swords and medals and gold braid and epaulets gleaming, they marched and rode solemnly behind the end of the Victorian era.

That was the real turn of the century.

The man who would come to represent the new century, the new era, was riding streetcars in Detroit as the horses pranced over the stones of London, the carriages rattled and the emperors strode with solemn step.

Henry Ford, for better or for worse, would in himself symbolize the first third of the new century, as much as any man could and far more than most.

171. Clara Ford, 1901. The fair automobilist in her diary took as much note of the mighty event as many an American:

January 22 Queen Victoria died today. Cut out dressing sack for myself. Edsel had hard time making letter E made it too much like L.

January 23 Edsel had big time coasting. Made new kind of salad dressing. Licking good.

January 24 Uncle George Ford died yesterday. Grandpa is not feeling well today. Coal stove went out and everything went wrong.

January 25 Met Henry on the crowded [street] car going home.

171.

January 26	Went to Uncle George's funeral. Saw Mr. and Mrs. Leslie go behind the house to count their money. They looked very funny.
January 27	Edsel and I went to S. School. Met Henry, went to vegetarian cafe for dinner, then went out home.
January 28	Coal fire out again.
January 29	Met Henry in streetcar. he had bad headache. Put brown paper and vinegar on his head and mustard plaster on back of neck.
January 30	Edsel made snow fort and decorated it with flags.
January 31	Ironed a little and packed grip for trip to Kate's.
February 1	Spent half hour with Henry then took train to Kate's.

Oliver Barthel, right-hand to Charles B. King, also worked half-time for Henry in the spring of 1901. King had come back from the Spanish-American War as a hero, to endure the normal, the historic difficulties of the American inventor: he triumphed over his problems of design and then was defeated financially. King, however, was of such kindly temperament, and his personal finances so comfortable, that he retained his good will toward men all his life.

Ford, in fact, was one of the very few American inventors who came out on top. Even Thomas Edison, who spawned inventions, spent the last half of his life a trifle short of cash, a step or two away from a bouncing check. Edison was revered, hailed, speeched about, protected, loved, decorated, his every birthday and anniversary filled with flags and plaques, but he died with only modest financial security.

With "Spider" Huff to work on the electrical problems, with Wills and Barthel to work on design, Henry had something of a research team. To carry out their notions he brought in a lathe hand, Ed Verlinden, from the Lauer machine shop, and a blacksmith, Charlie Mitchell. Strauss had given Henry up again and drifted away to a saner business.

Ford must have earned the respect and interest of outsiders, for although he had no manufacturing company, he was still treated as an auto manufacturer. He had made useful contacts with suppliers. For some time two vigorous young partners, Alfred P. Sloan, Jr., and Peter S. Steenstrup, who ran the Hyatt Roller Bearing Company, had solicited Ford to use their bearings. (Sloan, of course, would become the most famous of all General Motors chiefs.) And Charles Seiberling, head of a good little outfit known as the Goodyear Tire and Rubber Company, was hard after Ford for the tire business.

Sloan, in his memoirs, describes a visit to the Ford shop in the Cass Avenue building about this time; he noted with pleased astonishment that when the unheated building got too cold, Ford and Wills would put on boxing-gloves and gaily whale each other until they warmed up and then resume their studies at the drawing board.

Another casual visitor was Roy D. Chapin, later to become Secretary of Commerce under President Hoover. Chapin and an Oldsmobile engineer were driving one of the little Oldsmobiles toward the C. R. Wilson Body Works when a spring on the steering apparatus broke, "something that happened about once a week." They lifted the car around and kicked the wheels forward block after block until they reached a place where the engineer said the spring could be fixed. Wrote Chapin:

> A man came out, a quiet, kindly-voiced man; he inspected the spring and called an assistant who removed it and carried it into a small building adjacent to the Wilson plant, where the man repaired it himself. The man was Ford.

To return to Clara who is still in Jasper, awaiting Kate's baby. From her diary:

February 2	Edsel had fine time with Uncle Sam feeding cows and lambs and giving pigs chocolate ice cream soda as he calls it.
February 3	Snowed all day. Wrote a letter to Henry. Felt pretty lonely. Kate said she wished it was not Sunday so we could play cards.

Here is the letter Clara wrote that lonely Sunday:

> Dear Husband—
> I will write you a few lines today to let you know how we are. We got here all right. Sam was at depot to meet us got home at nine found Kate in best of health. It is storming hard mostly sleet. Edsel is cleaning the snow off the stepps, with the fire shovel. He follows Sam all over. Sam Edsel and Frank went down in the woods this morning and shot a rabbit. They have two pet lambs and he thinks they are fine. I have thought of you so much today. What are you doing? I suppose it seems strange for you to be staying there without us. Are you lonely? I am. I suppose I will have it bad if I have to stay two weeks. It is six o'clock and Kate is all right yet. I hope you will keep well. I felt bad to leave you when you were not feeling well. Write me soon. Good bye dearest—
>
> Clara

The diary:

> February 4   Sam Frank and Edsel went for cutter ride to Jasper. Played cards all night. Edsel had bad attack of chilblains.

That day Clara wrote Henry:

> Dearest
> . . . Last night the snow drifted so that they had to hitch up the big sleigh and drive it around to make paths. Edsel is as happy as a bird toddling around in the snow. I have taken some snap shots of him. He has been making some caves Sam picks him up and throws him up and lets him come down in a bank. Kate is starting dinner and is as lively as ever, but we dont know how long it will last. She says come if you possible can. I say so too. I put on Sams rubber boots this morning to go across this yard. I could hardly get through the banks.
>
> —C.
>
> Good bye honey

More excerpts from the diary:

> February 5   Kate baked bread mince pie and biscuits. She did not feel well after dinner so I did up the work. Edsel dug snow nearly all the day. Kate grew worse at night. Had doctor and nurse there by 12 o'clock.
>
> February 6   Kate's baby born at 9 a.m. None of us had been to bed. Had breakfast at 10. Dinner half after two. Kate and baby doing fine. Sam telephoned from Jasper to Henry.
>
> February 9   Took baby's picture with kodak. Henry came. Edsel and Sam went to Jasper to meet him. He had on a new automobile coat.
>
> February 10   Took snapshots of Edsel and sheep. Slept three in bed. It was pretty hot.
>
> February 11   Baked bread. Got great praise for my bread. My feet hurt so I can hardly stand on them.
>
> February 16   Kate got up for first time today. . . . Got a letter from Henry. It made me very lonely.
>
> February 17   Wrote to Henry and was very lonely.
>
> February 20   At half after three telegram came said Mrs. Ford: sick, come at once. Very much worried. Letter came at 5. Henry sick. Would give anything to get home tonight. [Jasper was only eighty miles from Detroit, but this was deep winter, and train service was occasional. This shows the isolation of the times.]
>
> February 21   Sam took us to Jasper to take train. Very nervous about Henry. Got home, and before train had quite stopped, Henry got in. Was never so glad to see him. Because I expected he would be in bed.
>
> February 22   Henry feeling some better. . . . Just resting and getting used to being at home. [This was at the West Grand Boulevard house, with Grandpa William Ford and Jane.]

February 23	Henry made toboggan of snow in back yard for Edsel.
February 28	Played cards with Mr. and Mrs. Beebe.
March 3	Edsel and I went to s. School. Edsel got book as prize for going steady. Henry Edsel and I took a nice walk. . . .
March 7	Met Henry. He took us to dinner. Played cards. Beat this time. Grandpa very much pleased.
March 12	Went downtown . . . to automobile works and came back on Belt Line with Henry. Grandpa and I beat at cards with Henry's help.
March 17	Henry took Edsel to S. School, while I got dinner.
March 23	Brought my geranium that Mrs. McElroy had kept all winter.
March 24	Went to S. School with Edsel. . . . All took a walk through the fields to the cemetery. Had lots of fun.
March 25	Edsel tried to do his chores. Emptied ashes, filled woodbox [tried to do Grandpa's chores]. Then Jane stopped him. Made him feel bad.

While their living together was convenient for Grandpa Ford, it wasn't much fun for Clara. Later that year, on December 3, she would write her brother Milton in Louisville: "Keeping house again and we are very glad to be alone."

April Fool's Day.	Tried to fool Henry but could not.
April 2	Jane Edsel and I went to hear recital of Little Lord Fauntleroy. It was very good.
April 5	Henry and Mr. Murphy went out with automobile to Farmington around to Orchard Lake on to Pontiac back home. Started half after two back at 6.

This was no doubt a key occasion. If Murphy had been paying the bills, this was probably the first real test ride on Henry's newest version of the fourth car, the "little car" (p. 124). This is why Henry worked so fiercely all winter, sleeping on a cot in the shop. And April 5 was probably the earliest date of good weather. Murphy must have been satisfied, for they kept on together.

There is no agreement on the number of cars that Henry made at the Detroit Automobile Company or in this later period. Some persons guess he produced only two, some say four, or a dozen, but Ford once said "nineteen or twenty" and again "about twenty-five."

Clara's diary:

April 6	Henry fixed me up a dose of brandy and rock candy for my cold. The dose made me laugh.
April 11	Went down town to get tickets for [the] Old Homestead. [This was the most popular melodrama of the time, a real never-darken-this-door-again-little-Nell thriller.] Henry bought me a pair of patent-leather shoes and a pair of black silk hose.
April 15	Went to RR crossing to meet Henry, he had Edsel's tricycle all painted up fine. Edsel is delighted.
April 20	Went downtown met Henry at Hudson's. Tried to change my shoes but could not. Got my money back. [Presumably the black patent-leathers had not been a success.]

On April 24, the archives show, the Moreton Truck Company hauled a load of furniture and a piano to the Fords at the West Grand Boulevard house. The charge was $3.50 and the bill was paid on May 20. Perhaps this meant that Murphy's approval had let them loosen up expenditures; perhaps only that William had moved back to Dearborn for the good weather. After April 2 Clara's diary no longer mentions Jane or the nightly card games with Grandpa.

The diary:

Henry came home to dinner. Took me and Edsel back on automobile.

This suggests that Henry did not regularly eat dinner at home, probably getting a bite near the "works," and also that he then drove his family down to the plant to watch him work at night.

| April 28 | Henry duck-hunting. |

May 7   Got all ready to iron, half past 10 Henry came with Mrs. McElroy on the automobile. Had some nice music.

May 15   Went down to McElroys on automobile.

There the diary ends.

In May the assets of the Detroit Automobile Company were finally disposed of. The team went ahead: Ford, Barthel in the evenings, Wills at odd hours, Verlinden, Mitchell, and Spider Huff, moving swiftly all the summer of 1901. They were building a racing car.

For Henry had decided he wanted to beat Henri Fournier's record for the mile (1 minute, 14⅘ seconds). He wanted to beat Alexander Winton, who held most records for distances up to twenty-five miles. He wanted glory because he felt that cash would follow glory—cash and backers. He wanted to learn the lessons speed would teach. And he was plainly smitten by the racing fever.

That fever is a little hard to understand now, when breaking the sound barrier is a daily occurrence and anything less than the speed of light no longer startles us. But in those days, and for years, auto racing was the Olympic Games, it was the "Stars and Stripes Forever," it was brass bands, death in the afternoon, pennants, hot dogs, hysterical cheers, women fainting, the World Series, heroics and heroes in capital letters.

Above all, racing was sheer sound; a set of noises that made thrills rip up and down spines. You would have to hear those sounds to know. They were unforgettable. This was long before engines had been refined smooth, small, deadly, delicate. Then, the way to make speed was to build engines big and heavy; the cylinders looked like kegs, the exhausts like stove-pipes; and the sounds they made, those great crashing rumbling roars that echoed for miles, pounding, snarling, grumbling coughs like a thousand tigers; those were what topped off the thrill of speed itself.

Those sounds are gone forever. They were never recorded; they vanished like the ricky-ticky-ticky, chuck-chuck-chuck of the smaller cars that preceded them; like the dong-dong of horse-car bells and the clop-clop-cloppety-clop of carriage and wagon traffic; like the "Extra! Extra! Wuxtreee Paper!" shout of newsboys in the night—all the American sounds heard no more, gone with the thunder of buffalo on the plains, that could be heard for more than fifty miles when all those miles grew nothing but sweet, thick buffalo grass.

When it came to sound, Ford built himself a sensational noise-maker. The two cylinders of the horizontal, opposed engine were actually seven inches by seven inches—so huge, so powerful its roar that he did not dare drive it through Detroit; the racket would have given horses and people heart failure. Ford always had to hire horses to tow it outside the city for trial.

Huff and Barthel solved the racer's ignition problem. They designed a special spark coil, and Barthel took it to his dentist, a Dr. W. E. Sandborn, who made special porcelain insulators for the coils: these were the first modern spark plugs, baked in Barton Peck's furnaces.

172. Bunting at the Wilson Works. Was it for the Fourth of July? One is not certain of the occasion. But this is the staff of the booming young C. R. Wilson Body Works, taken in the summer of 1901 at the Cass Avenue plant. The only three we know are F. A. Niedermeier, the good-looking young chap fourth from the left in the front row, who became important in the manufacture of Lincoln cars, Ford, second from the left in the second row, wearing what looks like a snap-on bow tie, and Fred Fisher, third from Henry's left. Ford's presence in the picture was accidental: he had just dropped in to watch the Wilson company make the floorboards for his new racer.

In July, Henry made his first trial run in the racing car. On West Grand Boulevard he went a half mile at the rate of seventy-two miles per hour; at least, he *thought* that was his time. But he found that timing racing cars was tricky business. If the time were true he was far ahead of every racer in the world; all the rest were sweating away to make sixty miles an hour. To be certain, he decided to design and build an electric timer.

173. Vacation, 1901. Right in the middle of designing the racer Henry suddenly took a full month's vacation, from about the middle of July to around August 18. All we know about it is in this picture: Clara on the left with a Gibson-

172.

173.

girlish hat and a long string of popular jet beads, Edsel in knee pants, bow tie and tiny cap, and Grandmother Martha Bryant in the stiff black proper to older women. The picture was taken at Niagara Falls, where they went by train; but the backdrop, of course, is the studio Niagara that the Falls photographers featured.

Now comes a sheer guess, and it is supported by what we know of Henry Ford: the Pan-American Exposition was thumping away full force at Buffalo. Is it not a hundred-to-one shot that he was there? I know of no record, no diary, no tickets, nor of anyone who recalls it. But Henry was an old hand at combining business and pleasure, and we know the Ford family record for expositions: one flutter of pennants atop a tent full of exhibits and it was full of Fords.

The guess can be stretched a little; perhaps Henry also used the occasion to tour factories, shops, suppliers in the East. Certainly he seemed knowledgeable about these things in 1903, and he had then been bound to Detroit for two years.

Buffalo was a glory of flags, inventions and pleasure that year. And it was there on September 5 that William McKinley, President of the United States, made a memorable speech, superbly written, only a fortnight after the Fords came back to Detroit. Among other important items, he shook Republican high-tariff men by proposing reciprocity in trade: "We must not repose in fancied security that we can forever sell everything and buy little or nothing."

He said: "We must build the Isthmian canal, which will unite the two oceans."
He said: "Gentlemen, let us ever remember that our real interest lies in concord, not in conflict . . . our real eminence rests in the victories of peace, not war."
He said: "The wisdom and energy of all the nations are none too great for the world's work."
He said: "No nation can any longer be indifferent to any other."
He said: "After all, how near one to the other is every part of the world."

And above all he said, as the first President of the United States to break with the Washington tradition of "no entangling alliances": "Isolation is no longer possible or desirable."

On the next afternoon, at four o'clock, he stood on a small dais in the exposition Temple of Music to shake the hands of his fellow Americans. On his right was Secretary George B. Cortelyou, on his left, John G. Milburn of Buffalo, president of the exposition. Across from him stood Detective Sergeant Ireland of the Secret Service.

A man with his right hand in a bandage approached; Ireland leaned forward to watch, but the man merely shook the President's hand with his left. Then came an Italian, swarthy, heavily-mustached, who held the President's hand and talked excitedly. Sergeant Ireland shoved him along, noting that next behind the Italian was a pale, calm innocent young fellow "of commonplace appearance," his right hand swathed in a handkerchief, and next beyond him a huge, smiling Negro. This was Big Jim Parker, six feet six inches tall, a waiter at a Buffalo restaurant.

As the Secret Service man urged the Italian on, the President extended his hand to the quiet young man. His name was Leon Czolgosz. He was born in Michigan, and was twenty years old. In Cleveland he had become an anarchist, a worshipper of the famous Emma Goldman, the anarchist queen of the times.

His handkerchief dropped from his hand, and he shot the President twice.

Detective Ireland was off balance, moving the Italian along. But Big Jim Parker moved like a giant cat. His great left hand smashed Czolgosz in the neck, crumpling him to the floor; with his right he grabbed for the pistol. Ireland leaped, too. He got the pistol as Parker and Czolgosz scrambled on the floor.

The President watched calmly, his pale deliberate face cool, a little contemptuous. Then he walked slowly to a chair and sat; finally he put his head into his hands. His vest was ripped off, then his shirt; a red stain was on the white linen.

The Temple was bedlam, the crowd crashing forward and back; the thousands outside pressed forward. Ireland and the guards somehow hurried Czolgosz out, dumped him in the very hack in which the President had arrived, and with the coachman lashing citizens with his long whip, they rushed him off to jail.

(Inside, the guards and the crowd were busily hammering the wrong man, as always: he had a three-day growth of beard and wore glasses, so he had to be an anarchist; actually he was another Secret Service man, Detective Foster.)

174. Cartoon, The Detroit News-Tribune. A contemporary cartoonist's attempt at presenting the assassination. Big Jim Parker seems to have been left out.

The news rocked Detroit as it did the rest of the nation. This was the third President shot in thirty-six years. Detroiters felt such special shame that Czolgosz had been born in Michigan that the relief was general when it was discovered he had moved to Ohio. Thereafter all Detroit papers referred to him as "the Cleveland anarchist."

McKinley, lying in Milburn's home in Buffalo, rallied strongly; after a week he was pronounced on the way to recovery. But gangrene had set in, and on Saturday morning, September 14, he died at 2:15 A.M.

There were funeral services in Buffalo, in Washington, and finally in Canton, Ohio, the black train steaming quietly through miles of mourners.

In all the national grief and anxiety, nearly everyone lost sight of McKinley's last speech, in which he had broken off from nineteenth-century American thought, from Republican protective tariffs, and that he had projected the notion that "isolation is no longer possible or desirable."

For more than two weeks the tone of the nation was serious, critical, philosophic; Americans re-examined their ideas. On the day of the McKinley funeral, Mayor Maybury ordered the saloons closed—but many residents rebelled at any infringement of their rights of thirst, and the saloons remained open, filled with thoughtful men discussing the state of the union. (Maybury, a devout believer in free speech, was already under strong attack for permitting anarchists to assemble and orate.)

One such thoughtful discussion was held at Ford's experimental shop on Cass Avenue.

Everyone had liked McKinley. What kind of President would the vigorous, strenuous young Theodore Roosevelt make? People felt a stir of excitement but also of uncertainty. As they were in quiet talk, serious Oliver Barthel handed Ford a slim little book. It was Orlando J. Smith's *A*

Short View of Great Questions; it presented the case for reincarnation. This book had a profound effect on Ford. In some ways a belief in reincarnation came to be as near a religion as he ever got. He did not *know* about the hereafter, he reasoned, but if there were such a thing, this seemed the most fascinating kind of hereafter possible: if one came back, how? In what form?

175. Where the piano went. The Fords had paid $20 more on their player piano—the piano they had paid on for years, which they had moved nine times; now it was moved once again. This is their eleventh home, 332 Hendrie Avenue (now numbered 968), between Hastings and Rivard. The entrance served two apartments; the left one of the two doors, just visible under the arch, was the Fords'. The window just left of the porch and the bay window above it were theirs.

When the Fords moved here in the fall of 1901, Henry was—comparatively—unknown and poor. When he left this house in 1905, he was —comparatively—famous and on his way to riches.

176. The racer. Henry at the wheel and Oliver Barthel (whom we last saw seated with King on Detroit's first motor-wagon, p. 73). Right-hand drive was standard. This photograph was taken on West Grand Boulevard, about fifty feet west of the intersection of Second Boulevard. This is the result of the Ford team's labors during 1901.

The engine developed twenty-six horsepower (Winton's racer was rated at forty, others were rated at up to seventy) with opposing cylinders of 7 x 7 inches, running at a normal speed of 650 revolutions per minute, capable of 900. *The Horseless Age* described it:

It is fitted with Mr. Ford's patented vaporizer with measuring device, ditto sparking device and a Huff induction coil with a new ribbon buzzer. The lead of the spark is changed manually. The vaporizer is operated mechanically [not by suction].

The vehicle has a patented reach and trussed front and rear axles, with equalizing rods attached to the latter. The patent on this construction has just been issued.

The vehicle being high-powered is built low, but the flywheel is 9 inches from the ground.

174.

175.

176.

177a.

177b.

178.

The tread is standard and the wheel base 8 feet; 36-inch wire wheels with 4-inch Diamond [Rubber Company] tires are used. The front wheel bearings are ball and the rear axle bearings roller [Alfred P. Sloan had made his sale]. Eight gallons of cooling water are carried and coils of copper-flanged tubes assist in the radiation of the engine heat. Enough gasoline is carried for a run of 250 miles. A tonneau can be attached to the rear of the body for touring. The weight is 2,200 pounds. Mr. Ford claims to have made a half-mile in 26 seconds and challenges any foreign machine to race him on an American road track.

177a, b. The rivals, Henri Fournier, the mile record-holder, in his sixty horsepower Mors racer; and the Winton forty horsepower racer.

The first serious article on "Style in Automobiles" appeared in the *Scientific American,* November 9, 1901, written by Hrolf Wisby. Here are excerpts:

Comparatively little is being done by the automobile makers toward guiding the public taste. . . .
We are daily happening upon horseless carriages of a horsey style for horsey people . . . this silly combination.
An automobile is not merely a vehicle bereft of horses.
Only a single class of automobiles is progressing toward a definite style, namely, the racing machines. . . . The racing automobile is constantly seeking new improvements.
The highest present development in American racing automobiles shows a distinct improvement over even the most graceful French patterns. . . . The American model has of late acquired a superior, original style of its own, considerably in advance of Gallic ideas.
The latest American racing automobile, the Ford, possesses features entitling it to credit as being the most unconventional, if not the most beautiful, design so far produced by American ingenuity.
It is a model that commends itself strongly to the automobile experts because of the chaste completeness and compactness of its structure. In this rarefied type of racer, the same neat tapering stern will be noticed as in the Winton;

the chauffeur seat has been shaved down to a mere toadstool perch and the forward condensers, instead of being enclosed in a pyramidal casing, have been placed in an inverted shield set at an angle with the air pressure so as to force air up under the pipes—a most ingenious arrangement.
The carriage element, so detrimental to a clear, unsophisticated style, has been avoided. . . .
No matter how we may choose to view this machine, it is an automobile first and last.

178. The way they rode. Spider Huff kneels on a shelf-like running board; when they hit a curve the icy-nerved Huff hung way out from the hand grips as ballast.

In the autumn, Ford and Huff made several speed trials, out Twelfth, back on Linwood, north of the Boulevard. Once they rumbled the machine out to Dearborn for a trial. William Ford left off running a cornhusker in the neighborhood to have the neighbors help scrape the old Scotch Settlement Road from Ten Eyck's woods to a point near the Homestead. Henry brought out his machine to try to break the mile record. The road wasn't good enough, but the neighbors had thrill after thrill betting on what would happen each time Henry hit the bridge over the creek. But no record was set.

179. Henry Ford, October 1901. Ford was now thirty-eight. Most of his contemporaries were soberly settled in their careers.

Marvin Buckberry reports the attitude of the farm neighbors in Dearborn:

We had all been on a church excursion to Tashmoo Park on the Tashmoo boat and when we arrived in Detroit in the evening in walking up the street to take the trolley car we came to the Lighting Plant where Henry had been working. . . . As we stopped and looked through the windows at the machinery running and admiring how nice everything looked, it was remarked by one of the party . . . "I think Henry would have been a great deal better off if he had stayed right here."

Henry was too busy to think about his lost career in the Edison Company. Kate Bryant wrote her brother Milton: "Clara's getting awfully fleshy and Henry is getting awfully thin."
He was getting ready for the great race.

179.

Daniel J. Campau, Maybury's political enemy within the Democratic party, was head of the Detroit Driving Club, which owned the Grosse Pointe Race Track, a mile course along the Detroit River. Campau, William B. Shanks, manager for the great Winton, and William Metzger had decided to promote the first auto race in Detroit.

180. William Metzger's shop, 1901. Known as "Smiling Billy," Metzger was a mustachioed, twinkle-eyed salesman who began as a typewriter dealer and became the ideal of the American bicycle dealer of the period: a promoter, a salesman, a friend to all, active in lodges, clubs, parades. (Later Metzger joined with B. F. Everitt, the carriage maker for Ford, and Walter E. Flanders, Ford's first real production boss, to put out the E.M.F. car.) The shop was on the east side of Woodward Avenue, near John R. Street.

The three promoters of the race could not afford a great array of purses and prizes, but they did promise a $1,000 prize for the big event, at a twenty-five-mile "World's Championship" sweepstakes open to all cars: electric, steam and gasoline, of any size. Five preliminary events were scheduled: a five-mile steam race, a one-mile race for all cars weighing less than 1,500 pounds, a one-mile electric race, a ten-mile race for machines weighing less than 1,000 pounds, a ten-mile race for machines weighing less than 2,000 pounds, and an obstacle race to follow the World's Championship.

The dirt horse track was banked at the turns in the hope that the racers would break the world's mile record, still held by Fournier at 1 minute, 14⅕ seconds.

181. The Bowl, the prize, the sweepstakes. Shanks, Winton's mechanic as well as manager, picked out a beautiful cut glass punch bowl set which "he figured would look well in the bay window of the Winton dining room," according to W. A. Simonds.

Detroit was excited. The *Free Press* wrote:

The event is the talk of Detroit's smart set. The boxes are almost all engaged and the display of feminine finery is expected to attract quite as much attention as the speedy machines.

One of the most promising contestors is the Detroit chauffeur, Henry Ford. His machine

180.

181.

was tried out on the boulevard recently and without great effort covered a half mile in 38 seconds.

The papers had missed that story. All the reporters were downtown covering a Detroit visit by the new President, Theodore Roosevelt; so were all the crowds, and above all, so were the police. Henry seized the opportunity to give his racer another speed tune up on the empty boulevard; the only observer was an elderly Irish policeman who saw no reason to interfere.

The list of entries was imposing. At first both W. K. Vanderbilt and Henri Fournier had been expected, but both were forced to withdraw. Nearly every other speed demon had posted an entry fee.

Henry put in his cash entry on the night before the race. He was still making changes in the racer, for he told Ann Hood: "Finished the racer the morning before the race," and by this he probably meant he had finished it to his satisfaction.

Every thirty seconds, the streetcar company announced, cars would leave for the race track. On the morning of the race the D. and C. steamer brought from Cleveland a whole boatload of the "mobes," as one reporter called them. Judge Phelan announced he would adjourn Recorders' Court, because of the numerous "requests from attorneys and others. . . . and as there is nothing else of importance on. . . ."

The weatherman forecast a light rain for the night before to make a fast track. Next morning the *Evening News* headlined: "Clouds Will Go!"

October 10 was the big day in Detroit. One of the department stores was having a sale of ladies underwear, heavy fleece lined, twenty-five cents. Many of the sportsmen attending the race were smoking two of the fancy cigars of the time, the John Drew and the Colonel J. J. Astor. The Colonel Astor was advertised as "the straight honest goods. No pictures with this cigar. No pocket knives with this cigar. No mufflers or neckties with this cigar. No trick purses with this cigar. No horse and buggy with this cigar. Nor automobiles."

On race morning a "giant" automobile parade chugged odorously through downtown Detroit. A reporter wrote: "There were more than 100 machines in line and not a horse in sight!"

The track's big grandstand was packed, with "a crowd on the lawn in front and a row of railbirds clear down past the three-quarter pole . . . fully 8,000 persons . . . a Blue Ribbon Day crowd."

The first races were dull. A reporter sniffed: "A bunch of little autos started off and soon were scattered all over the track." White, of Cleveland, won the event with no effort.

"The electric machines did not like the going [in the second race] and it took more than four minutes to circle the track." To most of the crowd a mile in *four minutes* just about summed up the case against electric automobiles.

The following races were as bad. Some of the entrants could not even get their machines to the track, some cars failed as they reached the track, and some failed at the starting post. Automobiles seemed to be more trouble than they were worth.

As smiling Bill Metzger heard the steady trickle of bad news he felt he must improvise to save the day. With true promoter's wit he announced a "special event: Alexander Winton would try to break the mile record!"

The agreeable Winton rolled out his machine and flew alone around the track three times in a great roar—and then the crowd roared, too, because his time for the three miles was announced as 3:42½, and on his second mile he had done a mile in 1:12⅘! The mile record had come to Detroit! (At that very hour, at the Empire City track in New York, Henri Fournier was doing six miles, with no mile slower than 1:08⅘, and with his fastest mile in 1:06⅘. Next morning the *Evening News* headlined: "GLORY SOON GONE.")

Now came the main event. But broken cars littered the park. The entry list of twenty-five cars for the main twenty-five-mile world's championship sweepstakes had finally dwindled to two: Ford and Winton. To their despairing disgust, none of the other racers could raise a rumble in their racers.

Ford rolled his car onto the track with trepidation. He knew it would start: he had delayed his entry until the machine was as perfect as he could make it, from the newly invented porcelain spark plugs to its patented reach rods. But he was simply afraid it would go too fast, especially around turns, and he hadn't once yet taken a curve in it. With envy and admiration, he had watched Winton whiz around. And he worried about his car as much as his own neck: he had put nearly $5,000 worth of materials into it and much time and effort.

Since the earlier events had taken longer than expected, the race had been cut down from twenty-five miles to ten.

182. Winton at the wheel. This is a later model than the one Winton raced in Grosse Pointe (that car is shown on p. 140), but this picture shows Winton in the pose then familiar to thousands of race-goers in Europe and the United States.

183. They're off. Winton and Shanks are in the leading car. The nerveless Scot took the lead at the start and held it easily for the first five miles.

Without brakes, of course, and an amateur at race-driving, Ford let up on the gas at the turns and also swung wide each time. Through two-fifths of the race he was actually just coasting. Spider Huff's eager head can be seen just below Henry's steering wheel; over the hood is draped a cloth with a huge number 4. The big wheel beneath Henry's seat is the flywheel.

184. Ford is out front. Ford's car was lower, a bit longer, but rated at only twenty-six horse-power against Winton's forty. But on the seventh lap his car began to creep up steadily: Henry was mastering his first racing curves.

A reporter wrote: "Right in front of the grand-stand, on the seventh lap, Ford forged ahead. Winton seemed to lose his power at once, his great racer began to smoke, and he was out of the race."

Another wrote: "For the first few miles Winton had the better of it. Ford seemed to be afraid of the turns and he lost on them right along, although he seemed to be holding his own or more on the straightaway. But Winton's motor got out of order and began to smoke. Then he dropped back, Ford winning easily."

Another wrote: "Ed Huff hung far out in his effort to ballast the car. After three miles Winton was a fifth of a mile to the good. . . . Then Ford on the sixth lap shot up perceptibly. . . . A thin wreath of blue smoke appeared at the rear of [Winton's] machine and it gradually increased to a cloud. Mr. Shanks, who was riding, poured oil on it but it did no good."

182.

183.

184.

The time was 13:23⅕ for the ten miles, about 1:32 per mile. The crowd roared for the "Detroit chauffeur"; we see Henry pounding hard down toward the finish line, only a quarter of a pole away, and Winton is lost somewhere in Ford's cloud of dust.

Clara wrote her brother Milton:

Henry had been covering himself with glory and dust. He rec'd a beautiful cut glass punch bowl for winning his first race. I wish you could have seen him. Also have heard the cheering when he passed Winton. The people went wild. One man threw his hat up and when it came down he stamped on it, he was so excited. Another man had to hit his wife on the head to keep her from going off the handle. She stood up in her seat & screamed "I'd bet fifty dollars on Ford if I had it!"

When the dust settled, two small boys came close to their new hero as he stood, greasy and dusty, beside the racer. They heard his breath whoosh as he said, "Boy, I'll never do that again! That tight board fence was right here in front of my face all the time! I was scared to death."

To reporters Ford said modestly: "Put Winton in my car and it will beat anything in this country."

It was to Helen Gore's mother that Clara Ford said after the race: "Well of all things to win, a cut glass punch bowl! Where will we ever put it?"

She finally decided to put it on a landing in the hall at Hendrie Avenue. It was very much out of place there, says Helen Gore; it was a huge bowl and they "were in very moderate circumstances."

Nothing more was ever heard of the $1,000 prize. It had been abandoned soon after the first announcement.

XVI. OLD 999

Henry Ford said that we made each other.
I guess I did the better job of it.
                    —BARNEY OLDFIELD

After the race, Henry had criticized his own steering, but Alexander Winton criticized Henry's steering gear. Winton wrote him:

> I will soon send one of our steering posts and attachments, as I think from what I remember of your steering apparatus that there was something wrong with it, and I noticed that you had to wind the wheel around once or twice in making turns.

Henry's backers thought he could steer them to quick wealth. They were in a new flush of enthusiasm. Right after the race they rushed around to form a new company: the Henry Ford Company. Papers were filed on November 30, 1901. Ford was named again as the company engineer; Black, White, Bowen, Hopkins and Murphy parceled titles out among themselves with Murphy, the wealthiest, as treasurer. Each of the six took 1,000 shares. To make their support real, the five put up $30,500 in cash on a $60,000 capitalization, with Henry's 1,000 shares valued at $10 each.

Clara wrote Milton:

> Henry has worked very hard to get where he is. That race has advertised him far and wide. And the next thing will be to make some money out of it. I am afraid that will be a hard struggle. You know rich men want it all. . . .

This sounds as if it were Henry's view. He doesn't seem to have taken the Henry Ford Company very seriously.

The backers had changed the name of the company but they hadn't changed their spots. Nor had Henry. The backers wanted to make cars and sell them for all the traffic would bear.

Ford had a completely different philosophy, which he spelled out later:

> Concretely, what I most realized about business in that year is this:
> (1) That finance is given a place ahead of work and therefore tends to kill the work. . . .
> (2) That thinking first of money instead of work brings on fear of failure and this fear blocks every avenue of business. . . .
> (3) That the way is clear for anyone who thinks first of service—of doing the work in the best possible way.
> The money influence . . . seemed to be at the bottom of most troubles.
> It was the cause of low wages—without well-directed work high wages cannot be paid. And if the whole attention is not given to the work it cannot be well directed. Most men want to be free to work; under the system in use they could not be free to work.
> During my first experience I was not free—I could not give full play to my ideas. Everything had to be planned to make money; the last consideration was the work.
> . . . During this time of reflection I was far from idle. We were going ahead with a four-cylinder motor and the building of a pair of big racing cars. I had plenty of time, for I never left my business. I do not believe a man can ever leave his business. He ought to think of it by day and dream of it by night. It is nice to plan to do one's work in office hours, to take up the work in the morning, to drop it in the evening—and not have a care until the next morning. It is perfectly possible to do that if one is so constituted as to be willing all his life to accept direction, to be an employee, possibly a responsible employee, but not a director or manager of anything.

Soon after the race, and before the new company was formally organized, Henry went to New York to the automobile show. Clara wrote Milton:

> He met Fournier the French racer, found him a fine young fellow. He met lots of personal friends and lots that knew him by reputation only and was given the glad hand by everybody.

Alfred P. Sloan wrote that his partner, Peter Steenstrup, saw Ford passing through the show, footsore and hot, and that Steenstrup called out: "'Come in. Where could you find a better place to rest? Sit down at the railing and see the show from a box seat.' Ford sat down, tilted back in a chair, his heels caught on the topmost rung, his knees at the level of his chin."

The picture is accurate: this was always a favorite Ford pose. And at the show Goodyear's Seiberling, mindful of the fact that Ford's racer had been equipped with Diamond tires, urged him to promise to equip his new racer with Goodyears.

185.

186.

185. The surrey with the fringe. This is the last time we see any Ford in a wagon or a buggy, except at a parade of antique transportation. This was one of Henry's snapshots and is inexplicable. Although Grandpa Melvin Bryant and Grandma Martha Bryant are in the surrey with Edsel, Henry's photography was not concerned with them; for some reason he wanted a picture of the door behind the surrey, for he took several other pictures of it; no one can suggest why. It seems to be a church.

We have a good insight into the Hendrie Avenue home life. Clara wrote:

We are keeping house again and very happy to be alone. We have a very nice cozy little house. We did not build on account of Henry building the racer. He could not see anything else. So we will have to put up with rented homes a little longer. We got Edsel a bicycle for his birthday. He rides it to school and thinks it is fine. He and Henry both have raglan overcoats. Edsel thinks he is as big as his father. You would laugh to see him imitate Henry. . . .

And Helen Gore told the Archives:

It had three rooms downstairs with a living room, a dining room and a kitchen. The stairway went up out of the dining room. I think there were two or three bedrooms upstairs. I remember there was a skylight in the hall, because we [Edsel and Helen] used to like to sit up there in the rainstorms and look at the rain patter on the skylight.

We used to go out to the Homestead for picnics. . . . The first time I saw baby pigs was out in the barn there. I remember one night we stayed and a big rainstorm came up. Mrs. Ford called me in the morning and said "Helen, come in my bed. I want to show you something." The rain had come through the roof and there was a spot on the ceiling and it was a perfect donkey. . . .

Mrs. Ford had no help at her home on Hendrie. She did all the cooking. . . . We always used to hang around her back door waiting for the big sugar cookies. . . .

Edsel used to have a little table in the kitchen and we used to have great fun when she would make soup. She used to put the alphabet in it. That was how I learned the alphabet. . . . We used to pick out the letters of the alphabet. . . . We used to take an ironing board and put it on a chair in the front room and use it for a slide.

These were things we did in the daytime. . . . Mr. Ford wasn't around then. We used to see him a little bit in the evening but he was pretty busy . . . and didn't have much time for play. . . .

When I was a tiny child and learning to talk my mother tried to teach me to say, "How do you do?" But the nearest I could come to it was "Ha doodle do?"

Mr. Ford used to say, "Ha doodle do?" to me every time he saw me and I used to say, "Ha doodle do?" back. As I grew older it didn't make any difference. It was still "Ha doodle do?" no matter where he saw me.

186. *The fifth car as it now is in Greenfield Museum. The beginnings of the famous planetary transmission are visible in the two foot pedals. In this car Henry went about as far toward simplicity of design as is possible. This was actually a pilot version of his next car; it was never even equipped with mudguards. But he toyed with this until well along into 1902, setting it up and tearing it down.*

187. *Edsel's letter to Santa Claus. The letter, famous since its discovery in the Ford Archives in 1951, has been reprinted as evidence of the "hard times" of the Fords. Now, of course, we know that such hard times as they had were the result of Henry's deliberate choice to work on his*

187.

cars. It would not be fair to dismiss lightly their ten straight years of rented houses, skimpy meals and lack of leisure, but neither would it be true to treat all this as heroic. As Clara had written, the only reason they did not build a house in 1901 was that Henry built a racer. Ford said plainly that "what money was left over from living was all spent on experimenting."

Edsel's strategy was like that of a West Point coach the day before an early-season game with some small private college. He was "crying poor," as they say.

The fact is Edsel had a fine Christmas. He had a Christmas tree, although Christmas trees were high-priced and in very short supply in 1901: there were only 15,000 for all of Detroit's population of 286,000.

His tree was decorated with popcorn and cranberries, which he and Helen Gore helped to string. There were lots of little globes of the world, said Helen, which were "very different." And Edsel came over to see Helen's tree at 336 Hendrie, which "also had a lot of glitter on it that year. I can remember the two of us sat in the front room behind my tree and ate all the candy we could off it."

That December, Ford and all other Americans were working in an atmosphere of tremendous prosperity. The big news was the Christmas bonuses in Wall Street—even the janitors at J. P. Morgan & Co. got a bonus equal to half their annual salary.

The boom was general, and Detroit felt it. Simon J. Murphy announced he would build a thirteen-story skyscraper, to be called "Penobscot." Stores boomed with the biggest Christmas rush the city may ever have seen. Some Detroit businessmen said the prosperity was "so great as to be actually embarrassing."

Cast-iron toys for boys, from the picking hen to little red fire engines, were never so ingenious. The big sellers in cardboard soldiers were "Boer & Briton" and "Philippine War," with popguns and corks provided.

The best-selling Christmas gift books were Kipling's *Kim*, George Barr McCutcheon's *Graustark*, the Horatio Alger and the Oliver Optic series, the *Little Colonel* series by Annie Fellows Johnston, and a title that sounds fresh today: *With MacArthur in Luzon*, a tale of the campaigns of General Arthur MacArthur, father of Douglas MacArthur.

The hero of war correspondents was Richard Harding Davis, who looked like the men in Charles Dana Gibson's Gibson Girl drawings. The big American authors were Mark Twain, William Dean Howells, Booth Tarkington and Ernest Thompson Seton. Only a few readers paid any attention to Henry James.

The most important columnist was Peter Finley Dunne with his Mr. Dooley. The sensational magazine was *McClure's*, which had begun to advertise its big shocker for the next year: Ida M. Tarbell's "The Real Story of Standard Oil," which would set off the whole era of trustbusting.

Piano scarfs in velour, damask and silk were big sellers. A compound known as "Rose-and-Cucumber Jelly" was advertised as best for women's complexions. But women generally were most interested in what beautiful Queen Alexandra would wear at next year's coronation. She had just diplomatically chosen the lily-of-the-valley as the ceremonial flower so as not to offend the Scotch thistle, the English rose, the Welsh leek, the Irish shamrock.

Women generally were a mass of clothes: they wore huge plumed hats à la Gainsborough, great floor-length raglan coats with puffed sleeves, and high-heeled kid boots that laced halfway up the leg.

Gift-giving men were daintily warned: "Fans, of course, are always acceptable, but woe to the young man who presents his sweetheart with a fan this year without a long rope of pearls or other jewels by which she may hang it around her neck."

In Westlawn Cemetery, in Canton, Ohio, a frail, pretty, disconsolate little woman, Mrs. Ida Saxton McKinley, had spent several silent hours each day through the autumn in the tomb beside the casket of her husband, the late President; a rocking chair had been brought here for comfort, and a rug laid on the chill stones of the vault to keep off dampness; now in hard winter weather she had finally been coaxed into cutting her daily visit to a few minutes.

High in the news that December was Guglielmo Marconi. On the Cornwall coast of England he had set up twenty poles, each 210 feet high; from them, on Wednesday night, December 11, his assistants sent wireless impulses 1,700 miles across the Atlantic to a station at St. Johns, Newfoundland: several times the men in Newfoundland clearly heard the three dots of the letter "S."

Even a picture had traveled over a wire; in Detroit old ex-Senator Thomas W. Palmer watched while his photograph was sent over 800 miles of wire in the studio of a Detroit photographer, C. M. Hayes.

The Roosevelt family was tearing the old sedateness of the White House to shreds. Within a few weeks after he had pledged to follow McKinley's policies "absolutely and without variance," the vigorous Teddy had replaced three Cabinet members and started dozens of quarrels. Word would soon creep around society that his daughter, "Princess" Alice, actually smoked cigarettes. His son Archie practiced walking on stilts in the very chamber where White House visitors waited to see his father, and fell enough times to crack almost as many distinguished shins in reality as his father did symbolically. In the East Room, after Christmas dinner, the President bounced gracefully about in the newest dance, the cakewalk, to the tune of "Whistling Rufus."

The somberest note in all the hustling prosperity of the time came from the French poet, Edmond Rostand, author of the play, *Cyrano de Bergerac*. Bitter at the deaths of hundreds of little Boer children in British concentration camps in South Africa, he wrote a sardonic "Christmas Ballad for European Boys and Girls," with these acid lines about the British Santa Claus:

> Their Father Christmas is not an old man with
> kind eyes,
> But a spectre,
> He brings not in his transparent hands to boys
> Toys and sweetmeats
> But little coffins of different sizes.

In Washington Lord Alfred Douglas protested because the Metropolitan Club barred him despite the fact, he said, he had only had an "indirect" mention in the trial of Oscar Wilde. But Michiganders were more interested in Coach Fielding H. Yost's greatest Michigan football team—first in the nation to score more than 500 points in one season.

And above all, Detroiters were much more interested in the theater. Henry and Clara Ford,

especially in earlier years, were inveterate theater-goers, vaudeville, melodrama, comedy, opera—anything at all. No doubt they went that season, no matter the pressure on Henry, and if so, they had a feast, for Detroit was one of the most profitable stops.

The vaudeville headliners in Detroit that Christmas week were James J. Corbett, ex-heavyweight champion of the world, who appeared in impeccable evening dress as "Gentleman Jim," and did a monolog of the latest jokes from Broadway, and Sandow the Strong Man, even stronger than when he was the hit of the 1893 World's Fair—now lifting a piano single-handed and also a huge white horse.

188. Young Miss Ethel Barrymore, so beautiful, so crisply haughty, opened in Detroit that week in her latest comedy hit, Clyde Fitch's Captain Jinks of the Horse-Marines. *One Detroit critic wrote: ". . . And you go home with the taste of delicate candied violets in your mouth."*

189. Maurice Barrymore.

190. Sarah Bernhardt.

191. Ellen Terry.

192. Maude Adams.

Years later, in his collections of Americana, Ford brought together much material on the American stage; these photographs represent a few among those discovered, and may represent particular memories of past delights.

These stars, I believe, played Detroit at one time or another; in fact, several appeared in Detroit during this very period. Julia Marlowe was being seen in *Barbara Frietchie*; E. H. Sothern was coming in a few weeks in *If I Were King*. Robert Mantell played a Shakespeare repertory that December; the four Cohans had just finished a successful week in young George Cohan's farce, *The Governor's Son*. There was quite a bit of Barrymore news; Maurice Barrymore was seriously ill, perhaps dying; young John Barrymore, reputed to loathe the stage, was a successful newspaper artist and had just won a scholarship to study [art] anatomy under George Bridgman.

But in Detroit the biggest theater thrill of all, even more exciting than young Ethel Barrymore, was the production of *The Count of Monte*

188.

189.

190.

192.

191.

Cristo with a full stage representation of the Chateau d'If. The stage manager of the spectacle had taken great pains preparing the moment when Edmond Dantès, in a weighted bag, is thrown into the angry sea but struggles to the shore to swear revenge. The sea waves effect, now seen for the first time, was managed in most modern fashion by air billows, whereas for generations the waves had been represented by small boys bobbing up and down under the painted canvas.

193. Letter from Henry. All that survives of the Henry Ford Company are a few fancy illustrated letterheads. They were found in 1953 in an old trunk stuffed with the correspondence between drug salesman Milton Bryant in Louisville and Clara in Detroit. For those who cannot penetrate the Ford script, this is what Henry wrote Milton:

January 6th, 1902

My Dear Brother

If I can bring Mr Fournier in line there is a barrel of money in this business. it was his proposition and I dont see why he wont fall in line if he dont I will chalenge him untill I am black in the face. as for managing my end of the racing business I would rather have you than any one else that I know of. My Company will kick about me following racing but they will get the advertising and I expect to make $ where I cant make ¢s at manufacturing. we are writing to Mr. Fournier

Henry

194. Picnic at Belle Isle. This is spring 1902 and one of Henry's most crystal-clear snapshots. The four women, left to right, are Clara, slim and smiling in her pleated white blouse with black bow-tie; Martha Bryant in her usual proper black, and Eva Bryant and Kate Bryant Raymond, with assorted sandwiches, cake and lemonade in hand. The four children are Mrs. Bryant's grandchildren: at the left are Wallace Bryant and Doris Bryant Henderson, then Edsel with milk-mug in hand, and Russell Raymond, the baby all the fuss was about in February 1901. Eva became Mrs. George Brubaker.

Much had happened since Henry's letter. After four months, the Henry Ford Company had died. Henry left the company on March 10. All

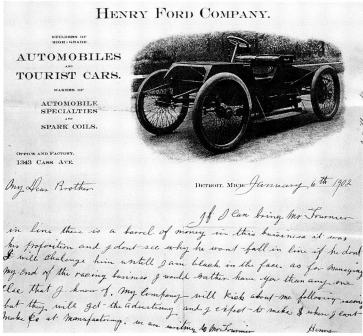

193.

194.

he took with him were the drawings of the design for his new racer, a $900 cash settlement, and Murphy's promise to drop the name "Henry Ford." The company's assets merged into those of the old Detroit Automobile Company, as the officers and stockholders were pretty much the same.

Murphy, Bowen and company had finally wearied. They had two real complaints: Henry's feverish preoccupation with racing cars and his persistent refusal to freeze the design of his passenger car so that manufacture could begin.

They had brought in the grandest of all the going experts in machine shop practice, Henry M. Leland, the venerable, white-bearded head of Leland & Faulconer, a firm with a national reputation for the highest quality, which tooled and finished its products to much closer tolerances than were then usually practical.

Leland was, it seems, somewhat haughty about Ford's engine, and his name carried such weight with Ford's backers that they began to look at Henry with a new eye, the way some first-nighters, who have liked a play, change their minds after they read the critical reviews.

The whole affair was quickly over. The backers quickly reorganized, took the name "Cadillac," and began almost at once to turn out a car, based on the Ford design, but powered by a single-cylinder engine made by Leland. This was the famous "one-lunger" that gave Cadillac its start. Seven years later, with Bowen as president, the company was sold outright to "Billy" Durant as one of the divisions of General Motors Corporation.

Henry moved his operations entirely to his half of Barton Peck's workshop at 81 Park Place, little more than a barn with some tools in it. He had Spider Huff, Harold Wills part time, Oliver Barthel part time, and the beginnings of a national reputation—as a racer.

Henry said: "In March 1902 I resigned, determined never again to put myself under orders."

To everyone else but Henry, his life seemed pretty mixed up in 1902. Without backers, he was going ahead with two big racing cars, continuing to revise the "Fourth" car, and beginning the design of a four-cylinder car.

But he found fresh money again.

On the day of the Ford-Winton race, one fea-

ture of Billy Metzger's improvised program had been an exhibition race against time by two famous cyclists, Tom Cooper and Barney Oldfield. The automobile-minded crowd had given them "scarcely a ripple of applause." But the two cyclists had watched the auto races with fascination.

Cooper, in both the United States and Europe, was as near to being the world's champion bicycle racer as was possible without a recognized central event; he had beaten everyone at every distance. This was worth real money then; he represented bicycle firms for high fees, much as golf champions today represent sporting-goods companies. He was sensible, handsome, young and well-to-do, and mightily attracted to Ford. He had gone west to manage a coal mine but could not get Ford and racing out of his head; toward the end of February 1902 he returned to Detroit and looked Henry up.

Cooper supplied the funds Ford needed; and their bargain was simple: instead of one racing car, Henry would build two identical monsters, with Cooper to own one of them.

Henry built the 999—named after a New York Central express train that Henry had seen on exhibit in the Chicago World's Fair of 1893—and the Arrow, also named for an express train.

195. Old 999. The 999 was the biggest, most powerful American car yet built. It was nine feet, nine inches long, with a tread five feet, two inches wide. It was rated at seventy horsepower or more and was probably the first American car to develop one hundred horsepower. It had four cylinders 7 x 7, vertical, in line; the wheels were thirty-four inches diameter in front, thirty-six inches diameter in the rear.

Said Henry: "The roar of those cylinders alone was enough to half kill a man. There was only one seat. One life to a car was enough. I tried out the cars. Cooper tried out the cars. We let them out at full speed. I cannot quite describe the sensation. Going over Niagara Falls would have been but a pastime after a ride in one of them."

But Henry got another kind of thrill from the 999. Until the 999, the automobile motor had been neatly boxed beneath the buggy-seat; enclosed, covered over, minimized; the essence of

195.

auto style was, as stylist Wisby had pointed out, to seem to be in a carriage bereft of horses; a carriage that moved without visible means. Now Henry boldly took the motor out from under the seat and planted it squarely between the front wheels, pushing the driver back to the rear. He had begun to do this in his first racing car, but more tentatively. You can see for yourself in the picture. The radiator cooling is in front; then the big cylinders in line, the sight-feed oilcup, the batteries (here is the true beginning of the modern dashboard), and then the tiller steering.

Barney Oldfield is at the tiller, Ford is wearing rubbers, for the snow, and a new deep curved-brim derby.

This is the fall of 1902. That is when Henry shaved his mustache. This is the period when the Ford Motor Company truly began.

With Cooper putting up money—we don't know how much—Henry cast around that spring and summer for racing opportunities, scattering challenges to Fournier and others. None of the races came off, mainly because Henry was always tinkering, always reluctant to freeze the design. Despite his flash-in-the-pan assertion that in racing he could "make $ where I cant make ¢s at manufacturing" he just never got around to getting his cars to the track.

Another reason was that he feared he would be killed in a race, although he didn't mind racing the 999 against time, as the *Detroit Journal* (September 18) reported, when he did a mile in 1:08:

> The oily appearance of the fence is nothing to the look of Chauffeur Henry Ford after he had made a few dashes around the track yesterday in his new speed machine which he and Tom Cooper have built. Mr. Ford was a daub of oil from head to foot. His collar was yellow, his tie looked as though it had been cooked in lard, his shirt and clothes were spattered and smirched, while his face looked like a machinist's after 24 hours at his bench.

Ford was not alone in the reluctance to compete. Tom Cooper himself was afraid to drive the 999 in an actual race. Then Cooper remembered daredevil Oldfield: "Nothing's too fast for him. . . . He'll try anything once." On came Barney Oldfield, cigar clenched in his bulldog

jaw. Ford and Huff met him at the railroad station.

Ford didn't dare drive the 999 through town. He went to one of his friends, "Night Owl John," who ran a little lunch wagon where Ford often ate while working nights; John agreeably drove his wagon home, brought his horses back, and towed the monstrous 999 silently through the streets to the Grosse Pointe track.

Oldfield took the tiller, and the nerveless Huff crouched behind him. The reason Ford had a tiller instead of a steering wheel? Henry gave a matter-of-fact picture of a frightening problem:

> You see, when the machine is making high speed, and the operator cannot tell because of dust . . . whether he is going perfectly straight, he can look at this steering handle. If it is set straight across the machine he is all right and running straight.

Oldfield practiced for a week for a big race, scheduled for October 25, 1902, little more than a year after the Winton race. Huff told him he was doing fine: "You can get more speed out of it than either Cooper or I." Before the race Ford worried about Barney's safety. But Oldfield told him: "Well, this chariot may kill me, but they'll say afterward that I was going like hell when she took me over the bank."

To Spider Huff, Oldfield said: "I may as well be dead as dead broke."

The race was for the Diamond Trophy; five miles, four entrants: Winton, a racer named Buckman, Winton's manager Shanks, and Oldfield.

The lead seesawed. On the third mile, Winton was hit by his old devil, mechanical failure; he dropped out on the fourth mile. Oldfield, spattered with oil, unprotected except for goggles, fought bitterly for the lead, rushing blindly around the turns through the dust with the tiller wrenched sharply askew. By the fourth lap he was in the clear; 999 was pounding home farther and farther ahead; he lapped Buckman and then lapped Shanks. He finished in 5:28 for a new American record.

The crowd carried Oldfield around on its shoulders. Men pressed cigars on him. On that day his name became synonymous with speed in America, and a wraith of his fame still lives whenever daredevils are discussed. Six weeks later he took the 999 around the mile in 1:01⅕—closest yet to the mile-a-minute goal.

Winton vowed he would build a new racer to get the record back. Said Ford:

> If Winton does lower this time, I'll build another machine that will go him one better if I have to design a cylinder as big as a hogshead. I am bound to keep the record in Detroit.

196. Henry and Edsel, 1902. Framed oval photographs such as these were as near as studio photographers of the period could come to the candid camera. Edsel affectionately holds on to Daddy, who has, for the occasion, given his hair a set of water waves that are picturesquely unattractive. Ford, who had little personal vanity, was for some reason unaccountably vain about his hair and correspondingly concerned with baldness. He often concocted strange mixtures to use as hair lotions: one of the weirdest was a solution of water, kerosene oil and old razor-blades. Henry's suit is the latest in the businessman's classy cut, worn buttoned only at the top, just below the three-inch choker collar. Since Henry is clean-shaven, this picture was probably taken in the autumn.

About the time that Henry Ford shaved off his mustache, so did a Detroit coal dealer, Alexander Y. Malcomson. This may have been by mutual agreement. They had just become partners, and out of that partnership would come the company that would make more money more swiftly than any other ever known.

With somewhat unscholarly relish, the extremely sober *Journal of Economic Review* discussed in 1952 the fabulous profits of the founders of the East India Company, of the men who organized the diamond-studded, gold-loaded Empire of India as a kind of enormous golden goose to enrich England. After searching all human economic history for a comparison to the way the gold rolled in from India, the *Journal* decided that the empire-builders' profits were *"almost* as spectacular as those of the early stockholders of the Ford Motor Company."

196.

157

197.

Right now there are thousands of opportunities to make fortunes. People just don't see them—that is all.
—HENRY FORD

197. Edsel Ford, 1902. This is the finest portrait study of Edsel as a child. He was nearly nine years old when this was taken. By the time he was ten he would be driving a Ford car, the first Model A, with easy competence.

To today's teen-agers, restricted by nervous elders, police, traffic laws, safety regulations and the actual perils of the highway, this is hard to believe. But there was less trick to learning to drive a Model A than there was to learning to ride a bicycle. Henry Ford taught many a child in later years to drive a Model T before they were ten years old—T's were as easy to drive as today's automatic transmission cars.

198. The Scotch plunger begins to operate. An advertisement like this at the time (November 23, 1901) was equivalent to throwing a brick through a plate-glass window. Full-page ads were rare and crowded with blocks of small type. This ad is most characteristic of Henry Ford's next backer. He was aggressive, hustling, impatient, and of tremendous energy.

199. Alex. Malcomson and wagons. This is 1901: the walrus-mustached little man at the left is Malcomson.

200. The historic coalyard, 1901. Before the office stands Malcomson, his wife, and three of their children. The young man at the right, arm outstretched to the muzzle of a white horse, is Malcomson's clerk, James Couzens. Here is where Malcomson and Ford founded the partnership that led to the Ford Motor Company. This is 1901.

Sunny Jim and the Coal Man

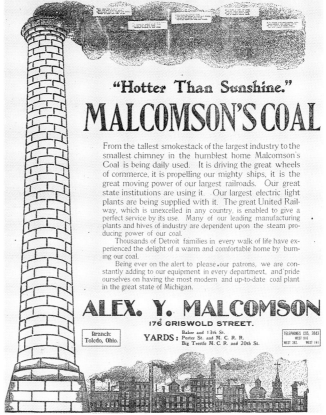

198.

199.

200.

Six days after the advertisement appeared, Mrs. Sarah Jane Malcomson died suddenly, leaving six small children and a grieving husband. As soon as he recovered from the blow, Malcomson hurled himself into his business with such vigor that he soon had bought up most of his competitors, one after another. He plunged, spreading himself thin, his credit extended as far as it would stretch; but he put together coalmine concessions, railroad concessions and delivery yards with a skilled hand. He was exceptionally swift in the ability to put men and situations together for profit, the same kind of chess-player's *combinative* ability that Henry had shown with men and machines.

As we saw earlier, the whole of Michigan Territory had been woodland and a naturally wood-burning country. The rise of industry brought the need for coal—coal fueled the boilers that made the steam that turned the turbines that made electricity. Lake boats needed coal, railroads needed coal—everything powered by steam needed coal. As the railroads cobwebbed the nation they became haulers of coal above all else.

Coal, most convenient for big furnaces, was also most convenient for kitchen ranges and parlor stoves. So around 1890 coal began to be really important in Detroit.

Alexander Young Malcomson was born on June 15, 1865, in Dalry, Ayrshire, Scotland. In 1880, at fifteen, he came to Detroit and got a job as a grocery clerk. He was small but big-boned; this gave him a rangy look, and his prominent nose, flung about as his head darted around in quick conversation, gave the impression of a strong bird pouncing. Before he was twenty he owned his own grocery store, but the grocery business was too slow for him. With an eye for the coming thing he set up in coal and wood. He was a natural advertiser and promoter, quick to please the small housewife customer as well as the largest industrial purchaser. He soon had big coal accounts, a fleet of new coal wagons, and he discovered something none of the other coal companies had thought of: that the true profit economics of the coal business lay in deliveries. Most Detroit coal companies used six horses to haul a huge wagon; Malcomson put three horses each on a number of smaller wagons and made more and faster deliveries.

When Henry Ford was chief engineer of the Edison Company he bought the coal for the furnaces from Malcomson and went over to check its quality every two weeks or so. On one of these occasions Malcomson's young clerk, James Couzens, asked: "Who's that man with the heavy mustache?" That was the first time Couzens saw Henry Ford.

At some time during the summer of 1902, Ford and Malcomson came together.

The Ford-Cooper agreement apparently broke up a little sourly, although the only real clue we have is a slighting reference to Cooper in one of Clara's letters to her brother Milton. Clara also reported that Henry had several offers to go into business but that she didn't think he would accept any of them. The probability is that Ford now realized that the only management he could satisfy completely was his own and that none of the offers would give him control or, at least, equal voice.

Henry now needed fresh money again, and he had gone through the whole first and second layers of Detroit's society of capitalists. And now we find in the background once again the figure of old ex-Senator Thomas W. Palmer, the kindly bulwark and the powerful political friend of the McMillans. Palmer had a great friend, William Livingstone, Jr., and it was Livingstone who now—and for many years to come—would take over the place of Palmer and of Maybury and of all the others as Ford's selfless, unofficial, unpaid consultant, friend and sponsor.

201. William Livingstone, Jr., was born in Dundas, Ontario, on January 21, 1844, and was now fifty-eight years old—a tremendous power in the background of all major Detroit affairs. He sometimes associated with the McMillans but on equal terms; he was a self-made man, quiet, sure, self-sufficient.

As a boy he went to a small Canadian academy and then learned the machinist's trade. At the age of twenty he "became identified with the shipping interests in the Great Lakes"—all the biographical material exasperatingly agrees with this phrase but does not tell us how, in what capacity, and how he rose. We do not know how, but steadily he "broadened the scope of his activities" and very quickly turned up as one of

the most important shipping men on the Great
Lakes, president of the Michigan Navigation
Company, the Percheron Steam Navigation Company, and stockholder in many associated companies.

Livingstone had the gift of getting men to
join associations to carry out his ideas: his prime
feat was to organize and develop the Lake Car-
riers Association, which he headed for more than
twenty years. This organization was basic in developing Great Lakes shipping; it most glitter-
ingly encouraged cities, states and the federal
government to dredge channels, build waterways,
and otherwise promote the interests of ship-
owners. A government-built channel for down-
bound vessels in the lower Detroit River, the
result of ten years of appearances by Livingstone
before Congress, was named for him.

Like the McMillans, he needed places to put
his money, so he helped organize, and later became president of, the Dime Savings Bank, and
in this capacity saved Henry Ford's financial life
in 1906.

He was a man of many interests and found
time to publish and actively manage the *Detroit
Journal*, by far the liveliest of the Detroit news-
papers at the turn of the century. The *Journal* is
still good reading today and seems old-fashioned
in only one sense: it actively practiced complete
freedom of speech and comment, particularly
about its competitors, whom it was wont to de-
nounce as "smug organs of hypocrisy and vilifi-
cation." In sum, Livingstone ran the brilliant
kind of newspaper that customers read with
horsewhip in hand. (It should be noted that it
was the *Journal* which ran the first story of Ford's
car.)

Livingstone was serious about developing Detroit, serving as president of the Board of Trade,
working actively in the Chamber of Commerce.
But his real pleasure over many years was an
attempt to beautify Detroit; he headed the city's
Parks and Boulevards Commission.

Politically he was an active Republican, serving by appointment of President Arthur as Collector of the Port; he was personally so popular
that once he was the only Republican to survive
a Democratic landslide in Wayne County. With
Palmer, the McMillans, and a few others, Livingstone made most of the Michigan Republican

201.

202.

203.

decisions—which meant that he helped set the course of the state's government from Lansing to Washington. And he was enough of a scholar and writer to compile and publish in 1900 a very respectable pioneer two-volume work, *The History of the Republican Party*.

In later years he became a two-term president of the American Bankers Association and was one of those men of active civic cast of mind who head all sorts of Liberty Loan Drives, committees and the rest.

As a memorial to his lifelong friend, he named one of his sons T. W. Palmer Livingstone. Another Livingstone son headed the City Lighting Plant from 1896 to 1899, while Henry was still at Edison. Livingstone himself was close to George Peck, the president of the Edison Company, and had innumerable dealings with both William H. Murphy and the McMillans.

Now, up to this point throughout Henry's various failures, Livingstone stands just outside the picture. He may have been a quiet counselor. Certainly he knew—because he was on the same boards—nearly all of the stockholders of the late Detroit Automobile Company; he must have been fully informed.

Further, as one of the bankers involved in the numerous extensions of credit given to Malcomson as he spread his coal business over Detroit, Livingstone was unquestionably profoundly interested in any new Malcomson venture.

Anyway, we see him here.

202. The coal office. At left, comfortable beside the cold coal stove, a base-burner, face aglow with a good cigar, sits William Livingstone, banker. Perched on a stool at the rear is Alexander Malcomson, owner of the coalyard office and prospective partner of Henry Ford. Pompous in the center, his cashier's eyes suspiciously alert for the slightest sign of a bouncing check or a counterfeit bill, stands James Couzens, coalyard clerk to Malcomson and now only a few years away from being a multimillionaire. On the right is a young man who has successfully defied five years of attempts at identification.

Now we do not know the occasion, nor the exact date, but since Malcomson is bare-faced, this has to be soon after Malcomson and Ford shaved their respective mustaches. And since Couzens is still present in working jacket in the coal office, it must be before he had moved to the Ford offices. The stove is unlit and the unknown young man is in straw hat, so the weather is warm: this places the picture at late summer 1902 or early summer 1903. (The calendars on both walls defy magnification.) But the grouping of these men at this time was significant. It is even possible that Ford himself took the photograph (although indoor shots in those days required cumbersome flash-power illumination) because he often attempted to photograph friends in interiors by natural light.

The earliest recorded formal coming together of Ford and Malcomson was on August 16, 1902, when Malcomson's lawyer, John W. Anderson, reported that Malcomson brought Ford to his office. This all ties together: Ford had already had dealings with Horace H. Rackham, and Anderson and Rackham were shortly to become law partners, as well as investors in the Ford Motor Company.

As his racing fever cooled, as the Cooper venture broke up, Ford and his team of Wills and company had continued to develop his newer ideas for a passenger car: they had roughed out a design for a pilot model and estimated that they needed some $3,000 to develop it. (By the time Henry was ready, the cost to Malcomson had become $7,000—Henry's perfectionism had set in again.)

The new design had picked up many notions from Henry's racing experiences; the engine particularly had profited and was now to be vertical (the best-selling Oldsmobile engine was horizontal), in an engineering attempt to reduce vibration and wear. This was true pioneering—automobile engines ever since have had vertical cylinders.

Malcomson was then driving a Winton and was enthusiastic about it to the point of wanting to invest in Winton somehow. But Henry must have reminded him of the Grosse Pointe auto race—which Malcomson had seen.

Anderson drew up a contract and the partnership was under way. At the same time articles of employment were drawn up for Wills, and most notably, Malcomson decided that the partnership would open a separate banking account under the name of James Couzens, his clerk. There were two reasons for this—Malcomson

wanted to hide as far as possible from his numerous bankers the fact that he was taking on another venture; and second, since he himself was so busy, Couzens could serve as the cold-eyed business watchdog. This was a fateful choice. It meant more to each of them than any of the three could have foreseen.

203. The second giant. This picture of James Couzens—there are notably few in all his long career in the headlines—was probably taken some five years later. But this shows the basic model of his face and his basic expression all his life: note how quickly—already, in six swift years—the rather arrogant youngster has settled into the very mold of the hardheaded businessman.

Couzens was a notable man, one of the true master organizers in American business history, and not far short of a financial wizard; later he became a great liberal senator in the days when the word "liberal" seemed to have a precise meaning.

But in the battle-scarred history of the Ford Motor Company, which is one long chronicle of fights among marvelously hot-tempered men, he was notable in another way: he had one of the finest red-hot tempers that ever broke up the Ford furniture. Henry Ford lost his temper seldom but thoroughly; Edsel almost never; but around them in the Ford hierarchy raged quarrels that shook Detroit for a generation. In a stormy scene Couzens' cold fury easily held its own—and when he smiled his annual smile the ice was said to break up on the Great Lakes.

He was strictly business from bump-toed shoes to derby hat. He organized the United States into Ford districts with desperate speed, planting dealers and parts depots in every hamlet. Before the company was two months old he was already planning the shipment of cars to England—although Henry had hardly finished assembling his first Model A car.

Our first view of James Couzens is on a winter midnight in 1890. The scene is the Detroit yards of the Michigan Central Railroad. A late afternoon sleet storm had turned to driving snow under a bone-biting northeast wind, and the trodden slush had hardened into rough ice.

Enter James Couzens, swinging a lantern in his left hand.

He was born on August 26, 1872, and is therefore now eighteen years old, a Canadian boy from Chatham, Ontario, determined to make his fortune in the States. He is called "the first white child born in Chatham," a joke arising from the fact that the little town was one of the Canadian termini for the Antebellum underground railroad and is the home of many ex-slaves.

James, from the start, is an eager beaver—but an extremely precise, methodical, careful one. At this moment in his young life he has only two distinctions: he is clean shaven when nearly every other male on the continent is fur bearing; and he never makes a mistake.

He crosses the ice-slicked railroad tracks in the bitter night, all set to begin his regular twelve-hour shift. His pay as a freight car checker: $10 a week. (There were no fringe benefits, either, unless you count the fact that he could sit in the warm track-shed when there were no more cars to check.)

He swings the lantern up until it rests on his biceps as on a stand and studies the first freight car. The number is almost obliterated by ice, but he notes it on his pad, sheltered from the driving snow by his lantern. Then he examines the seal on the car door; it is so caked with frozen sleet that it cannot be read. Taking off his mittens, he warms the seal in his hand, blowing on it until he can read the impression. Most checkers usually noted "indistinct," but not James Couzens.

Cards had to be tacked to the freight cars. It was hard to fumble for tacks in his pocket with a gloved hand; and so he had learned to carry a supply of tacks in his mouth. This was no impediment to conversation; he had no one to talk to, anyway. Some nights the frosty tacks stuck to his tongue. Now he made out a card, spat a tack on it, and with one quick drive of his thumb, nailed the card to the ice-glazed car.

This thoroughness seemed to escape the railroad's attention, but it attracted Alex. Malcomson. Malcomson liked the careful way Couzens checked the coal cars. Malcomson needed someone to answer the telephone at night in his branch coalyard near the depot. Couzens got

the part-time job. The pay was $2 a week, and now his total income was $12 a week.

Inevitably Couzens' stern perseverance even won him promotion on the railroad. After he had spent a mere five years on the night shift he was given a desk in the freight office. His new pay: $15 a week. But he lost the extra $2 from Malcomson, for he was now on the day side.

The hustling Malcomson was sympathetic but Scotch. He studied the new $15-a-week Couzens for two more years and then plunged with an offer. Would young Jim take over the management of his coal company office, including the entire bookkeeping? However, due to the great possibilities of advancement, the pay would be cut only slightly, to $14 a week.

Couzens must at this point have studied his own career. It was now 1897. He had been working hard for seven years. He was now making exactly $4 more a week than when he began.

The Michigan weather was mild that winter and the coal business was poor. In the spring of 1898 Malcomson had to fire one assistant, but out of fondness for young Jim he merely cut his pay (there is no record of how deep the cut). By the summer of 1898, Malcomson's spreading coal business had begun to pay off. In a generous moment he raised Jim's pay to $75 a month.

Inspired by this wealth, Couzens married Margaret Manning, his long-patient fiancée, on August 31. Then Malcomson bought the Crescent Fuel Company in Toledo and sent Couzens to break in its management. He was there a year at a new high salary: $100 a month. He saved his money, and saved it hard. Few men can have appreciated to a finer degree the exact purchasing power of a single dollar, penny by penny, than Jim Couzens.

By now James Couzens' lean years were almost over. Malcomson's quick eye for an embryo dollar had led his enterprises into a disorderly sprawl. On Couzens' return to Detroit, Couzens injected double-entry bookkeeping and modern management ideas into all of Malcomson's affairs, trying to keep him both organized and solvent. It was at this moment of ripeness that Malcomson and Henry Ford came together.

XVIII. A DOCTOR BUYS A CAR

Cash balance in the bank: $223.65.
—JAMES COUZENS, *July 11, 1903*

It is late in 1902. In a few months Carrie Nation will take up her little broad-bladed hatchet and begin smiting sin, which to her took the form of plate-glass windows in saloons. The homes of the land are swathed in portieres; parlor furniture has buttoned upholstery, but most people never use their tomb-like parlors. Good weather is spent on the porches, hundreds of thousands of people every evening creaking rhythmically in wicker rockers and porch-swings. All the best people have bought the latest Japanese import: little strips of glass that hang just inside and above the front door, where every entrance makes them tinkle pleasantly—the ancestor of the mobile.

On a little farm in Alabama, a stooped lean, gentle man, George Washington Carver, has begun to teach young negroes to grow sweet potatoes and peanuts and soybeans, to get them away from the curse of cotton, mules and credit. The biggest new song hit of the year is "In the Good Old Summer Time," but the hits of the last two years are still popular, for in those days songs did not wear out in a few weeks: "The Sidewalks of New York" and "Hello Central! Give Me Heaven, For My Mamma's There."

204a, b. Henry Ford's construction teams. Oliver Barthel left; he and Harold Wills did not get along, and in fact there was work for only one designer. But Henry added Gus Degener, a swift-moving, young, all-round mechanic; Dick Kettlewell, so eternally innocent that he immediately became the butt of all the practical jokes; and John Wandersee, a square-built loyal little man. Wandersee could not have guessed that day—October 17, 1902—that he would be the only one of them all to live through the whole furious first fifty years—in fact that he

204a.

204b.

would become the classic example of the lower-level Ford employee, serving in fantastic assignments, in dogged faithful bewilderment, through a thousand turnovers.

Wandersee has well described those days at 81 Park Place in 1902:

> They didn't have any model. They were just working on a car. It was just on the drawing board.
>
> We started on the car as soon as Degener came, in early November. The motor on the first car was in running order, on blocks, by Thanksgiving.
>
> Barney Everitt made the body. Walter Briggs was his wagon trimmer. [Briggs soon founded the Briggs Body Works, became a millionaire, and bought the Detroit Tigers baseball team. He is the father of "Spike" Briggs.]
>
> The chassis was made in the shop. There wasn't much to it. It was angle-iron the men put together. It was assembled shortly before Christmas.
>
> It was a two-cylinder car. It did not look like the Model A. One night, coming down Mack Avenue, Wills and Degener wrecked it. We kept it under the stairway after it was wrecked. That was about in May 1903. But it didn't make much difference—they already had the Model A on the way then. The first Model A for test purposes was assembled rather late in that May. It was right after the pilot car had been wrecked.
>
> Henry sometimes wore coveralls then. But that was the last time. After that he always wore a business suit. But he was into everything all the time, talking to each man.

Henry was doing a lot of talking then—and to many men outside the shop. He was raising the money to incorporate the Ford Motor Company.

It is time here to take a hack at a prime concern. Just how far did Henry Ford's vision go at that time? Did he envision as far back as 1902 the great miracle of the automobile as a liberator, as the instrument that would build the American road, as the single most powerful force for progress in the first third of the new century? Certainly he was sketching it out in boldest prophecy a few years later. But he was then well on his way, and so was the American road, although very few men saw the vast vision even then.

By the twenties Ford was generally acclaimed as the prophet who had first seen the vision of American emancipation brought about by the automobile: the end of the farmer's isolation, the end of the city man's fortress imprisonment. It was obvious enough then that Ford, more than any other man, had made this possible by producing a car with the four qualities which exactly fitted the American needs:

Light enough to handle easily and run inexpensively,
Rugged enough to overcome the terrible roads of the time,
Reliable enough to be depended on for hard service,
Cheap enough for every American to buy.

But did Ford do this by luck or by foresight?

The question that always engages a historian, of whatever caliber, is how much credit to give. The generals who bull through to a victory by numbers or by luck are of little account and no interest; we turn our minds to the Napoleons who had a battle plan, a grand strategy that saw far beyond the immediate conflict. The same is true of industrial captains. Of no interest to anyone are those worthy businessmen who merely do their work and make a profit; we pay attention only to those who have great plans that stretch beyond the store and the factory into vast operations. Success or failure is not the point; and morality is beside the point; we are as interested in a Ponzi, a Krueger, an Insull, as in a duPont, a Rockefeller. It is the breadth and sweep of a great strategic conception, win or lose, moral or immoral, that arouses us; Tolstoi's great canvas overpowers Chekhov's skill; Balzac's audacity in even programming the human comedy makes de Maupassant's life work seem like so many well-carved cherrystones.

Therefore, if Henry Ford is to be placed, it is important to discover how early, how far back, he saw the vision of the car as *something more* than a four-wheeled vehicle which he wanted to manufacture. Let me say at once that I am not certain when this was, but that I believe it was very early. Remember Fred Strauss: "He had the dream."

If we add up all the little things, the sum becomes quite impressive; it seems safe to credit Ford with a substantially greater vision than most of his contemporaries had.

The clue lies in his childhood preoccupation with taking the work out of farm work. Anyone who ever spent days following a team plowing through clayey land remembers fresh as dew the stumbling, wrenching struggle of the work, the monotony of the hours passing in slow minutes, the endless stretch of the furrows, the small area dug at the day's end, the great reach left to be done tomorrow—and the next tomorrow. To the nineteenth century the vision of a modern tractor was more sublime than Joan of Arc's vision of France.

205. Margaret Ford, later Mrs. James Ruddiman.

One Sunday in his farm days, after his mother had died, after he had served his Detroit apprenticeship and returned to the farm to work on the little portable road-engines, Ford was driving his sister Margaret home from church in Dearborn. It was a beautiful early spring day. The frost was not yet out of the ground, and the clay roads were almost impassable. The mud rolled up on the light buggy wheels in great soggy chunks; the horse snorted as he struggled heavily through the ruts. Slapping the reins, Henry talked to Margaret. She had accompanied Clara several times to watch Henry pull up stumps with his little machine; he reminded her of this, and of how he had been thinking of ways to lighten the farmer's work. The horse struggled on. The text of the sermon that morning had been: "Hitch your wagon to a star." Now Henry said: "That's what I'm going to do." And he told her that he had shifted his thinking toward some form of transportation that would enable people to travel around "easier, with less work." She listened doubtfully, hardly understanding a word. ("How could you get around without horses? After all, we had some very fine horses, of which we were very proud.")

But Henry repeated the sermon: "Hitch your wagon to a star."

His star, from boyhood on, had been a machine that ran on the road. His first steam road locomotive ran forty feet and stopped; his second never ran at all. Then, probably after many fail-

205.

ures and half successes, he made the little gasoline engine that ran on Clara's sink. Next he
tried to adapt it to a bicycle, almost immediately
gave that up for a quadricycle, building his first
car in the Bagley Avenue shed.

It is his thinking in the two and one-half years
between the kitchen sink and the Bagley shed
that must have been decisive. For what were
the prime characteristics of his first car? Above
every other consideration it was light in weight,
and therefore could run far and fast, notably
faster than the first cars of other auto pioneers.
It was definitely rugged; it was driven hard for
two years before Ford bought it back, and it still
runs smoothly, though nearly seventy years old.
It also answered the third essential: reliability.
Now these considerations and the fourth—cheap-
ness in manufacture—of course exactly met the
American problem and the American need.

The United States at that moment in its history
was very much like a group of rich feudal states,
connected only by the thin steel lines of its railroads. The resources of the Midwest, the Rocky
Mountains, the Far West and the South had not
really been tapped. Where there were communications—Boston to New York to Philadelphia, and, to a lesser extent, to Chicago—the
country was exploding with prosperity, power,
progress, as the minds and muscles of the land
were put together. But an incomprehensibly
greater strength was available, unused, slumber-
ing. The great giant lay asleep.

For transportation, the bicycle was a toy. The
day of wagons was past. The railroads did not
go everywhere and could not go everywhere.
America needed a network of roads enormously
greater than the world had ever seen, a network
at once as complex and yet as fine as the blood-
stream in a man; roads that would go over every
mountain range, through every swamp, across
every desert and plain, bridging every stream,
creek, branch, run, and river, roads that would
go everywhere and yet right down to every
front door in the land.

But all the roads ended just outside the cities
except for the flat places, such as between New
York and Philadelphia. Bridges were mainly railroad bridges, and the ferry business was still
big. The only great steel suspension all-purpose
bridge in the country was the Brooklyn Bridge.

*206. The vicissitudes of auto travel at the be-
ginning of the century.*

   a. The hills are steep and the roads are heavy.
   b. There are no bridges.

Most of the little cars, such as the curved-dash
Oldsmobile and the one-lung Cadillac, were just
not rugged enough for any substantial distance,
even on good roads. The big cars like the Pierce
and the Winton, were beautiful monsters, ideal
for fashionable idling about Newport, Boston,
New York and Washington, but hopelessly un-
suitable for ventures beyond city limits. For all
their size, they were fragile, and an owner whose
huge car had a breakdown on a lonely rural
road was not merely in an exasperating situation; his plight was pitiful. Even after he had
hired a farmer's team to pull him somewhere he
had to send by mail for parts and then try to
discover a mechanic not too ignorant to make
the repairs. Even these cars, the too-large and
the too-small, gave impetus to the demand for
good roads, neighborhood by neighborhood.

But what was needed was a car so obviously
all-round, so inexpensive, so reliable, that everyone could afford it; and then the demand for
roads would become national. This, clearly, was
the car that Ford had been working for years to
build. Thus far he had mainly suffered setbacks.
His backers had never had the same dream that
he had; he could never build the car they
wanted, and so far had not built the car he
himself wanted.

During 1903–06 he preached to every ear
he could reach his gospel of a cheap car, a light
car, "a car that workingmen could buy." He argued that a light car meant better engineering.
If the car was reduced in weight, it could be
pulled by a lighter engine. If the engine were
left large the car would be much stronger.

He argued his scheme of manufacture in 1903
to John W. Anderson:

The way to make automobiles is to make one
automobile like another automobile, to make
them all alike, to make them come through
the factory just alike; just as one pin is like
another pin when it comes from a pin factory, or one match is like another match when
it comes from the match factory.

206a.

206b.

To appreciate what that doctrine sounded like, you must realize that in those days most companies produced one sample handmade car and then took orders for more, producing according to advance orders. There were only a few exceptions, such as the Oldsmobile.

A small number of experts even at the time agreed with Ford. He was not the only man with a vision. But they were the minority. Many businessmen live by what they can see around them; high in practical sense, keen in operations, they cannot believe that their low powers of imagination, their lack of ability to visualize the future, are severe handicaps. Most businessmen at the time saw there were no roads and therefore could not imagine a nation with roads that led to every door; the market for cars was with people who had money for luxuries. They were sure of this: all the surveys showed that the trend was to the high-priced car; *and it was.* (Until 1907 the sale of high-priced cars would climb steadily; more than two-thirds of all automobiles cost more than $1,375 and up to $4,000.)

As always, the hardheaded businessmen thought: Why go against the trend? And the ancient, melancholy inevitable happened; they all went with the trend, and the trend went into oblivion; so did their companies, one by one, and all their hard money. Only the visionaries survived, the ones who had gone against the trend but toward the real market, and then at last it was clear that the visionaries were actually the hardheaded businessmen.

207. The Anderson letter. This document, perhaps more than any other in this book, will repay reading. No quick summary can do it justice. Here John W. Anderson, the lawyer, is planting a seed in his father's head—he's a doctor in La Crosse, Wisconsin—which he hopes will sprout a loan—$5,000?—to invest in the risky automobile business. The letter is careful, thorough, accurate in the main, and remains the clearest single explanation, in small compass, of the origin of the Ford Motor Company.

208. John S. Gray.

209. John W. Anderson.

210. Horace H. Rackham.

211. Charles H. Bennett.

212. John F. Dodge.

213. Horace E. Dodge.

214. Vernon C. Fry.

215. Charles J. Woodall.

216. Albert Strelow.

These nine original stockholders and Malcomson, Couzens and Ford are the founders of the Ford Motor Company. These nine and Couzens invested $28,000 in cash, and pledged $21,000 more in notes. For this they received $49,000 worth of stock. Ford and Malcomson split the other $51,000 worth of stock. The two partners put up no money. To cover their controlling interest, Ford and Malcomson turned over to the new company their machinery—which was not much; their patents—which were few and obsolete; and their partnership contract—under which Ford had now spent about $7,000 of Malcomson's money.

Henry Ford, therefore, put in neither cash nor realizable assets. Malcomson put in no new cash, but it was solidly understood that he backed them all. He was pledging his whole reputation, his coal business, his credit. In effect, Malcomson put in nothing but his faith in Henry Ford.

What Ford put in, and what all the investors were backing, was simply his know-how. All the backers knew this: the whole thing was plain talk on plain wooden tables in the coal office, the law office, Gray's bank office, the Dodge machine shop.

But to raise the initial capital was slow hard work over months. We must remember that a good many men in the first and second flights of Detroit capitalism had lost a lot of money in backing Henry Ford. And the mortality in the automobile business was already high. Jim Couzens sought new backers up and down the buildings of Detroit, and approached many a man as immovable as granite. After one particularly exasperating interview he came downstairs, sat on the curb with his feet in the street, and there fought down an impulse to burst into tears.

The truth is, Ford and Malcomson were com-

Detroit,June 4th.1903.

Dear father:

Horace and I have an opportunity to make an investment that is of such a character that I cannot refrain from laying the details before you for consideration.

Mr.Ford of this city is recognized throughout the country as one of the best automobile mechanical experts in the U.S. From the very begining he has been interested in their construction and developement. Years ago he constructed a racing machine which was a wonder,and since then has construct- ed others in which he has raced all over the country,Fast,and has won numer- ous contests on many tracks. I simply mention this to indicate his reputation as his name is widely known in automobile circles everywhere,and consequent- ly a very valuable and favorable asset to any automobile Co. Several years ago he designed,perfected and placed on the market a machine. A Co.was or- ganized,but not long after,desiring to devote his attention to a new model entirely,he sold out his patents and interest,and retired. The machine is known as the "Cadillac"(you will see it advertised in all the magazines) and is now being manufactured here by a large Co. The only condition Ford exact- ed in selling was that the Co.should not use his name in the Co.

He then turned his entire attention to the designing and patenting of an entirely new machine. Mr.Malcomson,the coal man,backed him with money and the result is they have now perfected and are about to place on the market an automobile (gasoline) that is far and away ahead of anything that has yet come out. He has had applications taken out on every new point he has de- signed and has just received word the 17 of them have been allowed,everyone of which are incorporated in the machine and,of course,cannot be duplicated in any other.

Having perfected the machine in all its parts,and demonstrated to their complete satisfaction and to the satisfaction of automobile experts,and cycle journal representatives from all over the country who came here to inspect it that it was superior to anything that had been designed in the way of an auto mobile,and that is was a sure winner,the next problem was how to best and most economically place it on the market. After canvassing the matter thor- oughly,instead of forming a company,with big capital,erecting a factory and installing an expensive plant of machinery to manufacture it themselves,they determined to enter into contracts with various concerns to supply the dif- ferent parts and simply do the assembling themselves.

So,they entered into contract with the Dodge Bros. here to manufacture the automobile complete--less wheels and bodies-- for $250.apiece,or $162,500.00,for the 650 machines,which were to be delivered at the rate of 10 per day,commencing July 1st.if possible,and all by Oct.1st. I drew the contract,so know all about it.

Now Dodge Bros.are the largest and best equipped machine plant in the city. They have a new factory,just completed and it is not excelled anywhere as an up-to-date and thoroughly equipped machine shop. Well,when this propo- sition was made them by Ford and Malcomson,they had under consideration of- fers from the Oldsmobile,and the Great Northern automobile Co. to manufac- ture their machines,but after going over Mr.Fords machine very carefully,they threw over both offers and tied up with Mr.F.and Mr.M.

Now,in order to comply with this contract,which was made last Oct.Dodge Bros. had to decline all outside orders and devote the entire resources of their machine shop to the turning out of these automobiles. They were only paid $10.000/on account,and had to take all the rest of the risk themselves. They had to borrow $40.000.,place orders for castings all over the country, pay their men from last October (they have a large force) and do evrything necessary to manufacture all the machines before they could hope to get a cent back. I go into this fully,so you may understand the faith that these experts and successful machinists have in the machine itself,in staking their whole business,practically,on the outcome,because under the contract if Mr.F. and Mr.M.did not pay for them,Dodge Bros.were to have the machines in lieu of the money-thus making the risk entirely theirs.

In addition to this,contracts for the remaining parts of the automobile- the bodies,seat cushions,wheels and tires- were made so that they are sup- plied as wanted. The bodies and cushions,by the C.R.Wilson carriage Co.at $52 apiece and $16 apiece respectively. The wheels by a Lansing,Mich.,firm at $26.per set (4 wheels). The tires by the Hartford Rubber Co. at $46.00 per set (4 wheels).

They found a man from whom Mr.M.rents a coal yard on the belt-line R.R.,with a spur track running into it. He agreed to erect a building,designed by Mr. Ford for their special use,for assembling purposes(which will cost between 3 & 4 thousand dollars) and rent it for three yrs.to Mr.F.and Mr.M.at $75.per month. This building has been all completed and is a dandy. I went all through it today. It is large,light and airy,about 250 feet long by fifty ft. wide,fitted up with machinery necessary to be used incidental to assembling the parts,and all ready for business. To this assembling plant are shipped the bodies,wheels,tires,and the machine from Dodge Bros.,and here the work- men,ten or a dozen boys at $1.50 a day,and a foreman fit the bodies on the machine,put the cushions in place,put the tires on the wheels,the wheels on the machine and paint it and test it to see that it runs "o.k.",and it is all ready for delivery. Now this is all there is to the whole proposition.

Now,as to the investment feature. You will see there is absolutely no money,to speak of,tied up in a big factory. There is the $75 a month rent for 3 years,and the few machines necessary in the assembling factory. All the rest is done outside and supplied as ordered,and this of course is a big saving in capital outlay to start with.
The machines sell for $750.,without a tonneau. With a tonneau,$850. This is the price of all medium priced machines and is standard. It is what the Cadillac and Great Northern sell for here,and what other machines elsewhere sell for. Now the cost,figured on the most liberal possible estimate,is as follows:

Machine--------$250.00	Fixed by contract	
Body----------- 52.00	" " "	
Wheels--------- 26.00	" " "	
Upholstering---- 16.00	" " "	
Tires----------- 40.00	(All these fixed by contract)	
Cost of assembling --------- 20.00	--- This includes wages,rent,in- surance and all incidentals at factory.	
Cost of selling---------------- 150.00	---This includes advertising,all salaries commissions,etc. 20% on each automobile.(It will be nearer 10 or 12.)	
Total cost.---------$554.00		
Cost of tonneau ------- 50.00		
$604.00		

Selling price,with tonneau--- $850.00		Without tonneau $750.00	
Cost price " "	604.00	" " "	554.00
	246.00		196.00
Throwing off $46.00	46.00		46.00
(For any possible extra contingency.)	$200.00		$150.00

On the seasons output of 650 machines it means a profit of $97.500,without a tonneau,and more in proportion to those sold with tonneaus,and of course the latter is almost always bought,as it adds so much to the capacity of vehicle.
Now,the demand for automobiles is a perfect craze. Every factory here, (ther are 3,including the "Olds--the largest in this country--and you know Detroit is the largest automobile in the U.S.) has its entire output sold and cannot begin to fill their orders. Mr.M.has already begun to be deluged with orders,although not a machine has been put on the market and will not be until July 1st. Buyers have heard of it and go out to Dodge Bros.and in- spect it,test it and give their orders. One dealer from Buffalo was here last week and ordered twenty-five:three were ordered today,and other orders have begun to come in every day,so there is not the slightest doubt as to the market or the demand. And it is all spot cash on delivery,and no guarantee or string attached of any kind.
Mr.Malcomson has instructed us to draw up articles of incorporation for a $100.000.00 limited liability company,of which he and Mr.Ford will take at least $51.000.00 (controlling interest) and the balance he is going to dis- tribute among a few of his friends and business associates,and is anxious that Horace and myself go in with him. Mr.Couzens,whom Spencer met,is going to leave the coal business,for the present at least,and devote his entire time to the office end and management of the automobile business--and he is a crackerjack. He is going to invest,as he expresses it,"all the money he can beg,borrow or steal"in stock. Mr.Dodge,of Dodge Bros.,is going to take 5 or 10 thousand,and two or three others,like amounts. Horace is going to put in all he can raise,and I do want to do the same if I can,because I hon- estly believe it is a wonderful opportunity,and a chance likely not to occur again. Mr.M.is a successful in everything he does,is such a good business man and hustler,and his ability in this direction ,coupled with Mr.Ford's in- ventive and mechanical genius,and Mr.Couzen's office ability,together with

(Copy #3)

fixed contracts which absolutely show what the cost will be, and orders already commencing to pour in, showing the demand that exists, makes it one of the very most promising and surest industrial investments that could be made. At a conservative estimate the profits will be 50%, with a good sinking fund in addition. The machines are turned into money as fast as delivered and indicate a return of the whole original investment practically by Winter, if nothing were turned into the surplus account. It is a well known fact that the Oldsmobile Works, with a capital of $500.000., cleared up a million dollars last year and are now preparing plans to double their capacity for next year, which indicates, as strong as anything possibly can, what the demand is throughout the country.

I went all over the Dodge Bros. plant and the assembling rooms today, and even into the room where the half dozen draughtsmen are kept under lock and key, (all the plans, drawings and specifications are secret you know) making drawings and blue-prints of every part, even to the individual screws, and was amazed at what had been accomplished since last October. Not another Automobile Co. has started and got its product on the market inside of three years before this.

Copy of letter written by
J.W.A. to W.A.A., June 4th. 1903.
According to envelope it was
mailed on the 5th. and received
on the 6th. of June, 1903.

207c.

208.

209.

210.

211.

212.

213.

214.

215.

pletely unable to raise any real outside money. They had surpassing difficulty in convincing even the nervous little group of Malcomson's friends. And this group had such difficulty in raising cash that the company started business practically without funds. Everything was on paper. Their total resources constituted one of the weakest shoestrings in American business history.

One Detroiter, Dr. Jacob Zumstein, actually did volunteer $500 for five shares. But it was too late—they had twelve pledges and he would have made a thirteenth stockholder. They felt they could take no chances on their luck.

None of them had the least awareness of being an economic pioneer. Most were prey to an intense, ulcerating anxiety; they could almost feel the hot breath of the sheriff, dispossessing them of their homes, throwing their children into the street. In plain fact, their total bravery—always excepting that of Ford, Malcomson and Couzens—would not add up to that of a pack of Cub Scouts on night patrol. They started out with deep forebodings, faint hearts and nervous stomachs.

This fear is why some of them sold out as soon as possible, hilariously happy to get their money back. This is why John S. Gray, the biggest cash stockholder, who had plunged in with a full $10,500 of hard cash, was still gravely worried about the venture three years later, just before his death in 1906. He had already gotten back his full investment and another $50,000 more. Yet the only thing that kept him from selling his stock—he was a grave and conscientious man—was that he could not in full honesty recommend to any of his friends that they buy it. He said solemnly: "This business cannot last." (By 1915 his estate had received $10,000,000 in dividends.)

216.

217. List of stockholders and their shares. A document in Couzens' handwriting. Who were these men of great faith?

John S. Gray was Malcomson's uncle. Anderson and Rackham were Malcomson's lawyers. Actually they served as his collection agency, dunning dead-beats for small coal bills. Vernon E. Fry was Malcomson's cousin. Charles J. Woodall was Malcomson's bookkeeper. James Couzens was Malcomson's business manager. Albert

Strelow was Malcomson's contractor, who had built his coalyards.

In short, Malcomson was very much like the small boy who starts out in business by selling magazine subscriptions to his mother's friends.

There is no profounder commentary on the state of Detroit faith in Henry Ford at this time. Five years before he had been backed by the most glittering array of gilt-edge capitalists that could be assembled in one room at the same time. Now the only men who could be coaxed or bludgeoned into supporting him were little fellows, friends and relatives of Malcomson, and even then Malcomson had to give each of them his word or his note that he would indemnify them against loss.

One outsider appears in the list, Charles H. Bennett. Bennett was president of the Daisy Air Rifle Company, an inventive mechanic himself.

The catching of Bennett as a backer was a piece of purest luck. He was on his way to buy an Oldsmobile when he decided to stop in first at his tailor's for a suit of clothes. As he was being fitted he talked to the tailor about the Oldsmobile. The curtains at the next booth parted and out popped the head of Frank Malcomson, the coaldealer's cousin. Said Frank Malcomson: "Pardon me; I couldn't help overhearing your conversation. Have you heard about the Ford car?" Bennett said courteously that he had not. Forthwith he was rushed posthaste over to meet Henry and the Model A. He took a ride and was so charmed by both car and inventor that he never did reach the Oldsmobile dealer.

The Ford car appealed to Bennett so strongly that for some time he considered a proposal to merge the air rifle and the car companies. (In later years one student of the automotive industries pondered this and suggested: "This would have worked out just dandy. At the start they could have given away one BB-gun with each Ford, and after the Model T came along, they could have given away one Ford with each BB-gun.") But wise counsel prevailed, and so the stockholders of the Daisy Air Rifle Company had to be content with their own fortunes.

But Bennett did pledge $5,000, though he was not carried so far away that he put in actual cash: he merely gave two notes for $2,500 each

2

Detroit June 16th 1903.

June 16	✓	Sundries Dr To Capital Stock			100000 00
	3	Alex Y. Malcomson	255 Shares	25500.00	
	4	Henry Ford	255 Shares	25500 00	
	5	John S. Gray	105 Shares	10500 00	
	6	John W. Anderson	50 Shares	5000 00	
	7	Horace H. Rackham	50 Shares	5000 00	
	8	John F. Dodge	50 Shares	5000 00	
	9	Horace E. Dodge	50 Shares	5000 00	
	11	Vernon C. Fry	50 Shares	5000 00	
	17	Albert Strelow	50 Shares	5000 00	
	10	Chas H. Bennett	50 Shares	5000 00	
	13	James Couzens	25 Shares	2500 00	
	14	Chas J. Woodall	10 Shares	1000 00	
June 26	50	Cash Dr To Sundries		18000 00	
	5	John S. Gray			10500 00
	6	John W. Anderson			5000 00
	7	Horace H. Rackham			3500 00
	11	Vernon C. Fry			3000 00
	13	James Couzens			1000 00
July 10	17	Albert Strelow			5000 00
	60	Bills Receivable Dr Sundries		19500 00	
June 26	8	John F. Dodge 3 Months Note			5000 00
	9	Horace E. Dodge 4 Months Note			5000 00
	13	James Couzens 4 Months Note			1500 00
	14	Chas. J. Woodall 4 Months Note			1000 00
	11	Vernon C. Fry Note			2000 00
	10	C H Bennett			5000 00

217.

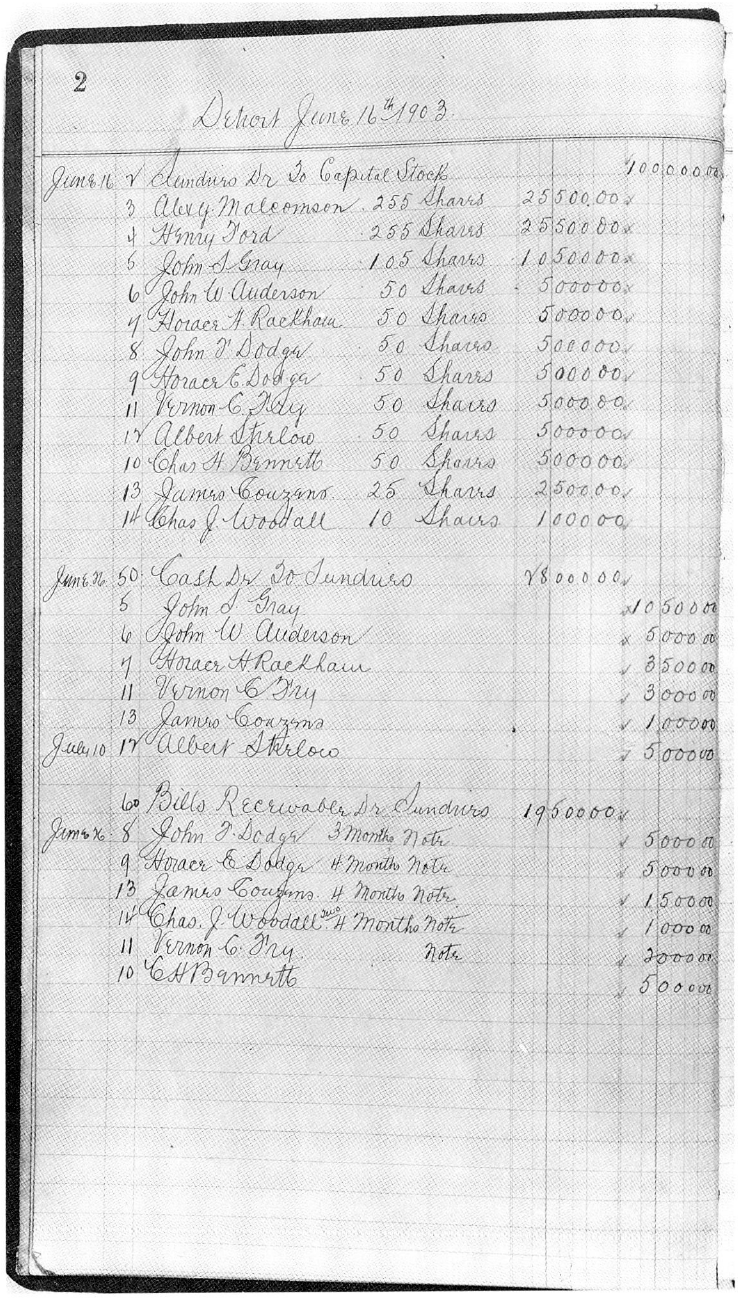

—one of them guaranteed by Malcomson. He was able to pay them off out of dividends in 1904, and hence never put in any real cash at all.

The only non-Malcomsonians, therefore, were Ford and the Dodge brothers. The Dodges made a really shrewd agreement. They had passed up the chance to manufacture more transmissions for the Oldsmobile because they liked the design of Henry's Model A engine. They were rough and tough horse traders, but known to be hardheaded, hardhanded but square in all their dealings.

This is the way the deal went.

The Dodges agreed to make 650 engines, chassis and running gears for the cars. To do this they needed to expand their facilities and hire more men, for the manufacture of the four-cylinder Ford was a lot more complicated than the making of the one-cylinder Olds.

John and Horace Dodge each gave a promissory note for $5,000 as payment for their stock; each then received 50 shares. But first they demanded, and received, $10,000 in cash for the engines they were going to make. This was supplied, apparently after tears, prayer and torture, by Malcomson's uncle, John S. Gray, on Malcomson's personal pledge to Gray to repay this. Gray, whose meager faith we know, knew only too well how his nephew's operations were overextended and how shaky was his credit at other banks; in effect he wanted to keep the whole disaster within the family. He put in another $500 for operating expenses and received 105 shares for his $10,500.

The Dodges were now well covered. They had given notes for $10,000 but they had it back in cash, which they were going to use for expansion and materials. And they were going to make a fat individual profit on each engine and transmission besides.

But they wanted further guarantees—and got them. Ford and Malcomson agreed helplessly that if the Ford Motor Company went down the drain in failure, the Dodges would have a prior right to payment; and even more, they could keep the motors and re-sell them to other companies.

With these locked-in guarantees of safety and with roaring enthusiasm, the Dodges plunged into manufacturing the engines.

Rackham had a time raising his $5,000. He had helped draw up the Dodge agreement in February 1903 and had been very much impressed, despite his natural quiet, mild conservatism, with his first real chance to mingle in weighty affairs and with men who talked freely of thousands of dollars.

For the partnership of Anderson and Rackham was very small potatoes indeed. Neither man had done well. Anderson had been a law clerk for some years before he discovered that the firm he labored for had no intention whatever of making him a partner in even the farthest future. He had then shopped for a partner and had found a strong one in George P. Codd. But Codd soon dropped him and went on to big things in politics, becoming mayor of Detroit in 1904.

Anderson, moreover, had a mild nature. The partners wrote their collection letters out in longhand, since they had neither secretary nor typewriter. Anderson could not bring himself to write a threatening letter; he pleaded gently with his group of debtors to let him know if they had any plans to pay their bills. As a result he hardly ever collected any money, and indeed spent the major part of his time writing letters to his clients explaining why he had made no progress.

Rackham, also, was too gentle for the profession. He had not handled a major case. He was dry, quiet, shy, pleasant, with but one iron facet to his character: he was an ardent prohibitionist, very proud that he had never touched a drop of liquor. (Later, when Ford had made him a multimillionaire, he built a superb golf course and clubhouse and donated it to the City of Detroit with one absolute injunction, that liquor never be sold or served there.)

Rackham, now forty-five, began to believe that he was close to his one chance to make a fortune. He discussed it with his wife. "But we haven't got $5,000," she protested. "No, but we have four acres of land out on Van Ness Avenue worth more than that. We can borrow the money."

Mrs. Rackham was greatly worried. She could see their sole nest egg of security gone in one quick puff of smoke. But she left the decision to her husband, and he went on wrestling. One day he had an idea. Why not see Henry Ford's old boss, George Peck, president of the Edison Illuminating Company, president of the Michigan Savings Bank, board member with the McMillans, and father of Barton Peck, in whose shop at 81 Park Place Henry was building the first Model A?

Said Rackham later: "Mr. Peck was a shrewd and farsighted man, and I wanted his judgment." What did Peck tell him? "You better keep out," said George Peck.

Still Rackham went on debating with himself. But at the crucial moment Couzens and Malcomson showed him "a bunch of letters"—we do not know what they were. And Rackham plunged, borrowing $5,000 from the bank of the reluctant George Peck. Actually he held out some, even then: he put in only $3,500 in cash and gave notes for the rest. (As it turned out, he was quickly able to pay the rest out of dividends. By 1919, when Ford bought him out, Rackham had received $4,935,700 in dividends, and he sold his $5,000 worth of stock for $12,500,000.)

A few days after Anderson wrote his father Dr. Anderson hurried to Detroit. Dr. Anderson had been a decorated Civil War surgeon, had developed a fine practice, and had become mayor of La Crosse, where he waged ceaseless war on the saloons, forcing through an ordinance which ordered bartenders not to fill the beerpails brought in by small boys for the lunch-hour refreshment of workers: this nearly wrecked the noon-hour saloon trade for La Crosse.

What brought Dr. Anderson on swiftly, however, was the fact that he had been deeply bitten by one of his son's earlier investments, a fire-sprinkler company in Chicago that had died in the slowest and costliest fashion. John Anderson, now thirty-five, had indeed suffered numerous disappointments.

Dr. Anderson knew better than to expect too much; his son had always been an optimist. But when he first saw the Ford Motor Company, his heart sank. He said later:

I came to see the factory about which I had heard so much. It was nothing prepossessing . . . just a little building on Mack Avenue in which the cars were being assembled from parts made elsewhere.

James Couzens was at the plant when we were there the first time, and he offered to drive us to town in his first Ford car. On the way he attempted to drive through a small park, but the car stalled at a little hill. After frequent attempts to cross the little hill, Mr. Couzens was forced to detour around the block. That was my first auto ride.

Despite this unfortunate first impression, he loaned his son $5,000. And blithe, optimistic John Anderson, who liked a long cigar and a tall glass, was very soon able to live in the highest style, for he eventually drew down from the Ford Motor Company the exact amount that came to Rackham, a total by the end of sixteen years of $17,435,700.

Henry Ford talked a good deal to Anderson. Once during the money-raising period he told him:

You need not fear about the market.
The people will buy them all right.
When you get to making the cars in quantity, you can make them cheaper, and when you make them cheaper you can get more people with enough money to buy them. The market will take care of itself.
We must make the cars simple. I mean we must make them so that they are not too complicated from a mechanical standpoint, so that people can operate them easily, and with the fewer parts the better.

This was accurate thought and accurate prophecy, at a time when almost every other automaker was convinced that the facts were diametrically opposed to this analysis.

James Couzens, in a very real way, was just about the poorest man of the lot. We have seen how he scraped his way up, how slowly his salary was raised. Like the others he had come to believe that this was his one great chance; like a religious convert, he was the most militant of all in his belief. He swore he would put in all his savings and every penny he could beg, borrow or steal.

The total did not come to much. His life savings amounted to $400. And he suffered, because he wanted 25 shares, which would come to $2,500.

First he went to his sister, Rosetta, a schoolteacher whose life had been just as difficult and frugal. Her life savings totaled $200, and he begged her to plunge with it all. She was tempted but finally wrote their father for advice: she would let him make the decision. The senior Couzens heard both sides and finally ruled like Solomon: split the $200: keep $100 in the bank and gamble with the other $100. (When the company made good, Couzens, instead of paying back his sister the $100, gave her one share of the Ford stock. From that one share she drew down $95,000 in dividends and sold it to Ford in 1919 for $260,000, a total of $355,000 for her $100.)

So now Jim had $500. Where to get the rest? Then his boss, Malcomson, made him a proposition: if he could bring the year's profits in the coal business up to $100,000, Malcomson would give him a $1,000 bonus, which he could then invest in the Ford Motor Company.

This split Couzens' personality right down the middle and set him working night as well as day, selling coal and Ford with both hands. We can only assume that if a backer refused to invest in the car, Couzens tried to settle for a ton of coal.

But try as he might, he could not quite hit the $100,000 profit mark. At the year's end the profits reached $90,000, just $10,000 short. As ever, Malcomson was deeply grateful and wholly Scotch: he gave Couzens a bonus of only $500.

Now Couzens had $1,000 and not a prayer of more. He went to John S. Gray and pleaded mightily, and that kindly but cautious man—probably glumly thinking "In for a penny, in for a pound"—let him borrow $1,500 from the bank on a rigid high-interest note. So Couzens had his $2,500 and could put himself down for 25 shares.

Albert Strelow was all important to the company, for they needed his building and his backing. But he was as flighty as a hummingbird; Ford and Malcomson had to strong-arm him, soothe him, and batter him repeatedly before they netted him. By all accounts he was the kind of investor who hangs around shaking his head in deepest gloom, muttering half-aloud, "How did I let myself in for this?"

Strelow was an important builder; in fact, he had built the Edison Illuminating plant in which Henry had worked. He employed a hundred car-

penters and painters, lived in a fifteen-room mansion and had a country home. William Simonds tells how Malcomson approached Strelow. The first proposition was very gentle: "Albert, I want you to let us have room for a shop in back of your place." Strelow asked why. Malcomson answered:

"We're going to start building automobiles."
"Who's with you?"
"Some of my friends. We're getting the money together now."
"But what's the automobile? Whose car are you going to build?"
"It's designed by a man named Henry Ford. You know him, I think."

Strelow thought, but couldn't remember Ford.
"Come with me and I'll show him to you." They went to 81 Park Place and shook hands with Ford. The two left. Strelow turned to Malcomson: "No, I won't do it."

But they had to have him.

218. The first factory. This is the Mack Avenue plant, where it all started. Strelow owned this building; it had been a one-story icehouse. The photograph was taken in 1904, after a second story had been added. Although they paid him $5,000 to construct the upper floor, Strelow was extremely reluctant, for he feared that the extra story would make the place unrentable after the Ford Motor Company had failed.

The plant was originally 72 feet by 172 feet, about a third of an acre. It stood on the corner of Mack and Bellevue, on a spur of the Michigan Central Railroad. Strelow insisted on $75 a month rent; he must have felt that he wanted some return, however slight.

On a hot, sticky Saturday night, June 13, 1903, after dinner, the twelve stockholders of the Ford Motor Company gathered in the Malcomson office of the drab old McGraw Building, which stood on the southwest corner of Griswold Street and Lafayette Boulevard. This is what they did:

Ford and Malcomson were credited with $25,500 each for machinery, patents and contract. Each got 255 shares; jointly they held control in the sum of 510 shares out of 1,000 issued.

John S. Gray paid $10,500 in cash and was named president of the Ford Motor Company. (The Dodges had been spending $10,000 of this since February 13.)

John Wendell Anderson turned over his father's $5,000 in cash.

Horace Hatcher Rackham put down $3,500 in cash, and notes for $1,500 more. (He paid $800 on January 28, 1904, $200 on February 5, 1904, and $500 in July 1904.)

Charles H. Bennett gave his notes for $5,000. (He paid the first note for $2,500, guaranteed by Malcomson, on March 24, 1904, and the rest on June 22, 1904.)

John Francis Dodge gave a note for $5,000.

Horace Elgin Dodge gave a note for $5,000. John's was due in three months, Horace's in four months. That night $7,000 was formally transferred to the account of John and $3,000 to the account of Horace. (Both notes were paid on January 28, 1904.)

Vernon C. Fry paid $3,000 in cash and gave a note for $2,000. (He paid $1,000 on his note on December 2, 1903 and the rest in January 1904.)

James Couzens paid $1,000 in cash and gave a four-month note for $1,500. (He paid off his note, having given himself more than a year's extension, on August 31, 1904.)

Charles J. Woodall gave a four-month note for $1,000. (He paid it off on September 17, 1903.)

Albert Strelow came to the meeting with only a promise to pay. He still hated to let his $5,000 go. (He finally got his money in on July 11, twenty-eight days later, when the company was poised on the brink of a bankruptcy that would have been remarkably quick even for those days.)

The company was nominally capitalized at $150,000, but only $100,000 stock was issued, the rest being held in the treasury.

Malcomson proposed that the new company be named the Ford Motor Company, and this was agreed. And they filed papers of incorporation at the capitol in Lansing.

Ford and Couzens went home together that night. Ford asked Couzens' advice on their salaries: "What do you think we ought to ask from those fellows?" It is the "those fellows" that is significant. To Ford the only important people were the doers, the operating staff; the

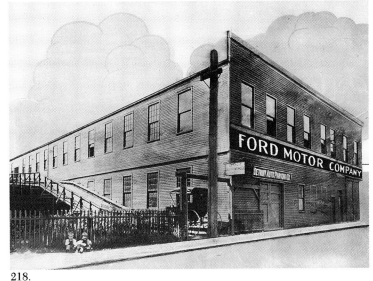

218.

backers and stockholders were merely a necessary evil.

On June 16, the Ford Motor Company started in business.

The Ford-Malcomson limited partnership was transferred to the new company on June 18. John S. Gray was president of the new enterprise, Henry Ford vice-president and general manager, and James Couzens the treasurer. There were five directors: Ford, Malcomson, Couzens, Anderson and John Dodge. Ford's salary was set at $3,600 a year, and Couzens' at $2,500.

Within a week they appointed a sales manager, Charles Wardle of Chicago, at $208.33 a month plus traveling expenses. But Couzens quickly discovered he could personally sell harder and faster at long-distance than Wardle could directly. So Wardle became the first man fired from the Ford Motor Company—the first name on one of the longest and most distinguished rolls of names in American industrial history.

219. The minutes of the directors meeting, Nov. 13, 1903, at which Mr. Wardle was discharged.

220. An early payroll. They all worked ten hours a day except Wills, Ford, and Couzens, who averaged from twelve to sixteen hours straight through seven-day weeks. Here are the names of Dick Kettlewell, the one they all played jokes on; Gus Degener, the swift mechanic who could do anything; John Wandersee, who began by sweeping up and became a photographer and a metallurgist.

221. Workers outside the Mack Avenue Plant of Ford Motor Company about 1903. Henry Ford does not appear in this photograph, but some of his assistants are recognizable—Leo Schultz, Al Aldrich, F. L. Rockelman, and Gus Degener. Said Wandersee years later:

> Up to June 16, 1903, no cars had come in except the experimental model. I would say the cars from the Dodge brothers started coming in early in July.
>
> The motor, the chassis, and the axles were all manufactured and assembled at Dodge brothers. All we did was put the wheels on and the body on.
>
> The body came on a hand truck and they picked it out and put it on. The fellows could

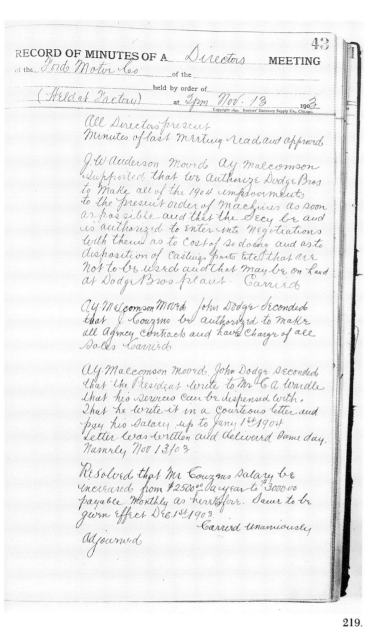

219.

lift a car body easy enough. After the car was assembled one fellow would take hold of the rear end and one the front end and lift the whole thing up.

They were assembled on the spot and driven out. One or two men would do each assembly. There were ten or fifteen spots for assembling. The testing was done right on the blocks. You'd have to get the motor started and run it so it would be fit to run. Sometimes the valves needed grinding and we'd do it right there. The Dodges didn't do any testing.

They used the second story for painting. Before that it was done in a barn down the alley.

The Dodges, by nature belligerent, kept things lively. Back in February, when they had outlined their exorbitant demands regarding payment for the engines they were to make, they had met for the first time a man with a jaw and a nerve as hard as their own. Young Jim Couzens had jumped up roaring: "We'll not stand for that!" John Dodge shoved back his chair and jumped up, too, jaw sticking out. He roared back: "Who in hell are you?" Couzens told him, in the same aggressive, toe-to-toe manner that had made him the most unpopular freight-car checker in the annals of the Michigan Central, and Malcomson had to step between them.

Many of the defects of the first cars were due to the haste with which the Dodges poured through their botchy work: the brothers paid their mechanics for piece-work, and the result was inevitably, to say the least, a lack of uniformity.

Ford's engine tester was one Fred Rockelman, who was just as choleric and quick-fisted as either Couzens or the Dodges. Rockelman went over to the Dodge shop to protest about the flywheels, which did not fit: they were too loose. After a few quick remarks by Rockelman, John Dodge strode forward to punch his head. "Go ahead!" roared Rockelman. "Throw me out! But that won't make us accept engines with loose flywheels." He walked over, grabbed a crankshaft, and thrust it into the flywheel easily, with his hand. The Dodges grinned. They all shook hands.

When Ford heard this he laughed. "Oh, those Dodges' bark is worse than their bite," he said. Ford always moved with easy poise in angry situ-

220.

221.

222a.

ations, joking, wrestling with the men down on the greasy floor. ("We always called him Hank or Henry," said one of those early-day workers, Fred Seemans.) But after the incident he cut down the Dodges' profits by insisting on large deductions for bad motors.

222a, b. Model A, 1903. This is the first car manufactured by the Ford Motor Company. It weighed 1,250 pounds and was relatively simple, light and efficient. It had a two-cylinder opposed engine, developed eight horsepower, and could run up to thirty miles per hour. As you can see, the steering wheel is on the right; the styling is based somewhat on the curved-dash Olds. The transmission was planetary, two speeds forward and one reverse. Two sets of six dry-cell batteries furnished the spark for the ignition. The wheel base was six feet.

222b.

It was not yet Henry Ford's dream car, but he was on his way. And no little credit should be given to Couzens, to Malcomson and the Dodges. With these forceful citizens hounding him, the perfectionist was forced to shift from creation to production; it is even likely that Ford would have gone on for years trying to build a car exactly to his liking—much like a lonely painter in a studio, endlessly repainting. But again and again Couzens set his jaw and refused to hear of a change in design: his slogan was "Get the money first!"

223. One-lung Cadillac, 1903. You can plainly see that the first Cadillac, produced by Henry's onetime backers of the old Detroit Automobile Company, was an almost exact duplicate of Ford's first car. This is the car that Ford had left with William H. Murphy and others. But in it Henry M. Leland had put a one-cylinder engine designed by Alanson B. Brush.

223.

The production philosophy of the two companies was entirely different. Cadillac made two of these cars by hand and sent them to New York with the ex-bicycle dealer, William Metzger. He exhibited them at the New York Automobile Show, and the style so enchanted New Yorkers that he got 2,200 orders! With these orders on hand, Cadillac then engaged in production. The Ford Company, of course, plunged in to manufacture long before they had an order for a car.

224a, b. The turning point: A few stubs from Couzens' checkbook. The entries are worth pondering. Here the Ford Motor Company almost went under before it got started. July 11, 1903 was the decisive day. On June 26 the company had $14,500 in the bank, and on the next day they received John Anderson's check, giving them a balance of $19,500. That was the actual total of the shoestring on which they began.

Voucher number one, in Couzens' hand, went to the Dodges. Next check went to the Hartford Rubber Works in Connecticut—$640 for 64 tires.

The money rolled out swiftly. By July 1 there was only $7,013.38 left in the bank. Then they paid the Dodges $5,000 more, spent $1.79 for blueprints, paid $1.15 to Western Union, and $7 (that's all) for fenders.

Jim Couzens ordered himself some office furniture: this came to $31.40. And what with one thing and another the bank balance dropped on down. By July 9 the Ford Motor Company had in liquid cash on hand exactly $595.47.

At the end of the first sixty checks Couzens had written away almost all of the money. On July 10 the balance was down to its lowest ebb: $223.65.

The little company had been in business only 25 days. Its capital was almost gone. The payroll had to be met and supplies paid for in cash.

The other investors had not yet paid in their money. But would they? Almost all of their notes had been guaranteed against loss by Malcomson's endorsement; and Malcomson, with all his enterprises and big profits, was yet desperately short of cash. Then they sold a car, July 15, 1903: that was the red-letter day, the turning point.

225. Dr. E. Pfennig, the first buyer of a Model A. (Couzens has misspelled the name in this account.) Most significantly, the first buyer of a Ford Motor Company car was a doctor, a doctor tired of hitching up his horse and buggy for emergency calls at night. This doctor was E. Pfennig, of Chicago, who paid the full cash price of $850 to the Illinois Trust and Savings Bank in Chicago. (Ford had only one dealer, and he was in Buffalo.)

By the very next week the balance rose to $6,486.44. By October Couzens passed around

the first dividend: 2 per cent. Next January he gave one of 20 per cent. And on the first anniversary of the company, June 16, 1904, the directors voted themselves a spanking 68 per cent dividend. With the other odds and ends of 10 per cent they had declared for themselves during the first year, the 68 per cent added up to exactly $100,000—the very amount they were supposed to have when they started.

They had made it. When Dr. Pfennig bought his car on that July day, the Ford Motor Company had done more than make its first sale. For Henry Ford had something more in mind. He had said:

I will build a motor car for the multitude.

It shall be large enough for the family, but small enough for the unskilled individual to operate easily and care for, and it shall be light in weight that it may be economical in maintenance.

It will be built of honest materials, by the best workmen that money can hire, after the simplest designs that modern engineering can devise.

But it shall be so low in price that the man of moderate means may own one and enjoy with his family the blessings of happy hours spent in God's great open spaces.

226. The company needed a distinctive symbol or design of its name to designate it. So Wills, once a commercial artist, drew up the flowing script that said "Ford Motor Company" which was used for all the years until Ford died.

It was July 1903. In Rome a great Pope, Leo XIII, at the great age of ninety-three, was dying. On his deathbed he said: "Oh, the weight of these robes! Can I hold out until the end?" On July 4 President Theodore Roosevelt sent the first round-the-world telegraph message: it was to Governor William Howard Taft of the Philippine Islands. The *Bookman*, the leading American literary periodical, featured the centenary of the birth of Bulwer-Lytton, with a long critical discussion of *The Last Days of Pompeii*.

Child-care hints featured the old advice: never wean a baby in summer time. It was reported that while Queen Alexandra of England never spent a penny more than $10,000 a year for her clothes, the Czarina of Russia spent more than

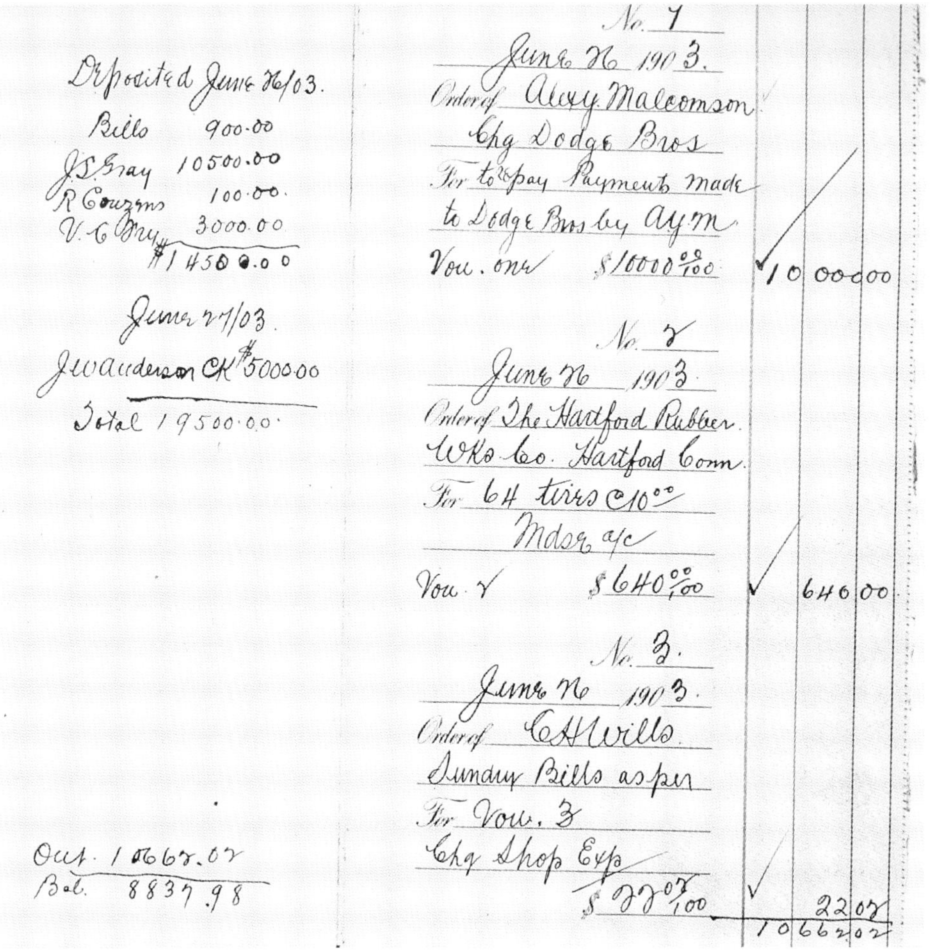

No. 1
June 26 1903.
Order of Alex y Malcomson
Chg Dodge Bros
For to pay Payments made
to Dodge Bros by A Y M
Vou. one $10000 00/100   ✓ 10000 00

No. 2
June 26 1903
Order of The Hartford Rubber
Wks Co. Hartford Conn
For 64 tires @ 10 00
Mdse a/c
Vou. ✓ $640 00/100   ✓ 640 00

No. 3
June 26 1903
Order of C H Wills
Sundry Bills as per
For Vou. 3
Chg Shop Exp
$22 07/100   ✓ 22 07
10662 02

224a.

225.

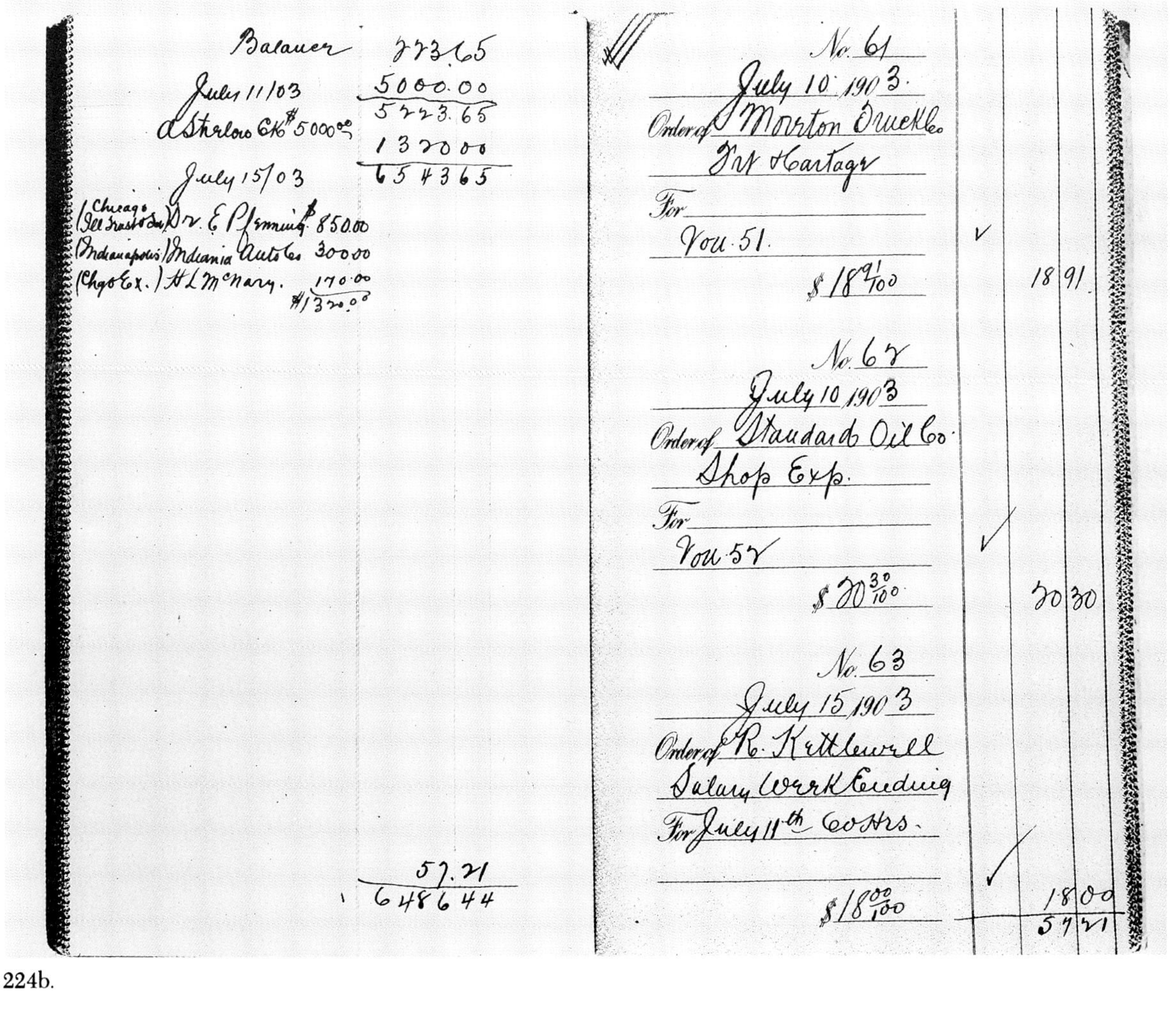

Balance   773.65
July 11/03   5000.00
            5773.65
A Sherlow Ck #5000 00   1320 00
            6543 65
July 15/03
(Chicago Del Sales Dept) Dr E Pfenning 850.00
(Indianapolis) Indiana Autos 300.00
(Chgo Ex.) H L McNary 170.00
        #1320.00

            57.21
            6486 44

No. 61
July 10 1903
Order of Morton Druck Co
Frt Hartage
For
Vou. 51
$18 91/100   ✓   18 91

No. 62
July 10 1903
Order of Standard Oil Co
Shop Exp.
For
Vou 52
$20 30/100   ✓   20 30

No. 63
July 15 1903
Order of R Kettlewell
Salary Week Ending
For July 11th Co Hrs.
$18 00/100   ✓   18 00
57 21

224b.

226.

227.

twice as much. And the Kaiserin of Germany never bought a stitch in Paris, dressing in simple clothes made in Vienna. Women's negligees for "graceful summer lounging" featured an English importation, the "breakfast, or coffee jacket," a cobwebby muslin bolero worn modestly over a tight-fitting silk slip.

The biggest family in Detroit was the Kennedys, nine grown-up sons and four daughters: they challenged any family of nine sons in Michigan to a baseball game. A Detroit doctor wrote a serious article on the close relationship of obesity to genius, citing Balzac, Victor Hugo, and Théophile Gautier. Wrote Dr. James Kiernan:

> The world and an overcoat could hardly contain the glory of Victor Hugo's belly. He burst his button-band every day. Rossini had not been able to see his feet for six years before his death—he was a hippopotamus in trousers. Balzac looked more like a hogshead than a man. Alexandre Dumas ate three breakfasts every morning.

The last chief of the Oneida Indians, the most powerful tribe of the once-mighty Six Nations, became an Episcopal priest.

When the Detroit Tigers beat their foes, the Chicago White Sox, at Bennett Park, now Tiger Stadium, in a fourteen-inning game by a score of three to two, a reporter wrote: "There went up a shout that even awakened the sleeping policeman in the Trumbull Avenue station."

And Calamity Jane—it was one of General Custer's captains who gave her that title—Calamity Jane Burke, the straightest shot in the plains, died in Deadwood, South Dakota, not far from the place where she had captured Jack McCall, the murderer of Wild Bill Hickok.

Detroit, once the sleepiest of towns on a Sunday, had become the gayest of cities: on the Sabbath beer gardens and dance halls dotted the outskirts of town, excursion boats plowed the rivers and the lakes. Belle Isle was thick with people from church time on. An anonymous *Evening News* reporter wrote: "To add to this Sabbathian hubbub there are the automobiles and bicycles shooting through the streets, vieing with the street cars in the clamor."

As yet, not one of those automobiles had been

made by the Ford Motor Company. But they were on the way.

Six months after the first sale of the Ford car, Henry Ford bought his first dress suit. He paid $65 for it.

It was July 1903 when the Ford first got into production. And on the thirtieth of that month Henry achieved his first forty years. His failures and years of experimentation were beginning to pay dividends. It may not have been "positively the most perfect machine on the market" as the advertisement claims, but it must have been dependable and it was versatile.

227. *"Boss of the Road." An advertisement from Frank Leslie's Popular Monthly of July 1903.*

228. *One of the versatile uses of an early automobile. This picture shows two "Fordmobiles," one being used as a stationary engine to run a buzz saw. Here logs are being sawed up—for firewood? It is at the Bryant farm on Monnier Road. The man at the right with the hat on is Melvin S. Bryant, next is Marvin R. Bryant. Henry Ford is feeding a log into the saw, and the young man is Edgar Leroy Bryant. The building was called "the Arch." The little white house is the home of neighbors, the Ed Richards.*

229. *A sign of the changing times. Horseshoers and machinists and blacksmiths are now becoming auto mechanics and repairmen. Shops of this sort were becoming numerous. The wagon in the front looks like a small omnibus.*

229.

228.

Titles in the
Great Lakes Books Series

Steamboats and Sailors of the Great Lakes, by Mark L. Thompson, 1991

Cobb Would Have Caught It: The Golden Years of Baseball in Detroit, by Richard Bak, 1991

Michigan in Literature, by Clarence Andrews, 1992

Under the Influence of Water: Poems, Essays, and Stories, by Michael Delp, 1992

The Country Kitchen, by Della T. Lutes, 1992 (reprint)

The Making of a Mining District: Keweenaw Native Copper 1500–1870, by David J. Krause, 1992

Kids Catalog of Michigan Adventures, by Ellyce Field, 1993

Henry's Lieutenants, by Ford R. Bryan, 1993

Historic Highway Bridges of Michigan, by Charles K. Hyde, 1993

Lake Erie and Lake St. Clair Handbook, by Stanley Bolsenga and Charles E. Herndendorf, 1993

Queen of the Lakes, by Mark L. Thompson, 1994

Iron Fleet: The Great Lakes in World War II, by George J. Joachim, 1994

Turkey Stearnes and the Detroit Stars: The Negro Leagues in Detroit, 1919–1933, by Richard Bak, 1994

Pontiac and the Indian Uprising, by Howard H. Peckham, 1994 (reprint)

Charting the Inland Seas: A History of the U.S. Lake Survey, by Arthur M. Woodford, 1994 (reprint)

Ojibwa Narratives of Charles and Charlotte Kawbawgam and Jacques LePique, 1893-1895. Recorded with Notes by Homer H. Kidder, edited by Arthur P. Bourgeois, 1994, co-published with the Marquette County Historical Society

Strangers and Sojourners: A History of Michigan's Keweenaw Peninsula, by Arthur W. Thurner, 1994

Win Some, Lose Some: G. Mennen Williams and the New Democrats, by Helen Washburn Berthelot, 1995

Sarkis, by Gordon and Elizabeth Orear, 1995

The Northern Lights: Lighthouses of the Upper Great Lakes, by Charles K. Hyde, 1995 (reprint)

Kids Catalog of Michigan Adventures, Second Edition, by Ellyce Field, 1995

Rumrunning and the Roaring Twenties: Prohibition on the Michigan-Ontario Waterway, by Philip P. Mason, 1995

In the Wilderness with the Red Indians, by E. R. Baierlein, translated by Anita Z. Boldt, edited by Harold W. Moll, 1996

Elmwood Endures: History of a Detroit Cemetery, by Michael S. Franck, 1996

Master of Precision: Henry M. Leland, by Mrs. Wilfred C. Leland with Minnie Dubbs Millbrook, 1996 (reprint)

Haul-Out: New and Selected Poems, by Stephen Tudor, 1996

Beyond the Model T: The Other Ventures of Henry Ford, revised edition, by Ford R. Bryan, 1997

Kids Catalog of Michigan Adventures, third edition, by Ellyce Field, 1997

Young Henry Ford: A Picture History of the First Forty Years, by Sidney Olson, 1997 (reprint)